# Woodworking for Beginners

*R.J. De Cristoforo*

**TAB** **TAB BOOKS**
Blue Ridge Summit, PA

FIRST EDITION
FIRST PRINTING

© 1993 by **TAB Books**.
TAB Books is a division of McGraw-Hill, Inc.

**Library of Congress Cataloging-in-Publication Data**

De Cristoforo, R.J.
    Woodworking for beginners / by R.J. De Cristoforo.
        p.    cm.
    Includes index.
    ISBN 0-8306-4324-9     ISBN 0-8306-3829-6 (pbk.)
    1. Woodwork.    I. Title.
    TT180.D338   1992
    684'.08—dc20                                    92-19907
                                                    CIP

TAB Books offers software for sale. For information and a catalog, please contact
TAB Software Department, Blue Ridge Summit, PA 17294-0850.

Acquisitions Editor: Stacy Varavvas Pomeroy
Book Editor: Annette M. Testa
Director of Production: Katherine G. Brown
Book Design: Jaclyn J. Boone
Cover Design: Denny Bond, East Petersburg, Pa.
Cover Photograph: Thompson Photography, Baltimore, Md.                HT3

# Woodworking
# for Beginners

## Other Books by the Author
The Portable Router Book
The Table Saw Book
The Jigsaw/Scroll Saw Book
The Band Saw Book
The Drill Press Book
Gifts from the Woodshop

# Contents

# Introduction

The camaraderie among woodworkers is legendary. When you become interested in the activity, you will join millions of craftspeople who enjoy the practical and therapeutic benefits of creating useful and fun projects with a natural material. A major appeal of the craft is the very nature of wood—the way it feels, its appearance before and after you have applied a finish, the infinite ways it can be shaped and joined, and the fragrances of the various species. All of these attributes contribute to the ambiance of a woodworking shop.

In its raw state, wood is only a board, a beam, or a panel, but with your creative attention it can evolve into an exclusive piece of furniture for your home or patio, a pull toy to intrigue a youngster, a miniature house to accommodate or supply food for birds, or interesting accessories for the kitchen. What you can accomplish is limited only by your degree of interest. Because of the revived interest in wooden objects, it's not unusual to find a person enjoying woodcraft while establishing a cottage industry for part-time, and even full-time, income.

The day of the professional woodworker whose intent is to create quality pieces that contrast, happily, with the clones of a production line is far from over. Many woodworking artists produce one-of-a-kind projects that rate museum exposure because of construction and design quality. On a commercial level, such exclusive pieces enjoy high prices. Not all of us plan our dedication to that extreme because it involves full-time application. However, anyone can produce pieces for personal use that can become family heirlooms.

Today's beginning woodworker has many more options in terms of tools, materials, and freedom to express ideas than yesterday's carpenter's apprentice, who was limited by the equipment, attitude, and design decisions of his master.

Traditionally, the student is initiated by becoming acquainted with handtools. This procedure is still a logical way to get started. Even though all woodworking operations can be quickly accomplished with readily available power tools, nothing brings you closer to the medium than using a handsaw to *crosscut* a board to length or to *rip* it to width, or to produce a *see-through shaving* from a board, using a chisel or a plane.

Actually, something of a turnaround is taking place today, since many good woodworkers who produce excellent projects are doing so voluntarily with handtools as "an extension of the mind and body." The philosophy is admirable, but not one that everyone needs to adopt. When viewing a quality project, it takes a very discerning eye to determine the method of construction. Whether the appeal of the project is increased by its having been made strictly by handtools is a moot point.

The amateur's home shop is affected by more factors then just how he or she might like to work. A full complement of handtools plus a workbench can occupy, for example, a corner of a garage, while a good assortment of stationary power tools would banish the family vehicles to the driveway. What happens most times is that the worker, after becoming acquainted with handtools, adds a few power tools that help him or her become more productive—more productive in the sense that a board can be cut faster on a table saw than with a handsaw.

Anyway, that's the direction of this book. Just as the careful aspiring artist learns about paint and brushes before he or she begins to paint, the woodworker should likewise establish a rapport with his or her medium—wood. This rapport is the basis of woodworking, regardless of where and how far the woodworker wishes to go.

Once involved, individual preferences affect future involvement and methods. And that's the way it should be. The ideal role for the woodworker is to be both a craftsman and an artist. We do make choices. We can be efficiency-minded to the point where the speedy end result is primary, or, at the other extreme, look down on what is practical as a hindrance to artistry.

Why not adopt both viewpoints? I personally feel that the broad-minded approach is part of the enjoyment of woodworking. A straightforward bookcase of knotty pine that is carefully assembled is as successful a project as an imaginatively designed showcase made of a rare wood from Tasmania.

Overall, it's important to enjoy working with wood. That's what woodworking is all about. Enjoyment also involves working safely. Always remember that tools don't think; that's your job. Adopt the two basic rules that ensure safety and accuracy with your projects: measure twice, cut once, and think twice before cutting.

# 1

# Layout

Layout has to do with measuring and marking material so it can be sawed to a particular length or width or to a shape that is required for a project's components. Many precise layout devices, some of which are shown in FIG. 1-1 can help when measuring, but accuracy depends on you as much as on the design of the implement. Tolerances in woodworking, which means the plus or minus error factor, are variable. Being over or under by $1/32$ or $1/16$ inch on the length of a storage shelf that will be used in the garage may not be crucial, but being so casual when forming a joint for a furniture project can cause problems. For example, when making a square or rectangular frame with mitered corners, a slight discrepancy in the angular cut will be duplicated eight times, resulting in a lot of frustration when you assemble the four pieces. Adopting an accurate layout habit regardless of the project's purpose is a primary rule.

## Layout tools

Lines that will be guides for sawing can be marked with a sharp, hard pencil (e.g., about 4H or 5H), but at times it's better to work with a utility knife like the types shown in FIG. 1-2. A knife makes a clean, fine line, but even more importantly, it can sever the surface fibers of the wood. The advantage is that the incised line helps to produce a smoother cut when you saw.

Marking a dimension point is as important as placing and reading the rule correctly. A common procedure is to place the rule flat and then make a short, heavy line to indicate the dimension. A more precise method is to hold the rule at a slight angle and to slide the point of the marker down the graduation line so

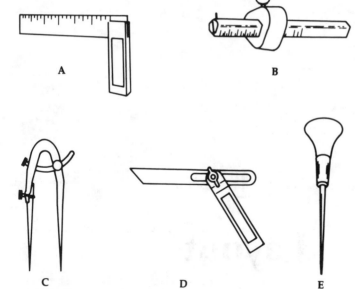

**Fig. 1-1** *A few basic layout tools: (A) a square; (B) a marking gauge; (C) dividers; (D) a T-bevel; (E) an awl.*

**Fig. 1-2** *Marking a line with a knife is often better than using a pencil. The knife forms a clean, slim line and severs the surface fibers of the wood. This helps to provide a clean edge when sawing.*

all you get on the work are small dots (FIG. 1-3). Of course this can be accomplished only when the rule has incised lines that serve as grooves in which the point of the marker can ride. This method is far better than using small scratches to mark dimension points.

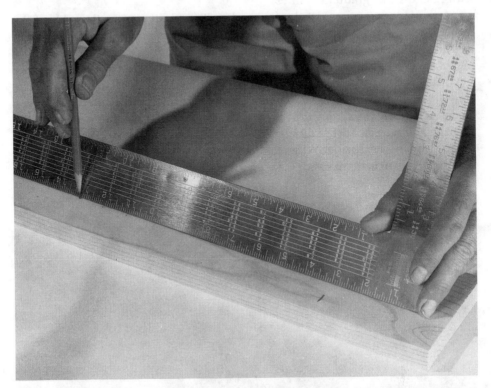

**Fig. 1-3** *Sliding the pencil down the graduation line of a rule leaves a small dot on the work. It's more accurate than keeping the rule flat and scratching a line.*

### Flex tapes

Flex tapes are today's most popular measuring instrument because they are compact, easy to use, and available in many sizes. Flex tapes are the rules that consist of a flexible steel blade that extends from and automatically recoils back into a small case. Common blade widths range from 1/4 inch to 1 inch and they can be as long as 100 feet. Those of excessive length are usually made of reinforced cloth instead of steel. Usual graduations are in inches, divided into 16ths and 8ths, but some flex tapes are also available in metric. Some flex tapes are marked in inches and metric so conversions can be made right on the job.

The blades are usually coved across their width to supply some stiffness when they are extended. Wide blades are bulkier but, when coved correctly, can span respectable distances without bending. This factor is more important for on-location jobs than it is for shop work. This tool should have a locking feature so the blade can be held at any extended position. Choose a flex tape that is at least 8 feet long; anything under that length is not adequate for a woodworking shop. You should be able to measure along the long dimension of a standard 4-×-8-foot plywood panel. Obviously, the tape you choose should be easy to read, with fine, distinct graduation lines.

A flex tape has a hook at the free end so it can butt against the edge of the object that is being marked or measured (FIG. 1-4). The hook might be designed to swivel or slide to-and-fro so the tape can be set for taking inside measurements. There is some debate about the merits of each type of hook, but the important factor is the accuracy of the measurement made with the tape. The swivel-type hook is moved aside when it's necessary to butt the end of the tape against a surface; the sliding type recesses into the blade. In either case, keep the hook end clean. Sawdust or dirt can interfere with the function of the hook, leading to errors in measuring. When taking inside measurements, the length of the case, which is usually marked, is taken into consideration (FIG. 1-5).

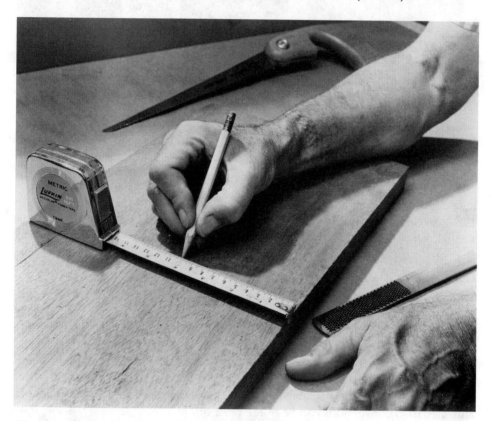

**Fig. 1-4** *The hook on flex tapes can bear against edges. Being able to lock the tape in an extended position allows using the tool in this manner.*

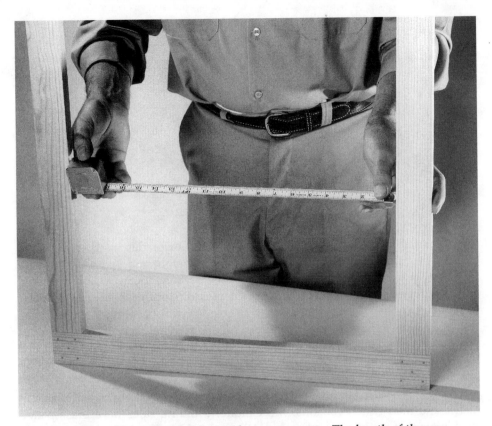

**Fig. 1-5** *Flex tapes can be used for inside measurements. The length of the case, which will be stamped, is taken into account.*

One of the advantages of a flex tape is that it can be used for more than straight measuring. For example, you can wrap it around a disc to measure its circumference. When reading the scale, look straight down on the graduation line. Errors can occur if your line of sight is at an angle, something like misreading a gas gauge or a speedometer when you don't view it head-on.

One caution about flex tapes. Retract them with care. Return springs can be strong enough to cause an extended tape to flip about as it is recoiled.

### Folding rule

The *folding rule* shown in FIG. 1-6 is more popularly known as a *zig-zag rule* because of the way it is opened and closed. A common unit will extend to 6 feet and fold to a compact 8 inches. An advantage of this tool is that it is fairly rigid even when fully extended. When the unit incorporates a sliding extension, as many of them do, it is handy for inside measurements. The reading on the exten-

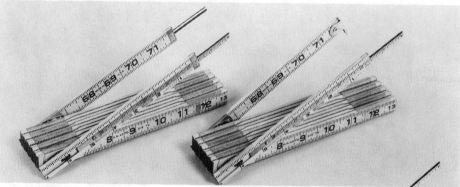

*Fig. 1-6*  *Folding rules are more popularly known as "zig-zag" rules.*

sion is added to the sum of the opened sections, or blades, as they are often called. Thus, this tool is handy for measuring the height and width of openings for doors, or drawers, and similar installations. Because the extension is removable, it can be used as a short rule or as a gauge to measure the depth of holes.

Carpenters like the fact that a few of the blades will stay at right angles to the rest of the tool so they can reach overhead for a horizontal measurement without having to climb a ladder or stool. Common graduations are in inches and sixteenths and will indicate 16-inch on-center stud markings. The latter information is appreciated by carpenters who are erecting house walls.

Folding rules are made of metal or wood and, like flex tapes, are available in metric and metric/inch versions. Most modern folding rules have brass plated steel joints that are lifetime lubricated. When this feature is lacking, you should occasionally place a tiny drop of light oil in each of the joints.

### Squares

*Squares* are used for measuring, marking, and checking cuts to be sure they are flat and at right angles to adjacent edges. A common practice is to mark the cutline with a square and then, after sawing, to use the square again to be sure you've done the job correctly. When it is used for checking, the blade of the square is placed across the surface of the cut with its handle against an adjacent edge. You can quickly determine the accuracy of the cut and its squareness by glancing around the perimeter of the blade. Errors will be obvious if you hold the work and the square so you get some backlighting. There are a variety of squares to choose from in woodworking. The following are the most commonly used.

**Try square**  The *try square* (FIG. 1-7) reigned supreme for a long time, being accepted as *the* marking and checking instrument. The fact that it is still listed in various designs in catalogs indicates that it is by no means passé. The try square has metal blades attached to a metal or hardwood handle that is fixed at a right angle. When designed so, it is pretty much a single-purpose tool, limited to 90-degree applications. However, there are versions, like the one in FIG. 1-7, that have the blade end of the handle cut at 45 degrees. In this case, the tool might be

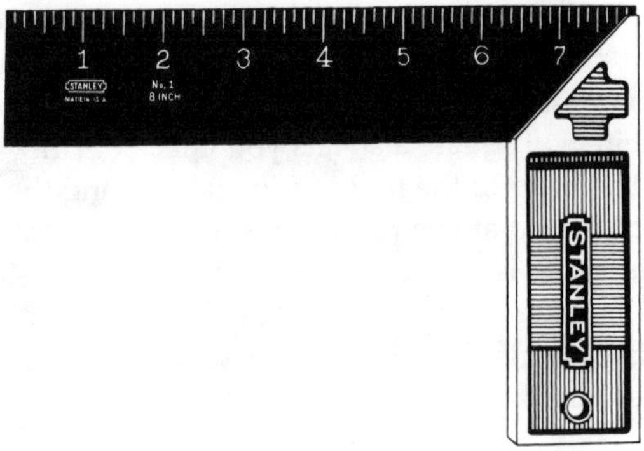

**Fig. 1-7** *Try squares have fixed handles. The handle on this unit is cut at 45 degrees so the tool can be used to check or lay out 45-degree angles.*

called a *miter square* since the added feature allows you to check or mark 45-degree angles.

Blades on a try square range from 6 inches up to 12 inches, with handles running from about 5 inches to 7½ inches, depending on blade length. Most commonly the squares have ⅛-inch graduations, but like most modern measuring devices, they are also available in metric. A good blade length for a woodworking shop is 8 or 10 inches long.

**Combination square** The *combination square* (FIG. 1-8) is more popular today for general shop use simply because it is has more applications than a try square.

**Fig. 1-8** *The combination square does more than a try square. For one thing, any of them can be used to mark 45-degree angles.*

It probably should be a first-buy tool for the woodworker and, since it is so versatile, it might likely be the only square you need buy. In addition to checking saw cuts and drawing 90-degree lines to an edge as you would with a try square, the combination square also lets you check or draw 45-degree angles.

The head of the tool is adjustable along the length of the 12-inch blade and can be locked at any point. This allows the tool to be used as a gauge when it is necessary to lay out a line parallel to an edge (FIG. 1-9). Since the blade is removable, it can serve as an independent rule or as a straight edge for marking or for guiding a knife when it is necessary to cut through thin material like veneer or poster board.

**Fig. 1-9** *Because the head of a combination square can be locked at any point on the rule, the tool can be used this way to mark lines parallel to an edge.*

Additional features of quality squares include a built-in bubble, so the head can be used like a level, and a short scriber, held in the handle by force-fit, and used as a marker.

The combination square is an important tool, so it makes sense to buy a good one. Avoid those that are heaped with other low-quality items in a bargain bin. In the long run, they are not "bargains." Respect the one you buy by keeping it clean and storing it carefully. An occasional wiping with a lint-free cloth and a drop or two of light machine oil is a good idea.

**Steel squares** The name *steel square* covers a variety of tools, all of which resemble the example in FIG. 1-10. There are *carpenter squares, rafter squares, mini squares,* even *a homeowner's square,* which is aluminum instead of steel. Many of these units are almost encyclopedic in terms of the information they offer. The *homeowner's square,* for one, has the following information stamped into its surfaces: board-feet equivalents; decimal equivalent table; metric conversion table; formula that tells how to square a foundation; 45-, 30-, and 60-degree angle markings; wood screw gauge table; drill sizes; common and finishing nail sizes; and a depth scale. All this informatiom appears in addition to the ⅛-inch graduations on its face and back. The applications of some of the squares are so extensive, they come with good-sized booklets to explain how to use them.

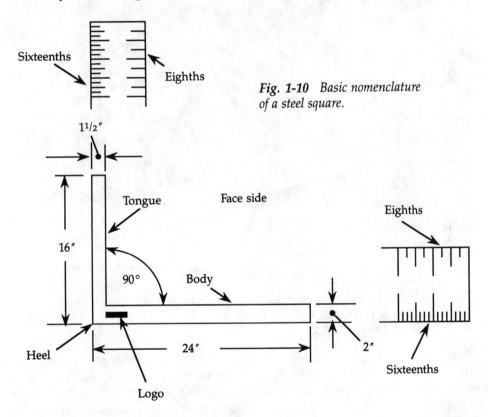

*Fig. 1-10  Basic nomenclature of a steel square.*

One major interest in a steel square is its size. Body or tongue can be used to draw long lines, whether at some midpoint or 90 degrees to an edge, and either leg can be used to check the flatness of broad surfaces. The tool is convenient for checking the squareness of inside and outside corners on large projects and for being sure that frames have right-angle corners.

Later in this chapter, I show how a steel square can be used to lay out angles.

## Marking gauge

The *marking gauge* (FIG. 1-11) is a fine tool for accurately marking lines parallel to an edge. The required edge-distance, the distance from the edge of the wood to a desired point on the board, is obtained by measuring from the point of the marking pin to the faceplate or head of the gauge. The reading can be taken directly from the scale on the beam. To measure with this tool, simply loosen the thumbscrew that locks the head only enough to allow the head to slide. When tightening the head, do not bear down heavily on the screw when securing position.

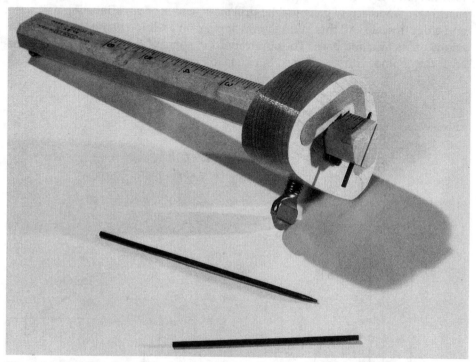

**Fig. 1-11** *Marking gauges are available in metal or wood and are usually able to function with a steel point or a strip of pencil lead. The beam on which the head slides is calibrated for direct readings.*

Likewise, do not tighten the screw too tight because you might strip the threads that are cut directly in the wood. Recheck the setting to be sure it is accurate after securing the head. Apply the tool with a gentle touch—its only purpose is to establish guide lines. Allow the marker, steel pin or pencil lead, to project only as much as it needs to contact the work. Place the gauge so its head butts against the edge of the work and so it rests on one of the flat faces on the board (FIG. 1-12). Always work so you are moving *away* from the marker's point. If you do otherwise, the point will probably dig in. Be especially cognizant of the projection of the marker when marking across the grain of the wood to avoid tearing surface fibers.

*Fig. 1-12* *The marking gauge is a fine tool for drawing lines parallel to edges. Move the gauge smoothly and hold it firmly against the edge of the work. The marker should project only enough to contact the work.*

At times, you may find it more convenient to push the tool rather than pull it. The layout and even the grain direction of the wood might have a bearing on this. Whether you push or pull, again remember that the tool is moved in a direction that is opposite the point of the marker.

The marking gauge is especially useful when lines must be duplicated, as is the case when marking cutlines for a *tenon* (FIG. 1-13). There's no room for human error here, because, once set, the gauge will mark as many lines as you need, all of them with the correct edge distance.

### Compass or wing divider

A *divider* is the term many metalworkers use for what most of us call a *compass*. A possible distinction between these two implements is that a divider has two integral metal points, while a compass has a single metal pivot point and works with a pencil or a strip of pencil lead for marking. One advantage of a wing divider, probably the most useful in a woodworking shop, is that it can be used either way. Its marking arm, or wing, can hold either a pencil or a metal scriber (FIG. 1-14). Call them what you will (I'll settle for compass), their basic function is

*Fig. 1-13* Once the marking gauge is set it can easily draw any number of lines that have exactly the same edge distance.

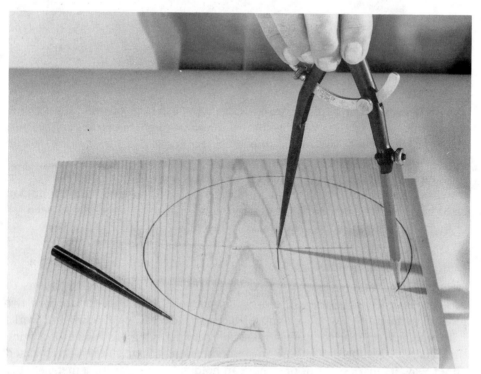

*Fig. 1-14* This type of compass can be used with either a steel scriber or a pencil.

to draw perfect circles and arcs. Like many tools, a compass will function beyond its basic application. It can be used, for example, to step off a line into any number of equal spaces (FIG. 1-15).

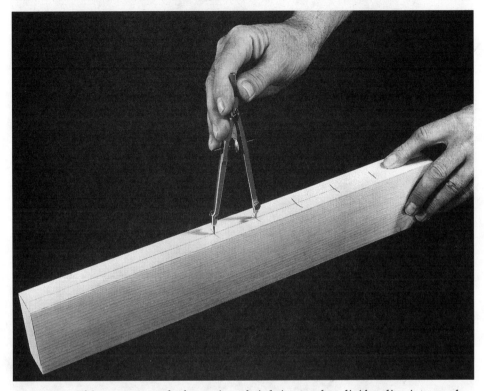

**Fig. 1-15** *This compass, a draftsman's tool, is being used to divide a line into equal spaces. You can work with any type compass to accomplish the same task.*

Setting a compass correctly can be done in one of two ways. One way, when drawing a circle, is to establish two points that are spaced to equal the radius of the circle. Then set the points of the compass on the marks. Another way is to set the tool directly by placing the points on the correct graduation lines of a rule. If you use the latter method, do not place one point of the compass at the end of the rule. Instead, place one point of the compass on the 1-inch line and the other point on a line that is 1 inch more than the radius you need. This way of working is more accurate, since holding a compass point at the end of a rule is difficult, and the starting end of a rule might be worn or damaged through use.

Another extra use for a compass is demonstrated in FIG. 1-16, where it is being used to mark a pattern that duplicates the shape of a piece of molding. Here, accuracy calls for holding the tool almost perpendicular and making sure that the line of the angle between the points is constant.

A compass has limits; the amount you can spread its wings determines the maximum radius you can establish for an arc or circle. If you wish to work

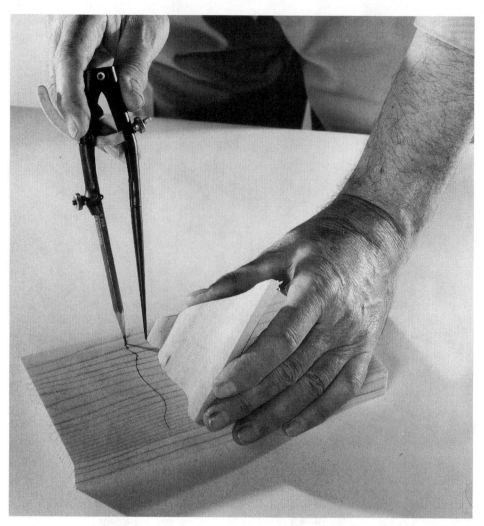

***Fig. 1-16*** *Duplicating the profile of a piece of molding is easy with a compass.*

beyond your compass's capacity, you need an instrument called *trammel points* (FIG. 1-17). Trammel points work in a similar fashion to the compass, but with this tool, separate points are made for attachment to a steel or wooden bar or a rule. The size of the layout is limited only by the length of the mounting component.

Since trammel points are not needed very often, they are not a priority purchase. Most of us improvise when it's necessary to draw an oversized circle. For example, drive a small nail to represent the center of the circle, then attach a pencil by means of a string to determine the radius of the circle. Caution, however, this method does not eliminate human error. A more accurate method is shown in FIG. 1-18. In the top example of the figure, the spacing of the nails driven

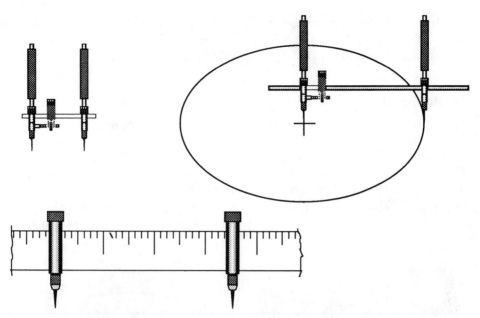

**Fig. 1-17** *Trammels allow drawing oversize circles or arcs. Those being used mount on a steel rod. The ones in the foreground are used on a yardstick or any strip of wood that has similar dimensions.*

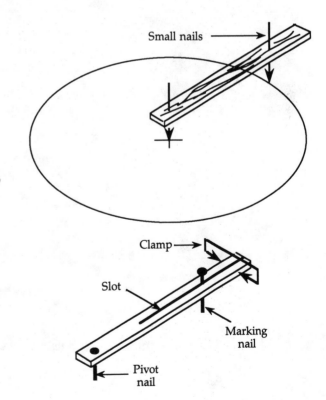

Small nails

**Fig. 1-18** *Pictured are two ways to improvise drawing circles that are beyond the capacity of a compass.*

Clamp

Slot

Marking nail

Pivot nail

through the bar establishes the radius of the circle. In the bottom example, the position of the marking nail is arbitrary so the tool is more flexible. The slot in the bar, which can be any length, is just a straight saw cut.

### Indentation tools

It's often necessary in woodworking to establish an exact location for, say, a hole. The most accurate way to do this is to draw intersecting lines with a square and to indent the intersection with an *awl* (FIG. 1-19). To be sure the drill bit will penetrate where it should, the indent is deepened a bit with a *punch* (FIG. 1-20). When using a depression tool, hold it at an angle so you can set the point exactly on the intersection. Then bring the tool to vertical position before applying pressure—hand pressure with an awl or a light tap with a hammer when using a punch.

*Fig. 1-19*  *An accurate way to establish locations for holes is to draw intersecting lines with a square and then indent the intersection with an awl.*

**Fig. 1-20**  *Deepen the indent formed with an awl by using a center punch to ensure that a drill bit will penetrate where it should.*

# Working hints

### Tracing

It's often possible to avoid doing a layout by using a project component as a pattern. This helps to speed up work by eliminating steps and, even more important, it helps you work accurately when developing parts that must *mate*, join or fit together. The thought applies when constructing joints, as is shown in Chapter 13, but it's also applicable when installing components like hinges. You can't go wrong when you hold the part firmly in correct position and then trace around it (FIG. 1-21). Forming the seat (called a *mortise* ) for the hinge will be done with a chisel, so it's a good idea to retrace the lines by using a square and a sharp knife (FIG. 1-22). The knife will sever the surface fibers of the wood so the mortise will have clean edges.

**Fig. 1-21** When laying out the location for a hinge or similar component, use the item itself as a pattern.

**Fig. 1-22** After tracing a component on the stock, go over the lines with a knife. This will make it easy to have clean lines when the depression for the hinge (the mortise) is formed with a chisel.

### Tricks with a square

Any diagonal line that is drawn from the 12-inch mark on the tongue of a steel square to a point on its blade will establish a particular angle. Figure 1-23 shows the graduations to use on the blade for most commonly used angles. Since the angles are complementary, they can be established from a vertical plane as well as a horizontal one. Just mark a perpendicular line from the tongue's 12-inch graduation.

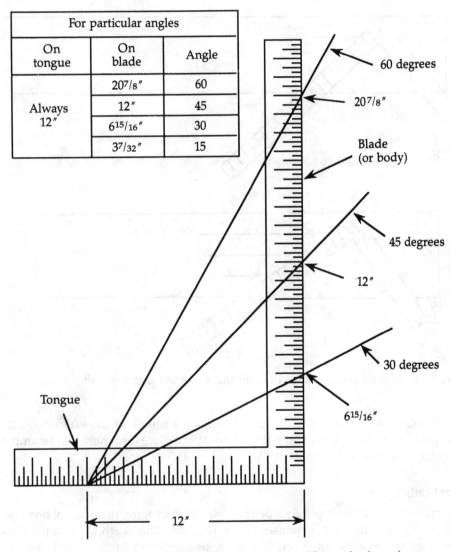

| For particular angles | | |
|---|---|---|
| On tongue | On blade | Angle |
| Always 12″ | 20⅞″ | 60 |
| | 12″ | 45 |
| | 6¹⁵/₁₆″ | 30 |
| | 3⁷/₃₂″ | 15 |

**Fig. 1-23** *A steel square can be used like a protractor. The angles formed are complementary. For example, the line that is 60 degrees from the horizontal plane is 30 degrees from the vertical plane.*

You don't have to worry about fractions when it's necessary to divide a board of odd or, for that matter, even width into a number of strips of equal width. Place a square, or a rule, across the board at an angle that will allow the diagonal line to be divided in even inches by the number of strips that are needed (FIG. 1-24). For example, assuming that you need to cut four strips of equal width from a board that is 11¼ inches wide, place the square at an angle that provides a 12-inch reading. When you mark the board at 3-, 6-, and 9-inch graduations, you will have equally spaced guide points.

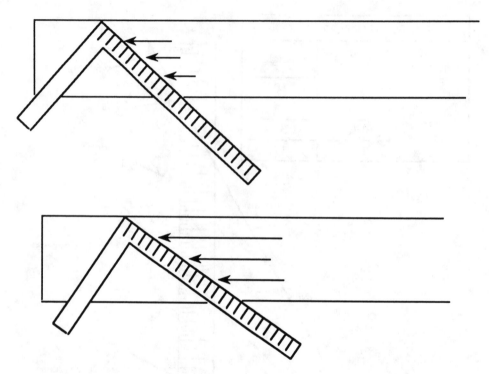

**Fig. 1-24** *A board of any width can be divided into equal spaces by using a square.*

You can find the center of any circle by using a square as shown in FIG. 1-25. The position of the square in Step 2 is arbitrary, but place it so there will be ample angular separation between lines "A-B" and "C-D."

**Duplicating patterns**

The traditional way to duplicate a pattern without damaging the original one is to use the squares method demonstrated in FIG. 1-26. This method is straightforward, allows making an exact, larger or smaller reproduction, and doesn't require artistic ability. Mark a sheet of tracing paper with squares of arbitrary size and tape it over the pattern or, if you wish, draw the squares directly on the pat-

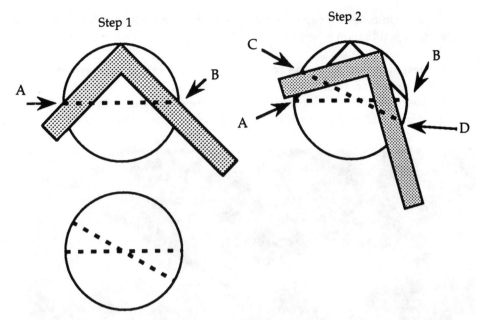

**Fig. 1-25** *The center of any circle can be found using a square. Step 1. Place the square as shown, mark points A and B, and draw the diameter. Step 2. Repeat step 1 with points C and D. Step 3. The intersection of the two lines marks the center of the circle.*

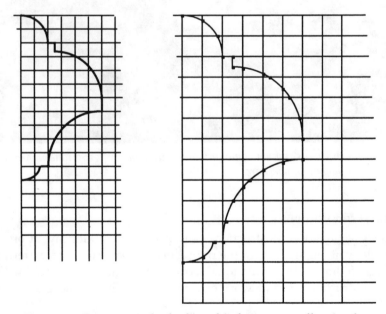

**Fig. 1-26** *Patterns can be duplicated in larger or smaller sizes by using the squares method that is pictured.*

tern. On a second sheet of paper, draw squares that are smaller or larger than the first ones, depending on whether you wish to enlarge or reduce the original pattern.

The next step is to mark the crucial points of the original pattern at similar points on the second sheet. The more marks you make, the easier it will be to connect them correctly. A tool that facilitates connecting the points when many curves are involved is the French curve used by draftsmen (FIG. 1-27).

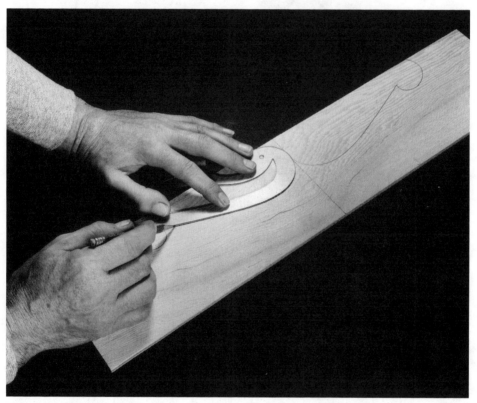

**Fig. 1-27** *French curves, which come in many sizes and configurations, make it easy to do the type of layout shown here.*

### Geometrical constructions

Many times, geometrical constructions can solve woodworking layout problems. For example, you might not have the right tool for a pattern or the pattern might be too large to draw with conventional tools. By becoming acquainted with geometrical constructions, layout work can be more easily and accurately accomplished.

Geometrical constructions sounds complicated, but, as you will see, it's just a way of using a compass, a rule, and a pencil to lay out particular forms or to establish accurate layout points. Figures 1-28 through 1-37 supply the nomenclature of various forms and show how to do some practical, commonly used constructions.

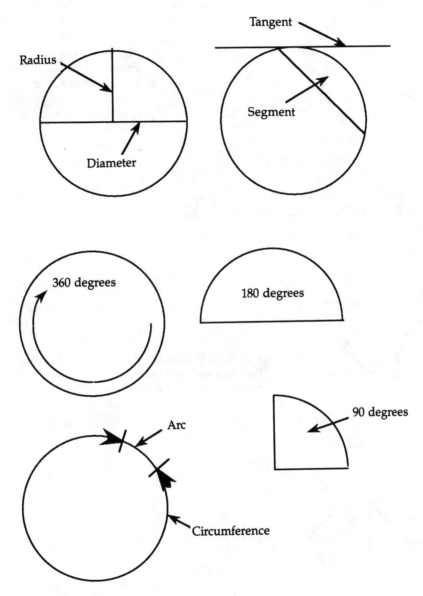

*Fig. 1-28   Nomenclature of a circle.*

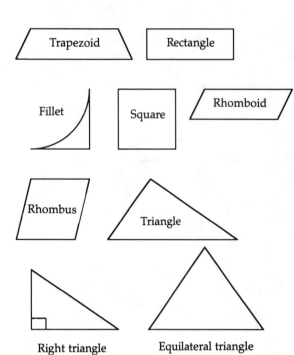

**Fig. 1-29** *Examples of geometrical forms. Note that a right triangle has one 90-degree corner, and an equilateral triangle has three equal sides.*

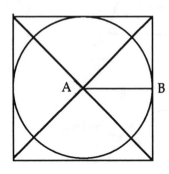

**Fig. 1-30** *Construct a circle in a square by marking the diagonals and then using the distance between A and B as the radius.*

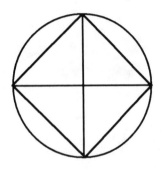

**Fig. 1-31** *Construct a square in a circle by marking perpendicular diameters and then connecting the ends with straight lines.*

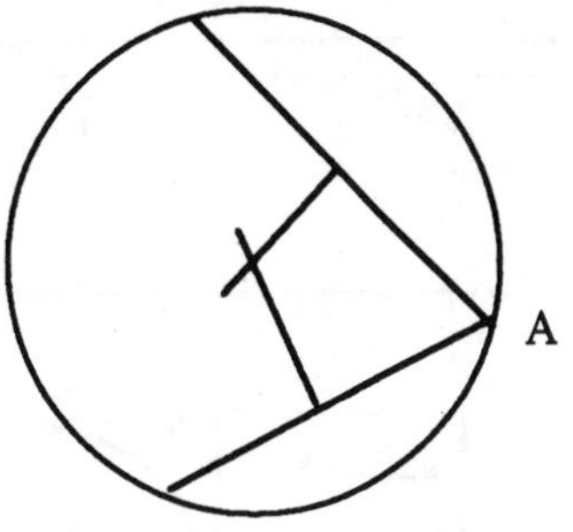

**Fig. 1-32**  *Find the center of a circle by drawing two arbitrary lines from a common point A, then constructing a perpendicular bisector for each line. The intersection at the bisectors is the center of the circle.*

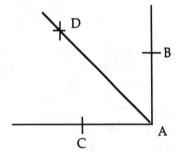

**Fig. 1-33**  *To bisect an angle, set a compass at point A and mark points B and C. From points B and C, strike intersecting arcs at D. The line from A to D bisects the angle.*

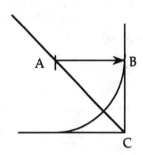

**Fig. 1-34**  *To round off a corner, bisect the angle, mark point A, and use the distance from A to B as the radius of the arc.*

**Fig. 1-35**  *Constructing a perpendicular: From the base point of the perpendicular, use a compass to mark points B and C at equal distances from A. From points B and C, strike intersecting arcs (D). The line from A to D is perpendicular to the base line.*

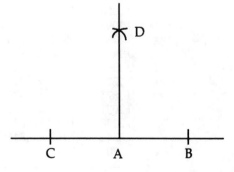

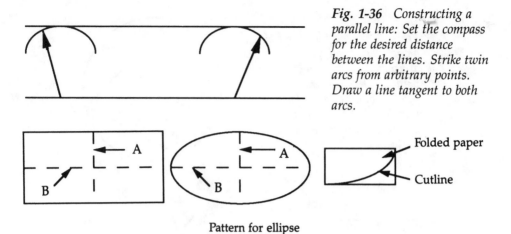

*Fig. 1-36* *Constructing a parallel line: Set the compass for the desired distance between the lines. Strike twin arcs from arbitrary points. Draw a line tangent to both arcs.*

Pattern for ellipse

*Fig. 1-37* *Making a pattern for an ellipse: Draw a rectangle using the major (B) and minor (A) axes of the ellipse. Fold the paper on both axes, draw and cut a suitable curve, and unfold the paper.*

## Decimal equivalents

Table 1-1 lists the decimal equivalents of common fractions. This information will be handy when you get to drilling chores and when you come across mathematical problems in your work. The formula for changing a fraction to its decimal equivalent is pretty simple. Just divide the numerator by the denominator. For example, to change $3/16$ to its decimal equivalent, divide 3.000 by 16. The answer is 0.1875.

### Table 1-1. Decimal Equivalents of Common Fractions

| | | | | | | | |
|---|---|---|---|---|---|---|---|
| $1/64$ | 0.0156 | $17/64$ | 0.2656 | $33/64$ | 0.5156 | $49/64$ | 0.7656 |
| $1/32$ | 0.0313 | $9/32$ | 0.2812 | $17/32$ | 0.5312 | $25/32$ | 0.7812 |
| $3/64$ | 0.0469 | $19/64$ | 0.2969 | $35/64$ | 0.5469 | $51/64$ | 0.7969 |
| $1/16$ | 0.0625 | $5/16$ | 0.3125 | $9/16$ | 0.5625 | $13/16$ | 0.8125 |
| $5/64$ | 0.0781 | $21/64$ | 0.3281 | $37/64$ | 0.5781 | $53/64$ | 0.8281 |
| $3/32$ | 0.0938 | $11/32$ | 0.3438 | $19/32$ | 0.5938 | $27/32$ | 0.8438 |
| $7/64$ | 0.1094 | $23/64$ | 0.3593 | $39/64$ | 0.6093 | $55/64$ | 0.8594 |
| $1/8$ | 0.125 | $3/8$ | 0.3750 | $5/8$ | 0.625 | $7/8$ | 0.8750 |
| $9/64$ | 0.1406 | $25/64$ | 0.3906 | $41/64$ | 0.6406 | $57/64$ | 0.8906 |
| $5/32$ | 0.1562 | $13/32$ | 0.4063 | $21/32$ | 0.6562 | $29/32$ | 0.9063 |
| $11/64$ | 0.1719 | $27/64$ | 0.4219 | $43/64$ | 0.6719 | $59/64$ | 0.9219 |
| $3/16$ | 0.1875 | $7/16$ | 0.4375 | $11/16$ | 0.6875 | $15/16$ | 0.9375 |
| $13/64$ | 0.2031 | $29/64$ | 0.4531 | $45/64$ | 0.7031 | $61/64$ | 0.9531 |
| $7/32$ | 0.2188 | $15/32$ | 0.4689 | $23/32$ | 0.7189 | $31/32$ | 0.9688 |
| $15/64$ | 0.2344 | $31/64$ | 0.4844 | $47/64$ | 0.7344 | $63/64$ | 0.9844 |
| $1/4$ | 0.250 | $1/2$ | 0.5 | $3/4$ | 0.750 | 1 | 1.000 |

# 2
# Safety

Safety is a habit to adopt immediately. It is important to accept that tools don't think; they will work on any material and that includes you. Shop accidents can be traced to casualness, to haphazardness, and to overconfidence, which frequently develops along with expertise. The latter thought is fact. Statistics show that as many, if not more, professional woodworkers are hurt than beginners. The degree of safety does not necessarily increase in proportion to the amount of time spent using a handtool or a machine.

Generally, we are less afraid of handtools than power tools. The noise generated by power tools makes us apprehensive. Handtools conversely, are quiet, so we're a bit more relaxed when using them; that state of mind can lead to problems. It's true that damage caused by incorrect use of a handtool might be less serious than being hurt by a power tool, but the point is there must be no damage at all. Smacking a thumb with a hammer, or lacerating a finger with a handsaw, or stabbing your hand with a screwdriver or knife are not life-threatening experiences, but they are far from pleasant. Regard every tool as a disinterested aid that requires guiding and deserves respect.

There is a correct way to use any tool. Often, and this applies more to power tools than handtools, manufacturers include detailed descriptions of the features of the machine and safety factors that apply specifically to the unit. Study the literature, especially where it relates to guards, and accept it as gospel.

Maintain tools in pristine condition and keep them as sharp as they must be to function properly. A dull tool is hazardous because it requires more pressure to perform, creating the possibility that your hands might slip. When using tools like knives or chisels, work so you will be pushing the implement away from your body. If you do slip, the cutter won't be directed at you.

While a screwdriver can be used to pry the lid off a can of paint, it won't do to try to use it like a chisel. Similarly, a crosscut saw is designed to cut across wood grain, but because it has teeth, it will also cut with the grain, although not as efficiently or as easily as a ripsaw. Wood chisels should not be used as pries nor should a common nail hammer be used to drive case-hardened nails or railroad spikes. The point is, use tools for the jobs for which they were designed.

## Proper dress

It may seem like overkill to have a special shop uniform, but it is important for both cleanliness and safety. Wear clothes that fit snugly. Billowing materials can snag against tools and can be caught by rotating cutters. Heavy, nonslip shoes, preferably with steel toes, are advisable. Gloves are not practical and anything like a necktie or scarf is a potential hazard. Rings, wristwatches, bracelets—any adornment—must not be worn when doing any kind of shop work. Provide a cover for your hair, regardless of its length, to protect against dust as well as for safety.

## Shop environment

Maintain the working area as you would a room in the house. Tables, benches, tool surfaces, and the floor, should always be free of litter. A shop-type vacuum cleaner, available in various sizes and price ranges, is an important piece of equipment. Most models have a port for the hose so the unit can also function as a blower to remove dust and dirt from tight corners.

Frequently remove the dirt and gummy substances that accumulate on tool tables. Cleaning solvents, used carefully according to the directions on the container, are often sufficient to return the table to proper condition. In extreme cases, you can go over surfaces with a pad sander or even emery paper that is wrapped tightly around a block of wood. Afterwards, wipe the table with a lint-free cloth and apply a coat of paste wax. The wax application should be repeated periodically to keep tables protected and to help workpieces move smoothly and easily on its surface.

Maintain the cleanliness of the shop as you work. It can be discouraging to find that you must do extensive cleaning before you can start a project.

## Caring for eyes, ears, and lungs

Most woodworkers do not need much coaxing to wear safety goggles or a face mask to protect their vision, but it's often a chore to convince them that their lungs and ears are also vulnerable to damage. It is accepted today that headphone-type hearing protectors are as necessary in a home shop or when using an outdoor gasoline-powered machine as they are in industry. Damaging high frequencies can be generated by electric motors and the cutters they drive, by air movements, and by the work sounds that are part of woodworking. The effects are cumulative; each exposure contributes to possible ear damage. Good hearing protectors will screen out damaging sound waves but won't interfere with normal conversation or shut out the normal woodworking noises you should hear.

Don't assume that you need a dust mask only when doing extensive sanding chores. Many operations, like sawing and drilling, can produce waste particles that you should not breathe in. Remember that a dust mask is only as good as its filter, so be sure to replace the filter or clean it, if that's the procedure, as often as necessary. Some dust masks are disposable, economical, and easy and comfortable to wear even in conjunction with safety goggles. Be aware though that not all products protect you against toxic fumes.

The products that are displayed in FIG. 2-1—safety goggles, face mask, hearing protectors, dust mask—are as important as any tools that are needed in a shop.

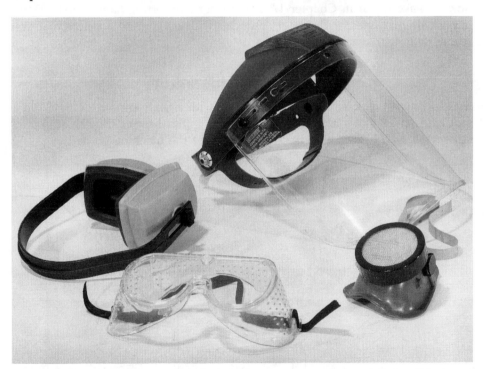

**Fig. 2-1** *Face mask, dust mask, safety goggles, hearing protectors—all should be in your shop.*

## Shop behavior

The primary rule of shop behavior is: Always be alert. The work you are doing and the tool you are using should have your complete attention. Don't do shop work if you are tired, upset, after taking medication, or while drinking alcoholic beverages.

The workshop is not the place for socializing. Don't combine working and visiting. Let friends and neighbors know that they must not barge into your shop, especially if they hear a tool running. You don't want to be startled.

Make the shop childproof. Store tools so they can't be used without authorization. It's okay for children to use some tools, but you should be there to supervise. It's also wise not to be generous in allowing others to use your shop and equipment. Remember that you are liable for their safety.

Don't stretch over the tool or your project regardless of the situation. You can be thrown off balance or place your body in a hazardous position. Have someone help you when you are working on a piece that is too large for you to control. Just be sure to explain the procedure to the helper so he or she will know how to cooperate.

Always provide adequate support for the work. Sawhorses (I'll show you how to make a pair in Chapter 17) are fine for supporting large panels. Don't handhold small pieces. It's safer, and you will work more accurately, if you secure them with clamps or a vise.

## Electrical considerations

Stationary power tools are usually supplied with a three-conductor cord and a grounding plug that should be used in a matching three-conductor grounded outlet (FIG. 2-2). If the outlet that is available for the machine is the two-prong

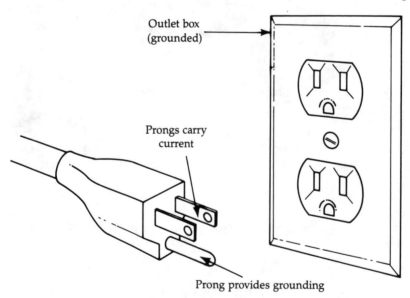

Outlet box
(grounded)

Prongs carry
current

Prong provides grounding

*Fig. 2-2   A three-prong plug is used in a matching grounded receptacle. Never remove or alter the grounding prong in any way.*

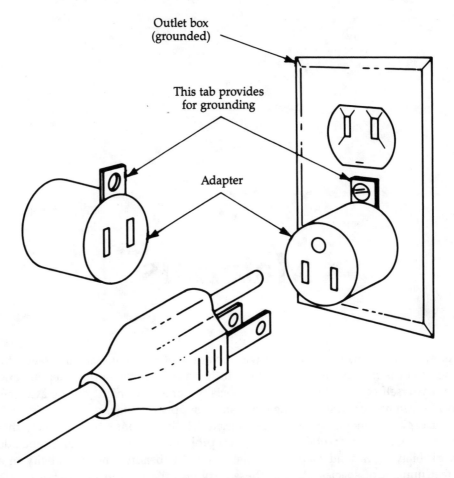

Outlet box
(grounded)

This tab provides
for grounding

Adapter

**Fig. 2-3** *An adapter that will receive a three-prong plug can be attached like this to a two-hole outlet. The tab on the adapter must make firm contact.*

type, an adapter can be used between the plug and the outlet (FIG. 2-3). *Never* remove or alter the grounding prong in any way.

There are several important factors to be aware of regarding adapters. First of all, always consider them a temporary solution, using them *only* if you are sure that the two-prong receptacle is correctly grounded. If the receptacle isn't grounded, the tool won't be either. If you have doubt about whether the system is correctly wired, have it checked by a qualified electrician. Incidentally, the use of an adapter is not allowed in Canada.

# 3

# Materials

Today's woodworkers are blessed with a variety of raw materials and ready-to-use products that are available at local lumberyards, home supply depots, and do-it-yourself centers. Furthermore, specialty items that might not be available locally, can be purchased through craftsman supply catalogs.

Despite technological advances in material "inventions," it's not likely that anything will replace wood as the primary project medium. Its attributes include workability with hand or power tools, durability, beauty, and availability in a great number of species. Add to these attributes the helpful products that are made from wood—like plywood and other type panels, ready-to-use turnings, and milled items like molding—and it's easy to understand why it's so popular.

Wood (lumber) is classified as *softwood* or *hardwood*, but the terms must not be taken literally. Actually, they are botanical designations that distinguish between evergreen-like needle-bearing conifers (softwood) and broad-leaf deciduous trees (hardwood). Pine, fir, redwood, and cedar are examples of softwoods; birch, maple, cherry, and oak are hardwoods. In terms of workability, fir, a softwood, is actually "hard" and poplar, a hardwood, is actually "soft."

## Lumber

*Lumber* designates wood that has been sawed from a log into usable sizes. How the sawing is done affects the visible grain pattern. The most economical system for softwood is called *flat-grain sawing*, in which the log is cut along its length to obtain the maximum number of pieces of various sizes with minimum waste.

Boards produced this way display conspicuous annual rings that appear as U- or V-shapes (FIG. 3-1).

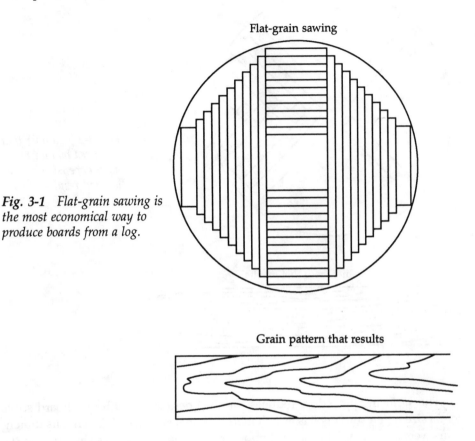

Flat-grain sawing

**Fig. 3-1** *Flat-grain sawing is the most economical way to produce boards from a log.*

Grain pattern that results

A second method of sawing is called *quarter-sawed* or *edge-grained*. With this method, the log is cut into quarters before it is sliced into boards. Lumber produced this way wastes more of the log, adding to the cost of the boards. Quarter-sawed boards have a grain pattern that appears more or less in straight lines (FIG. 3-2).

### Softwood

Lumberyards stock softwood lumber in boards of standard thicknesses and widths and in lengths that increase in increments of 2 feet up to, usually, 20 feet. Lumber is available as *rough*, meaning it hasn't received any attention after it has been sawed; *milled*, signifying ready-to-use products like flooring or molding; and *dressed* or *surfaced*, denoting the sawed board that has been planed smooth so it is ready to use.

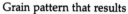
Quarter-sawed

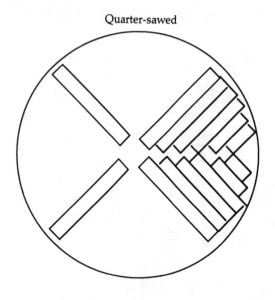

*Fig. 3-2   Lumber that is produced by quarter-sawing is more expensive because the method results in more waste.*

Grain pattern that results

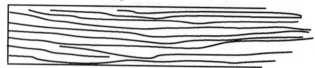

The surfacing procedure reduces the thickness and width of a board so its actual size when you buy it is less than its nominal size, which is what its dimensions were originally. You ask for lumber by nominal size, but as shown in TABLE 3-1, what you will receive has been reduced by planing. For example, if you ask for a 2×8×8, you will get a piece that measures 1¹/₂ inches × 7¹/₄ inches × 8 feet. Only the length will be what you ordered. If you wanted a piece that truly measured, for example, 2 inches × 4 inches, it would have to be custom planed from a board of larger dimensions.

There are various classifications and grades of softwood as noted in TABLE 3-2. These are factors to consider when choosing material for a project, especially since a cost factor is involved. There's no point in paying for wood that can be stained or finished naturally if the project will be painted. A way to save money when making a small project is to buy material that is less than ideal and culling out the good areas.

## Hardwood

Hardwood is available in random widths, lengths, and thicknesses. Table 3-3 shows common variations in thicknesses. Because hardwoods are expensive and

### Table 3-1. Nominal and Actual Sizes of Lumber

| Nominal size | Real dimensions |
|---|---|
| 1×2 | $3/4 \times 1^1/_2$ |
| 1×3 | $3/4 \times 2^1/_2$ |
| 1×4 | $3/4 \times 3^1/_2$ |
| 1×5 | $3/4 \times 4^1/_2$ |
| 1×6 | $3/4 \times 5^1/_2$ |
| 1×8 | $3/4 \times 7^1/_4$ |
| 1×10 | $3/4 \times 9^1/_4$ |
| 1×12 | $3/4 \times 11^1/_4$ |
| 2×2 | $1^1/_2 \times 1^1/_2$ |
| 2×3 | $1^1/_2 \times 2^1/_2$ |
| 2×4 | $1^1/_2 \times 3^1/_2$ |
| 2×6 | $1^1/_2 \times 5^1/_2$ |
| 2×8 | $1^1/_2 \times 7^1/_4$ |
| 2×10 | $1^1/_2 \times 9^1/_4$ |
| 2×12 | $1^1/_2 \times 11^1/_4$ |
| 3×4 | $2^1/_2 \times 3^1/_2$ |
| 4×4 | $3^1/_2 \times 3^1/_2$ |
| 4×6 | $3^1/_2 \times 5^1/_2$ |
| 6×6 | $5^1/_2 \times 5^1/_2$ |
| 6×8 | $7^1/_2 \times 7^1/_2$ |

### Table 3-2. Softwood Lumber Grades

| Grade | Description |
|---|---|
| **select** | |
| A | Almost perfect material—Does well when stained or finished naturally |
| B | Like grade "A" but will contain some small defects |
| C | Will contain defects but they can usually be concealed with paint |
| D | More defects than "C"—can be concealed with paint |
| **Common** | |
| #1 | Utility lumber that is sound and free of checks, splits, or warp—will have tight knots and some blemishes |
| #2 | Reasonably sound but will have end-checks, discoloration, and loose knots—should not have warp or splits |
| #3 | Medium-quality construction material—may have all defects—culling out bad parts causes waste |
| #4 | Low quality material with numerous defects, including open knotholes |
| #5 | Lowest on the quality chart—pieces can be used as fillers—considerable waste |
| **Structural** | |
| Construction | Top quality for structural applications |
| Standard | Similar to "construction" but with slight defects |
| Utility | Poor quality—usually requires strengthening with other structural components |
| Economy | Very lowest on the quality scale |

**Table 3-3. Nominal and Actual Thicknesses of Hardwoods**

| In the rough (nominal) | After surfacing (two sides) |
|:---:|:---:|
| 3/8 | 3/16 |
| 1/2 | 5/16 |
| 5/8 | 7/16 |
| 3/4 | 9/16 |
| 1 | 13/16 |
| 1 1/4 | 1 1/16* |
| 1 1/2 | 1 5/16* |
| 2 | 1 3/4 |
| 3 | 2 3/4 |
| 4 | 3 3/4 |

* Can be 1/16" variation. Hardwood thickness often called out in quarters, for example, 2/4 = 1/2", 5/4 = 1 1/4".

sometimes rare, the surfacing procedure does not reduce thicknesses as drastically as it does with softwood. While a rough 1-inch piece of softwood is reduced to 3/4 inch, a similar thickness of hardwood is planed to 13/16 inch. Hardwood thicknesses are often called out in *quarters*—the term meaning 1/4 inch. Thus, 5/4 equals 1 1/4 inch, 3/4 equals 3/4 inch, and so on.

The National Hardwood Lumber Association has established grade standards, shown in TABLE 3-4, to which producers adhere. The amount of clear or usable area in a board is what determines its grade. Hardwood is expensive, so be wise when making a selection. Choose less expensive grades for painted projects. A *select* grade is often adequate for cabinetwork because the interior is not visible. Also, study a cheaper grade when you are making a small project to see if it might contain enough "good" material for your work.

**Table 3-4. Shows Hardwood Lumber Grades**

| Grade | Description |
|---|---|
| *Firsts* | Very fine material for cabinetwork—the wood should be about 92% clear on both surfaces |
| *Seconds* | Rivals "firsts" for cabinetwork but needs to be only about 84% clear on both sides |
| *Firsts and seconds* | Lumber selection of first two grades but should include at least 20% "firsts" |
| *Selects* | One side is not graded but opposite side should be 90% clear—often used for cabinetwork but with some waste expected |
| *#1 Common* | Suitable for interior and less demanding cabinetwork—requirement is that it should be 67% clear on one side |
| *#2 Common* | Often selected for paintable work, some wall paneling and flooring—it should be about 50% clear on one side |

There are more grades of hardwood than those shown in TABLE 3-4. These grades consist of pieces that dealers cut apart to remove defects and sell as *shorts*, pieces that are usually narrow in width and short in length. These shorts are often suitable for small projects or project components.

**The board foot**

The *board foot* is the accepted unit of measurement for lumber. It indicates a piece of wood that has nominal dimensions of 1 inch × 12 inches × 12 inches. In a board foot, the amount of material, not the shape, determines quantity. For example, a 1 inch × 6 inch × 6 foot board equals 3 board feet, as does a 1 inch × 12 inch × 3 foot piece. To determine the board feet in any piece of lumber, multiply its length in *feet* by its thickness and width in *inches* and divide the result by 12.

Some materials are priced and called for by length only (linear foot). These include such items as trim stock, moldings, furring strips, and dowels. Lumberyards will often stack boards by size and post a price per piece.

# Plywood

Plywood has many advantages. It is real wood that is manufactured into large panels, usually 4 feet × 8 feet, that have great strength in relation to their weight. Most plywood is made by peeling logs on a giant lathe to produce veneers of particular thickness. The veneers are bonded in odd directions so the grain of one ply is at a right angle to the next one. This *cross-ply construction* provides strength that solid wood lacks. A board has strength along the grain but is comparatively weak across the grain. The cross laminations of plywood provide with-the-grain strength in both directions. Another important factor is the size of available panels. You can easily provide a one-piece top for a table or bench by using plywood. Because solid lumber has width limitations, using it to form a similar slab calls for gluing pieces together, which requires time and effort.

There are differences in the *cores* of plywood, the inner layer of wood onto which veneers are glued. The most common type of core construction consists of an odd number of veneers with variations in the number and the thickness of the plies. Lumber, or solid core plywood, has interior material that is much thicker in relation to the surface veneer or to the *cross-banding*, or cores, if any is used. The advantage of a solid core has to do with appearance and workability. Often, edges on plywood with a solid core are suitable enough to be left exposed, facilitating installation of dowels or hardware, like hinges. Veneer core plywood does not lend itself too well to such applications, and the edges are seldom attractive enough to be left as is.

Some of the methods for treating veneer core plywood are shown in FIGS. 3-3 and 3-4. As shown, plain or shaped strips of wood or suitable moldings can be glued on as covers, or adhesive-backed wood banding can be used. The banding, which is thin veneer, is available in many species to match surface veneers and in

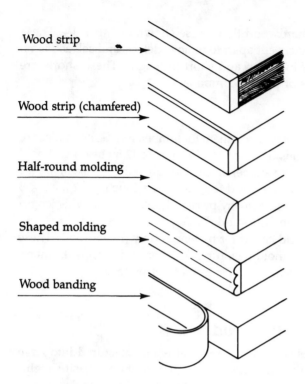

Wood strip

Wood strip (chamfered)

Half-round molding

Shaped molding

Wood banding

*Fig. 3-3* *Methods that are used to conceal plywood edges.*

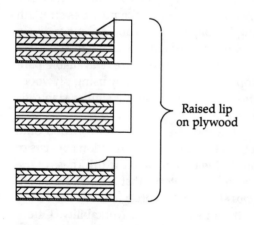

Raised lip on plywood

*Fig. 3-4* *Other methods that can be used to conceal plywood edges. They make the panel look thicker and can provide a lip.*

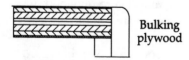

Bulking plywood

various widths. The banding requires heat for installation but it can be supplied by an ordinary household iron. This banding is very flexible and can be used on curved as well as straight edges.

### Plywood grades

Plywood is available for interior or exterior applications in the grades listed in TABLE 3-5. All panels are, or should be, stamped to reveal the construction. Softwood plywood might have surface veneers of Douglas fir, pine, redwood, and numerous other species. This type of plywood is suitable for cabinetwork, furniture projects, and various phases of house construction. Another important factor, in relation to the proposed project, is the choice of surface veneer, which also adheres to a standard grading program (TABLE 3-6).

#### Table 3-5. Plywood Grades

| Grade | Veneer quality | | | Applications |
| | Face | Back | Plies | |
|---|---|---|---|---|
| *Exterior* | | | | |
| A-A | A | A | C | When the project requires a good appearance on both sides—good for signs, fences, furniture |
| A-B | A | B | C | A good substitute for A-A if the appearance of the project on one side is not important |
| A-C | A | C | C | Has one good side—good for structural applications, fences, outbuildings |
| B-C | B | C | C | Utility projects—outbuildings, some fences, a base for other coatings |
| Siding 303 | C | C | C | Variety of surface textures and groove paterns—good for fences, screens, unique touches on projects |
| MDO | B | B-C | C | (Medium density overlay)—good for built-ins, signs, excellent base for paint |
| *Interior* | | | | |
| A-A | A | A | D | Door for cabinetry, built-ins, projects where both sides of the material will show |
| A-B | A | B | D | Can be substituted for A-A when back surface is not important |
| A-D | A | D | D | Face is finish grade—use for paneling, built-ins, backing for projects |
| B-D | B | D | D | Utility grade—okay for backing, cabinet sides |
| C-D | C | D | D | Structural uses and sheathing—unsanded—often used for subflooring |

### Table 3-6. Plywood Veneer Grades

| Grade | Description |
|---|---|
| A | Smooth surfaces—paintable—neat repairs are allowed—will take a natural finish on less demanding projects |
| B | Tight knots and circular repair plugs are allowed |
| C | Larger knotholes allowed (1″ to 1¹/₂″)—total area of blemishes limited by industry standards—some splits allowed |
| C (plugged) | Improved "C" veneer—width of splits limited to ¹/₈″—knotholes and other blemishes can't be more than ¹/₄″ × ¹/₂″ |
| D | Limited number of splits allowed—knots and knotholes can be as large as 2¹/₂″ |

### Hardwood plywood

Hardwood plywood is superior material with surface veneers that can range from mahogany, oak, walnut, and other familiar woods to the most exotic of imported species. Grades have been established to control the appearance and the quality of the product. The grading system, which can apply to one or both of the surfaces of the panel, is as follows:

- #1—custom grade, is free of defects but the surface of the panel, so long as color and grain are carefully matched, can be more than one piece.
- #2—departs from the custom grade in that matching is not considered overly critical.
- #3—is suitable for a painted project, but a clear finish is not recommended since some blemishes, like streaks or stains, are allowed.
- #4—a utility grade, will have knots and might show discoloration.
- #5—often referred to as a "backing grade," has negative appearance elements such as large knots and even splits.

### Unusual surfaces

Plywood panels with textured surfaces, like the example in FIG. 3-5, can be used to add decorative touches to many projects. Although textured plywood panels are designed for use mostly as wall paneling and house sheathing, there is no reason why they can't be used for projects in or outside the house. A plant container, for example, will be more attractive if its surfaces are textured.

Another product of interest is *Medium density overlaid* (MDO), a type of softwood plywood with baked-on phenolic resin surface. Although the material is intended for use as a house siding, its exceptional paintability makes it suitable for in-the-shop projects.

# Hardboard

*Hardboard* is made by cutting logs into small chips that are then, by a special process, reduced into separate fibers. The fibers are formed into a wet blanket, or *mat*,

**Fig. 3-5** *Various types of textured plywood are sold as house siding, but that doesn't negate their use for in-the-shop projects.*

that is subjected to tremendous pressure and heat. *Lignin,* an organic substance forming the essential part of woody fiber, bonds the mat into a dense, uniform panel that is tough, durable, and resistant to moisture and abrasion. Since the panel is free of grain or knots, it has strength in all directions. This type wood can be planed and drilled, and its smooth, hard surface is excellent for painting.

Hardboard is available as *standard, tempered,* and *service.* Standard is the basic panel. The tempered variety has been treated with chemicals and heat to make it stronger, more durable, and highly resistant to rough treatment and extremes in weather. The service panel is economical, but it has less density, is lower in weight, and has less strength than the standard.

Hardboard panels that are designated as *S2S* are smooth on both sides, whereas panels labeled *S1S* have a screen impression on one surface. Common panel size is 4 feet × 8 feet and its thickness range is from 1/16 inch to 3/4 inch. Hardboard is suitable for furniture, cabinet components, and tops of counters and workbenches. There is more to the product, too. It can be embossed in various ways, and treated to simulate the grain pattern of species like oak, walnut, cherry, and others. A product you are probably familiar with is perforated hardboard. Such hardboard panels have uniformly spaced holes for metal or plastic fixtures for hanging tools or other items.

Filigree panels, which can be used for special effects, are also available. These panels are die-cut to show patterns like cloverleafs, diamonds, rosettes, and so on. These are often used for projects like dividers, screens, grilles, louvers, and accent panels.

## Particleboard

Particleboard and hardboard are closely related in that they are both made of wood and manufactured by similar processes. Particleboard, however, is made from large particles of wood instead of fibers. Many materials that might be considered waste, like wood shavings, chips, and sawdust, are *recycled* to make particleboard.

The raw material is mixed with a resin-type adhesive and, after being formed as a mat, is heated and pressed into dense panels that are smooth on both sides. The most common has a medium density, but there are options for special purposes. The standard panel size is 4 feet × 8 feet and ranges in thickness from 1/8 inch to 2 inches.

Particleboard is economical, free of grain, strong, and offers a good base for finishing with paint. A popular application is as a base material for veneers and plastic laminates. Particleboard is easy to work with in the shop using hand or power tools, but it will not hold nails or screws as well as lumber or plywood, especially if the fasteners are driven into its edges.

## Ready-mades

The term *ready-mades* is used to designate commercial products that can be used as is, as project components. Some, like dowel pegs, serve a utilitarian purpose, being designed for use in, for example, *edge-to-edge joints*. Others, like those listed in FIG. 3-6, are available when you choose not to make them or when you are limited by available equipment. These products are available individually, but it's economical and more practical to buy a variety of them in a kit complete with storage bins, like that pictured in FIG. 3-7. Standard moldings, some of which are shown in FIG. 3-8, can also be viewed as ready-mades.

These days, not having a lathe does not prevent you from including wood turnings in your projects. Many supply centers display a variety of turned components like the ones shown in FIG. 3-9. Some have a specific application, like those made as components of stairway rails. Whatever their prime purpose, they can be modified, when necessary, to satisfy another need, such as using a baluster with its top area removed as a leg for a table.

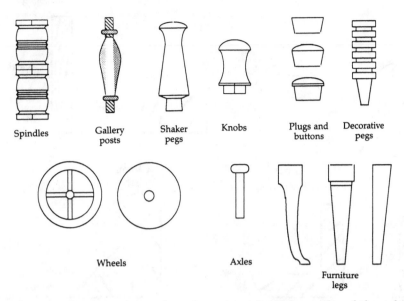

Spindles    Gallery posts    Shaker pegs    Knobs    Plugs and buttons    Decorative pegs

Wheels    Axles    Furniture legs

**Fig. 3-6**  *Ready-mades, such as these pictured, can be purchased through craftsman supply catalogs if not available locally.*

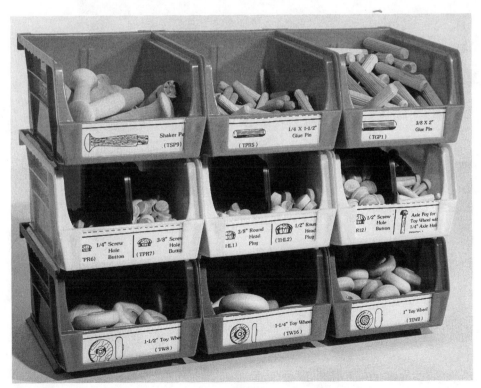

**Fig. 3-7**  *Buying ready-mades in kits is economical and practical.*

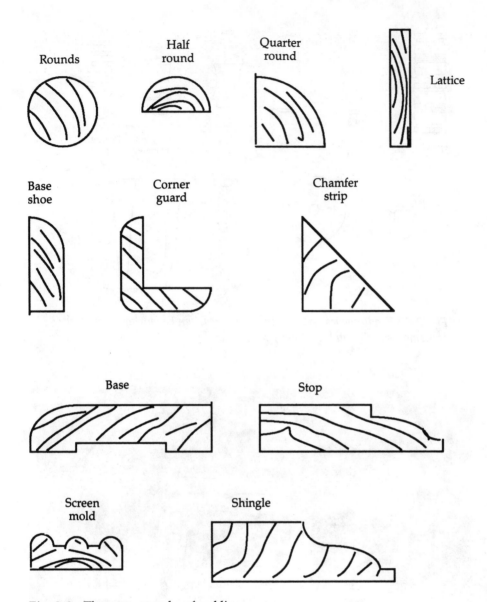

Rounds

Half round

Quarter round

Lattice

Base shoe

Corner guard

Chamfer strip

Base

Stop

Screen mold

Shingle

*Fig. 3-8  These are examples of moldings.*

**Fig. 3-9**  *The beginning woodworker doesn't have to depend on a lathe, not when ready-mades like this are available.*

# 4

# Sawing by hand

The modern, efficient saw had its start with the advent of the iron age. The steps in the development of steel, plus the sophisticated technology in treating the material, have resulted in the super handsaws that are now available. Some of the more commonly used saws are shown in FIG. 4-1. It is true that any saw will cut any wood, and there is definitely an overlap of function among some concepts, but using the *right* saw for particular applications leads to easier, more quality work. It isn't necessary to acquire a plethora of saws immediately. Start with essentials like a *crosscut* and a *ripsaw*, both of which look like the one in FIG. 4-2. Add others as they are needed.

## Saw blades

A saw can sever wood because it has *teeth*. It cuts more freely and is easier to use because the teeth are *set*. The teeth are alternately bent in opposite directions away from the body of the blade. This results in the *kerf*, the groove formed in the wood when sawing, being wider than the thickness, or gauge, of the blade (FIG. 4-3). Sawing can be done without blade-set, but stroking the tool is more difficult because the blade rubs constantly against the sides of the kerf.

Relief for the blade can also be provided by a manufacturing technique called *taper-grinding*. This innovation may be found on high-quality, expensive saws where the back edge of the blade is thinner than the toothed edge. A cross-section of the blade would resemble a very thin triangle. Such a saw might even have a secondary taper running from the handle end to the toe. Taper-grinding makes it possible to minimize the degree of set on the teeth, resulting in a saw

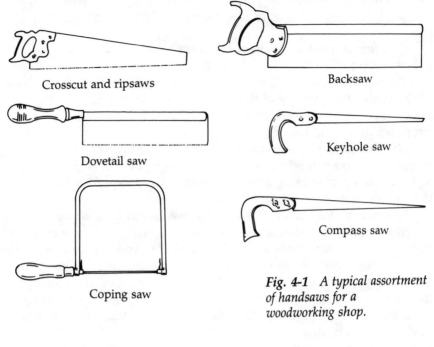

Crosscut and ripsaws

Backsaw

Dovetail saw

Keyhole saw

Coping saw

Compass saw

**Fig. 4-1**  *A typical assortment of handsaws for a woodworking shop.*

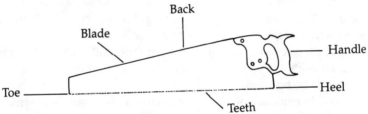

Back

Blade

Handle

Toe

Heel

Teeth

**Fig. 4-2**  *Nomenclature of crosscut and ripsaws.*

**Fig. 4-3**  *The kerf is the width of the cut made by the saw blade. It is determined by the gauge of the blade and the amount of set on its teeth.*

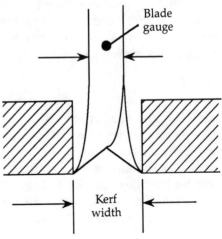

Blade gauge

Kerf width

that produces smoother cuts. The design also contributes to effective distribution of blade thickness, which helps to achieve good balance and flexibility while cutting.

*Crowning* is a design element that isn't found on all handsaws, but many experts regard it as a sign of special quality. A silhouette of a crowned saw shows that the teeth follow a gentle arc instead of a straight line from the toe to the heel of the blade. The purpose of the arc is to obtain maximum cutting effect with minimum drag. Fewer teeth come into contact with the wood, but those that do, cut faster, deeper, and easier.

My personal feeling, regardless of whether a crowned saw cuts faster, is that it contributes to a natural stroke. This reduces fatigue and helps you saw in good style. Good, clean stroking promotes proper use and prolongs the keenness of the cutting edges.

Personal reaction to a tool is a factor that is part of woodworking. Given a selection of tools with similar characteristics, you will most often choose the one that appeals to you visually and that feels good in your hands as you work.

The degree of flexibility that a quality saw should have is achieved by a manufacturing process called *tensioning*. The blades are rolled and hammered along the center areas to provide a built-in tension that keeps the blade straight and in good balance. By conducting the following simple test, you will reveal if the blade has been treated correctly. Simply brace the toe of the blade against some convenient stop and bend the blade by pulling up on the handle. Set a straight edge across the blade at its center point and sight to determine if there is a slight bow across its width. If the bow appears and is uniform, you can assume that the tension is right. An uneven bow will indicate poor quality. The tension feature is important because it's the saw's spring-back effect that helps to keep the blade straight when it is being used.

The best visible evidence of good workmanship in a saw is the finish on the blade and handle. This is an area where you can make a judgment by sight and feel. A good polish on the blade augments the relief created by tooth-set and taper-grinding, thus minimizing friction. Some manufacturers are now offering saws with either a conventional finish or an added non-stick coating. The latter treatment makes a saw more costly, but it practically eliminates saw maintenance chores and contributes considerably to smooth stroking.

## Saw teeth

Essentially, the number of teeth per inch, or *points per inch* (PPI) on a saw blade determines whether a saw cuts "coarse" or "fine." To know the true number of teeth per inch, just subtract one from the PPI (FIG. 4-4). What's important in this area is that the greater the PPI, the smaller the teeth will be. More and smaller teeth lead to slower cutting, but smoother results. That's why tools like the *backsaw* and the *dovetail saw*, which are used mostly for forming joints that must be precise, have a lot more PPI than conventional crosscut or ripsaws.

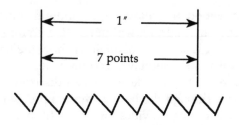

**Fig. 4-4** *The number of saw teeth per inch is one less than the points per inch.*

Also relevant is the fact that the less PPI, the larger the teeth. This allows deeper *gullets*, the space between the tips of adjacent saw teeth, creating larger waste chips. Large teeth also help when sawing green or wet wood.

Teeth on saws are designed to cut in a particular fashion, depending on whether they are made to cut across the grain of the wood or parallel to it (FIG. 4-5). For example, the teeth on a crosscut saw are shaped like sharp, pointed knives so they sever wood fibers cleanly. Conversely, the teeth on a ripsaw have square instead of pointed cutting edges. Each tooth on a ripsaw works like a tiny chisel; thus, it is easier to saw with the grain with a ripsaw. Examine the waste from sawing operations and you will see that a crosscut saw produces sawdust, while a ripsaw spews out small chips of wood.

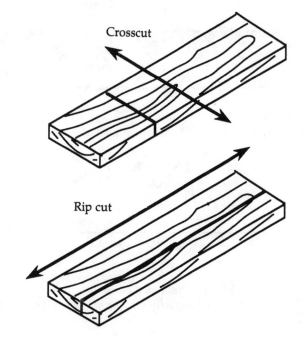

**Fig. 4-5** *Basic saw cuts are the crosscut, made across the grain of the wood, and the rip cut, made parallel with the grain.*

## Saw handles

It may seem picayune to talk about the handle on a saw, but a poor handle—one that isn't centered and comfortable to grip—can affect how you work and the quality of the cut. A good handle is contoured to fit the hand and large enough so you can grip it without feeling cramped.

A visible sign of quality is how the handle is attached to the blade. On good saws, the assembly is accomplished with tubular nuts and bolts. If you were to remove the handle you would discover that the shank on the nuts extends half-way through the handle and fits precisely through holes punched in the blade. This design provides for a snug fit that won't loosen through use. Any saw that has a handle attached with, say, wood screws, isn't worth purchasing.

## Types of saws

### Crosscut saw

Crosscut saws always have more PPI than ripsaws. If you view the teeth head-on, you will see the configuration that is shown in FIG. 4-6. If you sight along the length of the teeth, you'll notice that a V-groove runs down the center. If the saw is correctly set and filed, the groove should be straight enough so you can slide a needle along its path.

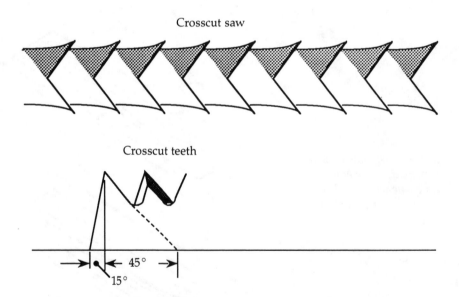

**Fig. 4-6** *The teeth on a crosscut saw have sharp points that sever wood fibers. When correctly set, they form a V-groove through which you can slide a needle.*

The most widely chosen saw by experienced woodworkers is probably the crosscut design because it comes closest to being all-purpose. It does the optimum job when cutting across the grain and when doing angular sawing, as in *miter* cuts (FIG. 4-7). It cuts adequately *with* the grain, but a ripsaw is certainly

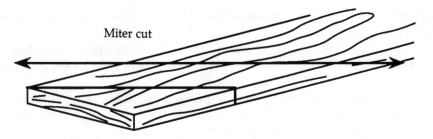

*Fig. 4-7  A miter cut is one that is made at an angle. It is essentially a crosscutting operation.*

quicker for such cuts. A crosscut saw is a good tool for sawing plywood, particleboard, and hardboard because its small teeth do minimum damage to surface veneers.

Blade length, which is the distance from toe to heel, ranges from 16 to 26 inches, with PPI running from 7 to 12. Blade length affects cut-speed simply because short strokes go along with short blades, creating a longer cut time. A reasonable first choice would be a saw that is 24 or 26 inches long, with 8 PPI. It won't cut as smoothly as a saw with 12 PPI, but it's a fast cross-cutter and can be efficiently used for ripping. A short saw, say, 16 inches long (often called a *toolbox saw*), is a handy extra, good for use in tight places and for storing in a tote box for work done outside the shop.

**Crosscutting**   Always saw along a cutline marked on the work with a square and maintaining the kerf on the waste side of the stock (FIG. 4-8). Have the work firmly supported and, when possible, place the board so the annular rings,

*Fig. 4-8  Always saw to a line that is marked with a square or a straightedge. Be sure the kerf is on the waste side of the stock. If you saw on the opposite side or on the line you will reduce the length of the part you need.*

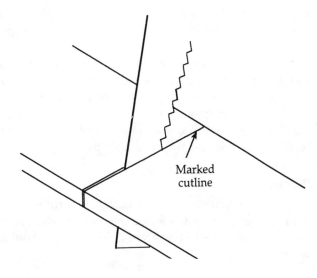

Marked cutline

which can be seen on its end, arc downward. This will minimize the splintering or feathering that can occur along the edges of the kerf. Take a stance so your line of sight is parallel to and a bit to the left or right of the blade depending on whether you are left- or right-handed. The idea is to have a clear view of the cut-line and the action of each stroke.

Grip the board so your thumb can be used as a guide for placing the saw correctly. Hold the saw at about a 45-degree angle (FIG. 4-9) and start the kerf by making a few short strokes with the teeth nearest the handle. Then, gradually increase the length of the strokes until you are using almost the full length of the blade. Shorten the length of the stroke as you approach the end of the cut. Hold the waste so it won't voluntarily drop off and cause the wood to splinter before the cut is complete.

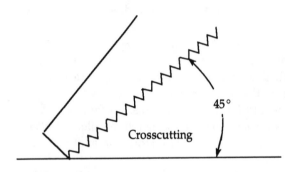

**Fig. 4-9**  *Crosscutting is most efficient when the saw is stroked at about a 45-degree angle.*

A common error is to force the saw, applying excessive pressure to coax the teeth to cut deeper and faster. This can cause the blade to buckle and to move off the line. It also produces rougher cuts and could damage the teeth. Be gentle with the tool; allow it to cut at the pace for which it was designed. Efficient sawing action requires very little pressure, not much more than the weight of the saw itself.

Sometimes, the grain of the wood tends to lead the saw off the cutline. If this should occur, give the handle a slight twist, only enough to counteract the negative grain factor, in the opposite direction as you continue to stroke.

The guide strip, shown in FIG. 4-10 can be used to help ensure accurate sawing. The strip, which can be tack-nailed or clamped to the work, will keep the blade on the line and help you hold the saw vertical as you stroke.

### Ripsaw

The teeth on a ripsaw differ radically from those on a crosscut saw. If you view the teeth head-on, you will see the configuration shown in FIG. 4-11. Each tooth looks and works like a miniature chisel, chipping out its own small portion of the wood.

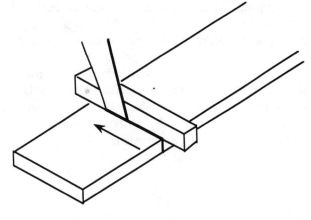

**Fig. 4-10** *A guide strip, tack-nailed or clamped to the work, ensures straight cuts and squares edges on the work.*

Ripsaw

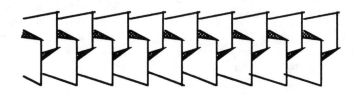

Rip teeth

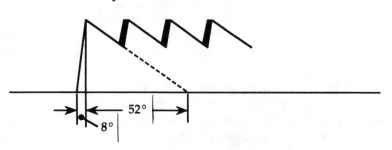

52°

8°

**Fig. 4-11** *The teeth on a ripsaw are filed straight across the face. Each tooth looks and works like a tiny chisel, chipping out its own share of the wood.*

You can check out a ripsaw for quality, but you don't have to make any judgments in terms of size. Most manufacturers offer only one size—26-inches long, with $5^{1}/_{2}$ PPI. This standard size and design has been proven to be the most efficient for sawing parallel to the grain of the wood. One added feature on some ripsaws is the deletion of one point at the toe of the blade. The reason being that this allows kerfs to be started more easily by making a few short strokes with the finer teeth.

**Ripping**    While crosscut saws cut on both down and up strokes, a ripsaw cuts mostly on the down stroke. This suggests a particular kind of stroke action, but it comes naturally if you just allow the weight of the saw to supply most of the tooth contact.

Start ripping as you would when crosscutting but get the kerf started with the forward end of the blade with short strokes. Use the saw at about a 60-degree angle and start making full-length strokes as soon as the starting kerf is established (FIG. 4-12). Smoother cuts will result if you use the blade at about a 45-degree angle when sawing thin stock.

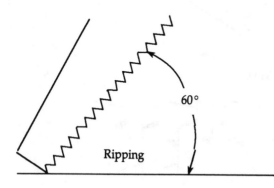

Fig. 4-12    *A ripsaw works best when it is stroked at about a 60-degree angle. This can be reduced to about 45 degrees when sawing thin stock.*

A technique used by many carpenters is to move the blade in a vertical arc as they stroke. This technique is particularly useful on hardwood because fewer teeth contact the work and stroking is easier. In any case, remember that excessive pressure will force the teeth to penetrate more deeply than they should. This will cause the teeth to clog and the blade to buckle. Muscle has nothing to do with achieving cut-quality.

The guide-strip method suggested for crosscutting is also suitable for ripping. Actually, it might even be more applicable since rip cuts are usually long. Speaking of long cuts, it's not unusual for the kerf to close after you have sawed into the board some distance, causing the blade to bind. This problem can be rectified by slipping a slim wedge of wood into the kerf to keep it open (FIG. 4-13).

The most comfortable way to do ripping is to support the board at about knee height so you will be well above the work. Situate the work so the waste will be outboard of the support. If you use sawhorses for support (instructions for making one are in Chapter 17), do not work so you are sawing between the bearing points. The board will likely bend and bind the blade.

## Backsaw

A major application for a backsaw is making the precise cuts that are required when forming wood joints. For this reason, it has many fine crosscut teeth, and a stiff blade that is reinforced along its back edge with a metal spine (FIG. 4-14).

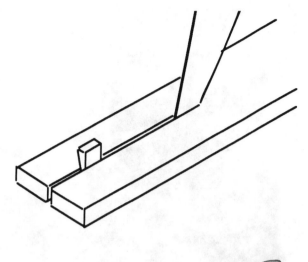

**Fig. 4-13** *It's not unusual on long cuts for the kerf to close and bind the blade. A slim piece of wood or even a screwdriver placed at the start of the cut keeps the kerf open.*

**Fig. 4-14** *A backsaw has small teeth, a stiff blade, and a reinforcing spline along its top edge.*

Common sizes include blade lengths that run from 12 to16 inches, with widths (the distance from the base of the spine to the teeth) running from $3^{3}/_{16}$ inches to 4 inches. The width feature is important because it determines how deep the saw can cut. A good first choice is a 14- or 16-inch unit with 13 PPI. The backsaw is similar to a *miter box saw*; however, the latter is longer, as much as 30 inches, wider, up to 6 inches, and designed for use in a commercial accessory called a *miter box* (FIG. 4-15). This particular miter box is a sophisticated, costly unit, but there are others like those in FIG. 4-16 that can be used with a backsaw, that are more reasonably priced.

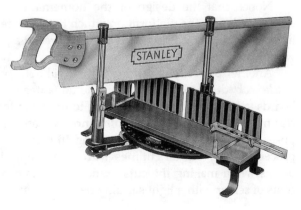

**Fig. 4-15** *Example of a sophisticated miter box. Units like this are usually used with miter box saws which are longer and can cut deeper than backsaws.*

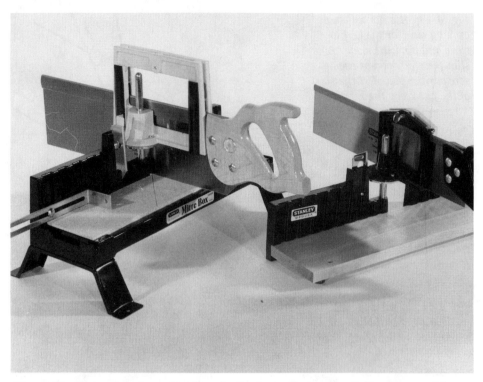

**Fig. 4-16** *Pictured are two examples of miter boxes that are available at reasonable prices. These are used with backsaws.*

Although a backsaw can be used efficiently freehand, and sometimes it must be used so, it's a good idea to take advantage of the accuracy a miter box provides whenever possible. If you can't, or choose not to buy a miter box you can make your own version by following the plan shown in FIG. 4-17. You probably have seen units like this on sale in bargain bins. Don't be tempted. Those I have checked out are poorly made and often lack accuracy.

Notice that the design of the homemade version has the front upright extending below the platform on which the work rests. This is done to provide a lip so the box can be gripped in a vise or braced against the edge of a workbench while you are sawing. The miter box is shown in use in FIG. 4-18.

Another project you can make that will help you saw more accurately is the *bench hook* (detailed in FIG. 4-19). The advantage of this design is that it allows boards to be sawed that are too wide to fit in a miter box. Custom-made accessories must be constructed carefully and accurately if they are to serve their purpose. These are projects where taking 10 minutes to do a 5-minute job is good procedure. Lay out all cutlines with a square and a protractor and use guide blocks when making the cuts. Sand the parts carefully and give them several coats of sealer with a light sanding between applications and after the final one.

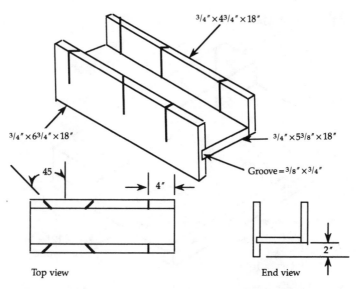

**Fig. 4-17** *Pictured are plans for a miter box that you can make yourself. This one provides for forming left- and right-hand 45-degree miters and square cuts. Assemble the box with glue and #10 × 1¹/₂" screws.*

**Fig. 4-18** *The lip on the front side of the miter box allows it to be gripped in a vise or held against the edge of a workbench. Here, the project is being used with a miter box saw.*

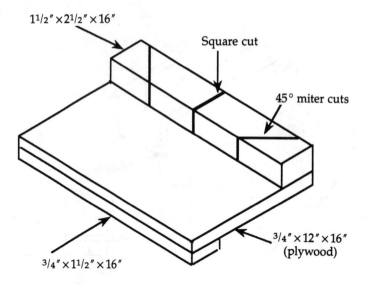

$1^{1}/_{2}'' \times 2^{1}/_{2}'' \times 16''$

Square cut

45° miter cuts

$^{3}/_{4}'' \times 12'' \times 16''$
(plywood)

$^{3}/_{4}'' \times 1^{1}/_{2}'' \times 16''$

**Fig. 4-19**  *The bench hook is used like a miter box but its generous base allows you to saw wider pieces of wood.*

### Dovetail saw

The dovetail saw is a smaller, more delicate version of the backsaw (FIG. 4-20). It's usually available in a 10-inch length and, because it is meant for precise, smooth sawing, has 15 PPI. The name of the tool suggests its basic function, which is to form the slanted cuts that are required for the classic dovetail joint (FIG. 4-21).

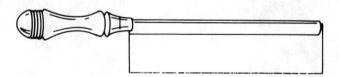

**Fig. 4-20**  *The dovetail saw is a delicate version of the backsaw. Handles are shaped like those used on files and are in line with the tool's spline.*

However, it needn't be limited to this single application. Its size and the fine kerf it produces make it especially useful for sawing small, thin pieces of wood or veneers. Although the dovetail saw isn't intended for use with a miter box, there's no reason why the tool can't function in a similar fashion if you scale down the miter box to suit it. The idea is often adopted by, for example, model makers and others who enjoy making dollhouses or miniature wood structures of any sort.

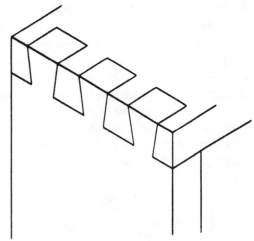

**Fig. 4-21** *The dovetail saw's major use is forming the slanted cuts that are required for dovetail joints.*

## Curve cutters

The primary functions of the *coping saw* (FIG. 4-22) are to shape uniform or irregular curves and to make internal cutouts without a lead-in cut from an edge of the stock. The latter function is possible because the blade is removable. This makes it possible to insert the blade through a hole drilled in the work before it is secured in the frame. A typical application would be forming an oval or circular opening in a one-piece picture frame.

**Fig. 4-22** *A typical coping saw. Blades for coping saws are either looped or have cross pins that engage notched "chucks" at each end of the frame. The chucks can be turned to allow the blade to cut in any direction.*

A typical coping saw blade is $6^3/8$ inches long. Their widths are available from $1/16$ to $1/8$ inch and with PPI ranging from about 10 to 20. Thus, you can select a blade that is appropriate for the job at hand. For example, a thin blade with many teeth is appropriate for fine sawing, while a heavy blade with fewer teeth is more suited for heavy stock and faster sawing. The design of the saw allows the blade to be rotated in the frame so you can adjust sawing direction to suit the cutline. Because of this feature, you can do intricate cutting, like that required for *scroll saw work*, that would not be possible if the blade had a single position. *Spiral* blades are a recent innovation. They will cut in any direction regardless of how they are positioned in the frame.

*Compass* and *keyhole saws* are taper-shaped from heel to toe (FIGS. 4-23 and 4-24). The difference between these two saws is primarily in the size of the blade—the keyhole saw being slimmer and with a sharper point. Because of their design, either saw can start a cut from a small, drilled hole. Thus, for example, you can make a cutout of just about any shape in the center of even a fill-size plywood panel. This, however, is not a limitation. The saws can be used for other jobs like forming scalloped edges on a valance, sawing discs from heavy stock, or cutting straight edges where a larger unit would not be suitable.

**Fig. 4-23**  *A compass saw can form an internal cutout with just a small hole where the point of the blade can start.*

**Fig. 4-24**  *Compass and keyhole saws look alike and have similar applications. The major differences are in the size of the blade and the sharpness of its point.*

A *nest of saws* consists of, usually, three interchangeable blades and a single handle. This is a good way to buy this type of saw because it is more economical than purchasing the units individually. A popular choice for general home and workshop use includes: a 16-inch, 8 PPI utility blade; a 12-inch, 8 PPI compass saw; and a 10-inch, 10 PPI keyhole saw. Another wise choice is a 16-inch blade with crosscut teeth on one edge and specially shaped teeth on the opposite edge that make the blade usable for light pruning chores on trees and shrubs.

# 5

# Sawing by machine

Increasing the scope of the woodworking shop by adding a powered sawing tool like the table saw is a logical step. When you compare crosscutting or ripping by hand with the same jobs done on a machine, you will be impressed with how much faster the work can be done, and with less effort. In fact, all the routine cuts that are shown in FIG. 5-1 can be done more easily with an assist from a power saw. Accuracy, however, is still the operator's responsibility. The machine does not compensate for human error, but it will cooperate by producing square and straight cuts automatically, if the relationship between its components, namely the *miter gauge, rip fence*, and *saw blade*, is correctly established.

The secret to using a woodworking machine efficiently and safely is to view it as a nonthinking device. It is disinterested in how you have measured for a cut and, by the same token, what you place in front of its cutting accessory. If you respect the tool and accept right off that you are the responsible guiding force, you will have taken a major step toward quality production and happy woodworking.

## Table saws

Table saws—despite differences in size, weight, and horsepower—have the same essential characteristics. They drive a circular saw blade that is vertically adjustable and that, with a few exceptions, can be tilted; they employ a miter gauge for crosscutting; they have a fence for ripping operations; and they use a guard, usually a see-through type, that covers the blade as you are sawing. Other features, like those called out in FIG. 5-2, are part and parcel of table saw design. While the

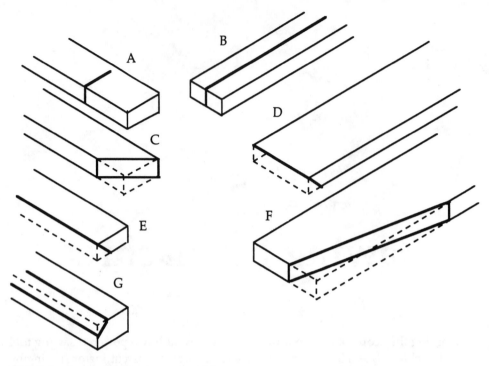

**Fig. 5-1** *Some of the basic woodworking cuts that can be accomplished on a table saw: (A) crosscut; (B) rip cut; (C) miter; (D) cross miter; (E) rip miter, or bevel; (F) taper; and (G) chamfer.*

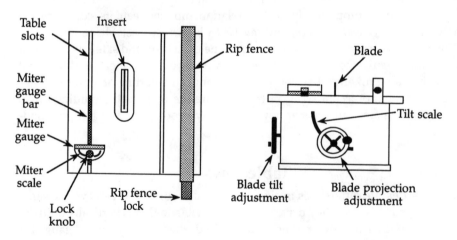

**Fig. 5-2** *Nomenclature of a table saw.*

location and the shape of the controls, like the rip fence lock and the tilt mechanism, may differ, they all operate to control essential adjustments.

Most saws work with a 10-inch diameter blade and conform to the standard of being able to saw through a 2×4 whether the blade is vertical, for a square cut, or tilted to 45 degrees for a bevel. Even today's so-called compact or *benchtop* machines, like the new Skil system shown in FIG. 5-3, meet this criterion. The size of a saw is called out by the diameter of its blade. You might not see much difference in the overall size, table area, or floor space requirements of various machines. For example, the Delta 10-inch Unisaw, which is something of a tradition in the saw field (FIG. 5-4), doesn't require much more floor space than a benchtop tool that is mounted on a commercial or homemade stand. However, space requirements are affected by table extensions that you may wish to add for additional work support. For example, the main table of the Unisaw measures about 27 by 28 inches, but its length can be extended to better than 6 feet by adding an extra-cost extension. A factor influenced by table size is the maximum distance that can be established between the *rip fence* and the saw blade. The greater this distance, the easier it will be to make cuts on panel materials like plywood. Some machines

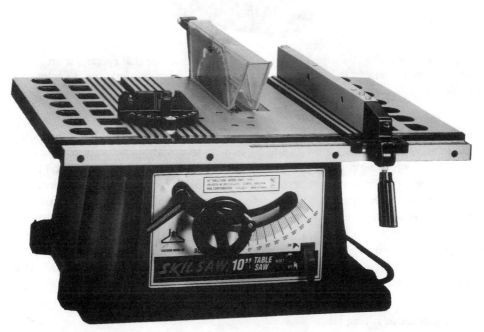

**Fig. 5-3** *Skil Corporation's new benchtop saw operates with a 10-inch blade and has all the features of larger machines. The table is die cast aluminum and measures 17⁵/₈ inches × 26⁵/₈ inches. The machine is expected to sell for about $200.*

**Fig. 5-4** *The Delta 10-inch Unisaw is a floor model machine that operates with a 2- or 3-horsepower motor. Its table measures 27 inches × 28 inches , but with an extra-cost extension, it can be extended to more than 6 feet.*

are equipped with bars or tubes on which the rip fence rides that are longer than the table's width. Thus, ripping capacity is increased without actually adding table area. Why is ripping capacity important? Well, for example, I work quite a bit today with 4-foot- × -8-foot panel materials, requiring 24 inches distance between blade and fence to cut the panel in half lengthwise, and 48 inches distance to halve the panel across its small dimension.

Table size also affects *crosscutting capacity,* which is the distance from the blade to the front edge of the table. If the distance is 12 inches or more, then it is easy to establish good support when crosscutting a standard-size board, that measures 11$\frac{1}{4}$ inches wide.

### Tilting arbor or tilting table

To do crosscutting or ripping so the cut slants (i.e., *cross miters* and *bevels* ), it's necessary to tilt either the table or the saw blade. When the tool has a tilting arbor that allows the blade to be tilted to a particular angle, the work stays on a horizontal plane. When the table must be tilted for angular cuts, the work is still flat on the table, but on the same plane as the tilt.

The question of which design is best is not as debatable as it once was. For one thing, you would have to search hard today, especially among saws that are available to amateur woodworkers, for a unit that is not designed with a tilting arbor. Exceptions are found among multipurpose machines like the Shopsmith where the design does not allow incorporating a tilting arbor (FIG. 5-5).

*Fig. 5-5*  *The Shopsmith multipurpose power tool operates with a tilting table.*

There is no doubt that a tilting arbor is desirable for many sawing operations, but for either type, accuracy depends chiefly on how carefully adjustments are made and how the wood is controlled during the cut.

## Alignment

Alignment refers to the relationship between the adjustable parts of a table saw. Since the components—namely, the table, saw blade, miter gauge, and rip fence, must cooperate in various ways, it is essential to organize them for precise settings. For example to crosscut so the severed edge will be square to the long edges of a board, the angle between the miter gauge and the saw blade must be 90 degrees. For the severed edge to be square to the board's surfaces, the angle between the blade and the table must also be 90 degrees (see FIGS. 5-6 and 5-7).

*Fig. 5-6*  *When the miter gauge is used for a routine crosscut, the angle between its head and the saw blade must be 90 degrees. It's okay to check the setting against a table slot if it's been determined that the saw blade and table slots are parallel.*

*Fig. 5-7*  *When the saw blade is in its normal position, the angle between it and the table must be 90 degrees. Make this check with the blade at its highest position and be sure to rest the blade of the square between teeth on the saw blade.*

If the table slots in which the miter gauge slides are not parallel to the saw blade, there will be a heeling problem (a condition that will cause excessive vibration, inaccurate cuts, and early dulling of the blade). If the rip fence is not parallel—misadjusted so that distance B, as shown in FIG. 5-8, is less than distance A—it will be difficult to make rip cuts and the possibility of *kickback* (the tendency of the blade to throw work back toward the operator) will increase.

**Fig. 5-8** *The rip fence is adjusted so it will be parallel to the saw blade. Distance B equals distance A. There are some exceptions to this rule.*

There can be some slight variation in methods of adjustment among table saws, but the relationship of components and how to check for accuracy is standard. The first step is to check the tool's owner's manual for specific instructions. Accept the manual as gospel for the particular machine. See FIG. 5-9 for adjustments that apply to any saw.

Check these factors carefully and regularly as you use your saw. Do not have the tool plugged in when you are checking alignment or making corrections; as a matter of fact, unplugging your tool when it is not actually being used is wise.

Since you don't have any control over how the saw blade mounts on the arbor, I suggest that the alignment checks start with being sure that the table slots

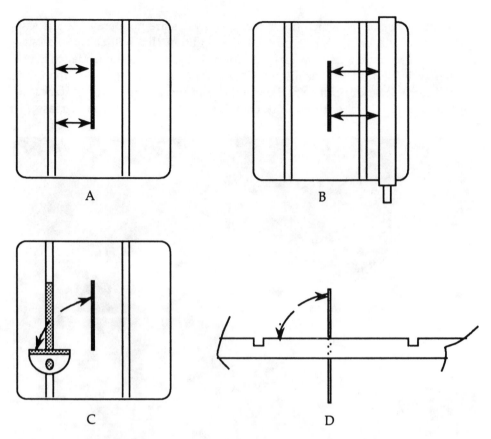

*Fig. 5-9   Be aware of these factors when checking the alignment of a table saw: (A) blade parallel to table slots; (B) rip fence parallel to blade and slots; (C) miter gauge square to blade when at 90 degrees; and (D) blade square to table when at 90 degrees. Follow the instructions in the owner's manual when making adjustments.*

are parallel to the saw blade. There are various methods to use, but a simple, reliable system starts with the setup shown in FIG. 5-10. Raise the blade to maximum projection and then clamp a slim rod or something similar to the miter gauge so it barely touches one saw tooth. If the blade has set teeth, choose one that points toward the miter gauge. Mark the tooth with a felt pen and then rotate the blade by hand until the tooth is at the rear of the insert. Then, advance the gauge to see if the rod touches the tooth as it was at the start. If there is a gap or the rod is forced against the tooth, the table must be rotated to the right or left to set it correctly.

On some saws, the adjustment is accomplished by loosening the bolts that secure the table to the substructure and then nudging the table a bit until the slots and blade are parallel (FIG. 5-11). On other saws, it may be necessary to adjust the internal mechanism that is secured to the underside of the table. The owner's manual will describe the correct method.

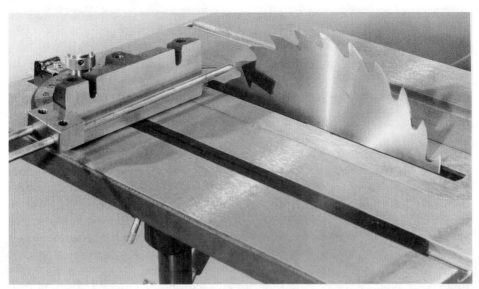

**Fig. 5-10** *This is one way to check for parallelism between the saw blade and the table slots.*

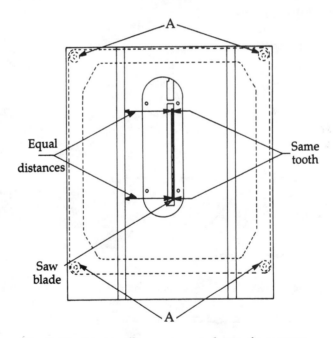

**Fig. 5-11** *It's usually necessary to loosen four corner bolts so the table can be rotated left or right to adjust for parallelism between the blade and table slots. The owner's manual will reveal if there is a different method to use.* Delta International Machinery Co.

The rip fence is secured to a base that rides on rails or tubes of some sort. When several lock bolts are loosened, the fence can be swung to the left or the right so it can be set parallel to the blade. The blade-tilt mechanism will have adjustable *auto-stops* to control the blade's 0- and 45-degree positions. Since the fence design and the tilting arrangement might vary with each machine, it's best to make any necessary adjustments by following the manufacturer's instructions.

**Saw blades**

The table saw is used for the same type of wood cutting that is done with hand-saws, so, because sawing with power doesn't change the characteristics of wood, it is logical that there are as many tooth designs for circular saws as there are for handsaws (FIG. 5-12). The all-steel *combination blade* or *all-purpose blade* is an exception. Such blades, available in a variety of tooth designs, can be used for crosscutting, ripping, and even mitering, but they are primarily convenience blades because they don't produce the best results in any of the cutting categories. Many combination blades have a tooth configuration and deep gullets that make them more suitable for ripping than for crosscutting or mitering. Despite this, they should not be shunned because they are a fair choice for routine carpentry, construction work, and general sizing cuts. Generally, combination blades are a poor choice for sawing plywood.

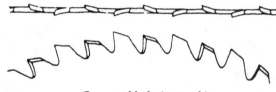

Crosscut blade (set teeth)

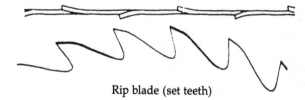

Rip blade (set teeth)

**Fig. 5-12**  *The teeth on typical all-steel circular saw blades.*

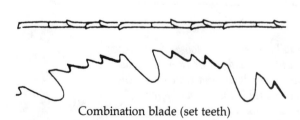

Combination blade (set teeth)

Another type of combination blade adopts the *hollow-ground* concept. Like handsaws, most all-steel blades get clearance in the cut because of set teeth (FIG. 5-13); however, with the hollow-ground concept, the blades are not set, so they produce smoother edges whether crosscutting, ripping, or doing angular sawing. They have clearance in the cut because the gauge of the blade is recessed in concave fashion from the points of the teeth to somewhere near the center of the blade (FIG. 5-14). This type of blade works efficiently only when its projection above the work is greater than is required for conventional blades (FIG. 5-15).

*Fig. 5-13* How a saw blade with set teeth gets clearance in the cut. Without this feature, the blade would do as much rubbing as it does cutting.

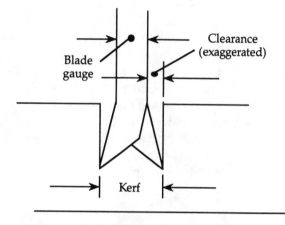

*Fig. 5-14* Hollow-ground blades work without set teeth. They get clearance because an area between the teeth and the center of the blade is ground thinner than the blade gauge.

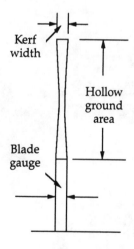

Without this consideration, the blade will not have clearance. The result will be excessive friction that will cause burn marks on both the blade and the work.

Many special *plywood blades* combine the characteristics of the crosscut and hollow-ground blades. They have many, very small teeth with minimum set or

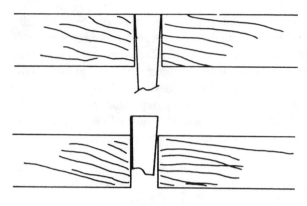

*Fig. 5-15* Hollow-ground blades require more projection above the work than blades with set teeth. Low projection (top) can harm the saw and cause burn marks on the wood. High projection (bottom) provides the necessary clearance.

none at all, and a limited recessed area at the perimeter. Limiting the recess provides more bulk in the body of the blade, which keeps it more rigid while it is cutting, but it also dictates the maximum thickness of stock it can cut, which is usually ³/₄ inch. Plywood blades are specially tempered to resist the abrasive action of the glue lines in the material.

**Tungsten carbide teeth** *Carbide tipped* saw blades, like the example in FIG. 5-16, are super cutters that are now generally available in as many concepts as you will find in all-steel blades. Basic ones are combination units and those specifically for crosscutting or ripping. Carbide tipped blades cost a lot more than other

*Fig. 5-16* Blades with carbide tipped teeth stay sharper much longer than all-steel blades. The blade has expansion slots that guard against distortion that can be caused by overheating.

blades, but when they are correctly used and maintained, they will hold keen cutting edges 20 to 30 times longer than steel blades. Another asset is that the teeth on these blades cut a kerf that is wider than the blade's gauge. Because the teeth are not set (FIG. 5-17), they produce cuts that are much smoother than those made with comparable all-steel blades.

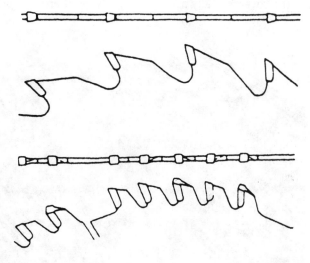

**Fig. 5-17** *The teeth on carbide tipped blades do not have set. They obtain clearance because the cutting edges of the teeth are wider than the gauge of the blade.*

Not all carbide tipped blades are manufactured to optimum standards, so it's important to check the following factors before buying:

- The size of the carbide tips. The larger the tips, the more times they can be sharpened before they must be replaced.
- The braze connection that holds the tips in place. If *pit marks*, or tiny holes, are evident, the blade has not been manufactured to high standards.
- The way the tooth is mounted. It should be seated in a special niche instead of just butted against an edge (FIG. 5-18).

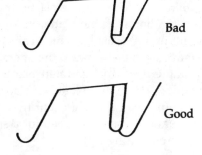

Bad

Good

**Fig. 5-18** *The teeth on a quality product will be set into a special niche, not just brazed to an edge.*

An important factor is that, while tungsten carbide is a very tough material—second only to diamonds in hardness—it is also brittle. Banging the teeth against hard objects can damage them. Handle, use, and store them with care.

### Guard

The guard shown in FIG. 5-19 is a fairly common design for table saws. In addition to the cover, usually a see-through type, there are *splitter* and *anti-kickback fingers*.

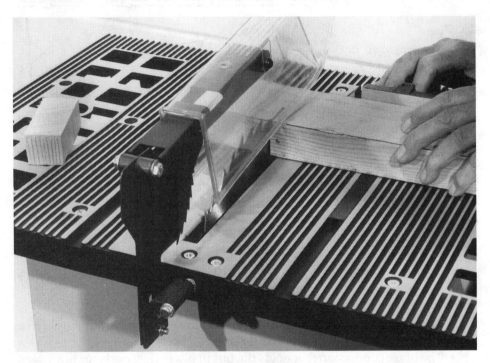

*Fig. 5-19*  *The guard on the saw should lift easily when you are crosscutting or ripping. It is provided for your protection, so maintain it in good working order.*

The cover serves mainly to keep hands away from the rotating blade but it will also deflect any flying debris that might be caused, for example, by the saw blade encountering a loose knot in the wood.

The splitter, which might be plastic or metal, projects above the table, behind and directly in line with the blade. Its purpose is to keep the kerf from closing and thus binding the blade, which can result in kickback (the tendency of the blade to move work back toward the operator). An anti-kickback device may consist of a single or several serrated blades that mount on the guard assembly behind the saw blade. The blade, or blades, are spring-loaded so they normally ride on the surface of the work, but they will dig in to hold the wood should a kickback situation occur. The need for a splitter is more apparent when ripping than when crosscutting.

Mount the guard carefully, following the manufacturer's instructions, and maintain it in perfect working order. There are some table saw operations, one of them being *dadoing* (cutting a groove in your stock), when the standard guard can't be used. At such times you must be especially alert and use extra care to ensure safety.

NOTE: Some of the how-to illustrations in this book show routine sawing operations being done without the guard in place. The photos are posed this way only for the sake of clarity and are not to be viewed as normal procedure. Accept the guard as a valuable safety factor.

## Uses of a table saw

### Crosscutting

Crosscutting is done primarily to bring stock to a specific length or to square the end of a workpiece. To make a simple crosscut, place an edge of the stock firmly against the head of the miter gauge and then move the gauge and the work, as a unit, past the saw blade (FIG. 5-20). Most workers prefer to use the gauge in the left-hand slot, but the table does have two slots, so a choice can be made depending on preference, the size of the work, and by the nature of the cut. You may find in some situations that using the gauge in the right-hand slot will provide more support for the work.

**Fig. 5-20** *Crosscutting is done by holding the work against the miter gauge and then moving gauge and work past the saw blade.*

The general rule is to use one hand to move the miter gauge and the other to keep the work secure. A good stance is directly behind the gauge so as to avoid being in line with the saw blade. Always keep your hands well away from the cut area. This means, for one thing, that you must not try to crosscut pieces that are too small for safe handling. Use a handsaw.

Move the work at a reasonable speed and without pausing until the cut is complete. How fast you can saw is affected by the design of the blade and the hardness of the material. Feed-speed, how fast you move the work, should be just enough to allow the blade's teeth to cut as they should. It's a good idea to slow up a bit toward the end of the cut to minimize the feathering that can occur when the blade exits the work. Don't remove the part that's been cut off until you have turned off the machine and the blade has stopped turning.

Remove the rip fence from the table when you are crosscutting, or lock it well away from the cut area. You don't want cutoffs to be trapped between the blade and fence. Also, don't allow scrap pieces to accumulate on the table.

**Miter-gauge extension** A miter-gauge extension provides extra support for the work and helps you saw more accurately. The most elementary concept is simply a straight piece of wood, mounted onto the miter gauge, that is much longer and a bit higher than the head of the gauge (FIG. 5-21). Most miter gauges are designed to accept extensions. The attachment method might be nuts and bolts that pass through holes or slots in the head of the head of the gauge, or just roundhead wood screws. Some manufacturers even offer an extension as an accessory.

*Fig. 5-21*  *An extension is just a long piece of wood that is bolted or screwed to the face of the miter gauge. It provides extra support for workpieces and makes it easier to saw accurately.*

When the extension is secured, move forward to cut a kerf an inch or so high (see FIG. 5-21). The kerf will serve as a guide so work can be positioned for accurate crosscutting. Use a square to mark the cutline on the work and then align the mark with the kerf so there will be no doubt as to where the cut will occur.

**Cutting to length**   Many projects require several components that are the same length. You can provide them by marking individual pieces and then placing them for the cuts, but this leaves room for human error. It's wiser to devise a setup that will gauge the length of the pieces automatically. A simple, but effective method is demonstrated in FIG. 5-22. Clamp a thick block of wood to the rip fence near the front of the table. Adjust the rip fence so the distance from the face of the block to the saw blade equals the length of the parts you need. Then, butt the end of the work against the block and move it forward to make the cut. You can cut as many pieces as you like, knowing that each will be the same length.

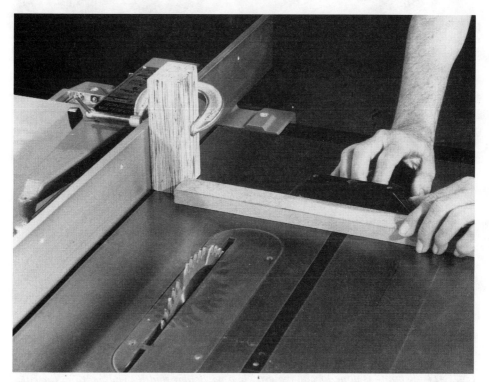

*Fig. 5-22*  *An example of a demonstrated method that automatically gauges the length of cutoffs.*

The rip fence itself must never be used as a stop to gauge the lengths of cutoffs because the cutoffs could become trapped between the fence and the blade, causing them to be twisted and tossed up or back at you. The only role for the rip fence in this application is as a support for the stop block. Using the block provides room between the fence and the blade so the cutoffs won't be captured.

## Ripping

Ripping is the operation that is used to saw material to a particular width. The workpiece is passed between the locked rip fence and the saw blade (FIG. 5-23). In order for the operation to go smoothly, the rip fence and the saw blade must be parallel. However, there is an exception to the rule. Many operators will offset the rip fence so that distance B (see FIG. 5-24) is a fraction more than distance A.

**Fig. 5-23** *Ripping is done to saw material to a particular width. The width of the cut is determined by the distance between the blade and the fence.*

The reason given for the idea is that it allows easier ripping and smoother cuts because it avoids having the "rear" teeth of the blade continuing to rub on the work after the "front" teeth have done the cutting. If you use this method, remember that the fence will have to be readjusted when it is used on the other side of the blade. If not, the offset creates a closed angle between the blade and rip fence, causing the work to bind, and possibly kick back:

**Fig. 5-24** *Some operators adjust the fence so that distance B is a fraction longer than distance A.*

The front rail on many saws is stamped with a scale that can be used to position the rip fence for the cut-width, but its accuracy might be questionable. It's usually wiser to use the scale for an approximate setting and make the final adjustment by actually measuring between the blade and the fence. Measure from the side of the blade facing the rip fence. If you measure from the outboard side, the width of the cut will be reduced by the width of the kerf. If the blade has set teeth, measure from one that points toward the fence. Also, if the fence has been adjusted to provide some offset, take the measurement from the front of the blade.

Rip cuts are started by placing the work firmly down on the front edge of the table and snug against the fence. Usually, the left hand controls the work at the start while the right hand moves the work forward. Once the work is engaged with the blade, the left hand is moved away unless the material is wide enough to allow the hand to help without coming close to the blade. Feed the work steadily until it is past the saw blade. There is no return on a rip cut. The *pass* is complete when the work has passed the blade. Many operators hook the fingers of the feed hand over the rip fence while moving the work forward. It's a wise precaution that guards against slipping.

The fundamental safety rule when doing table-saw work is never to allow your hands to come close to the blade. It's a rule to be especially aware of whenever you are ripping narrow stock. When there isn't enough room to move the stock safely with your hand, the wise alternative is to use a safety device called a *push stick*. Too often, workers will use a piece of scrap as a pusher. It's better than fingers, but won't do the job as efficiently or with maximum safety. It's better to make a special push stick, like the one in FIG. 5-25, that you can retain as a permanent accessory. Two ideas for push sticks that you can make are offered in FIG. 5-26.

*Fig. 5-25* *Always use a push stick when making rip cuts that are not wide enough for safe use of your hands.*

## Miter sawing

There are some frustrating chores in woodworking, and cutting a good miter joint is one of them. The sawing itself isn't any different from other jobs, but the

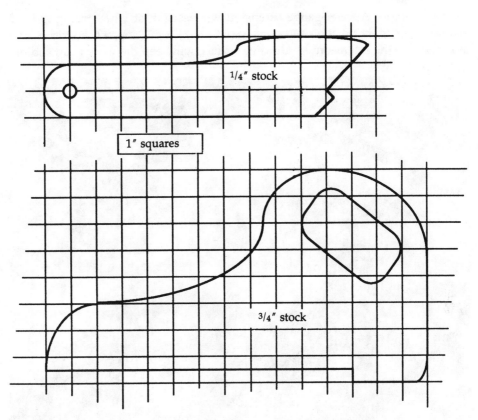

**Fig. 5-26** *Two designs for push sticks that you can make.*

problem is that you won't get away with the least amount of error. If, for example, you are "off" a fraction of a degree when cutting a 45-degree miter, the parts will come together okay, but the angle they form will not be 90 degrees. The single, slight error is multiplied eight times when you have cut parts, say, for a square or rectangular box or frame. The total error becomes frustratingly evident at assembly time. Don't be discouraged, though. The secret to perfect miters is being extremely careful when adjusting the miter gauge and making test cuts on scrap stock before you saw good material.

To do miter sawing, rotate the head of the miter gauge and lock it at the angle you require. Then, as in crosscutting, hold the work firmly in position against the gauge as you make the pass. It's a good idea to mark the cutline on the work with a protractor or triangle so you can judge the accuracy of the cut as you saw.

Two factors that can contribute to inaccuracy even though you've been careful with setting up are: the action of the saw blade will tend to pivot the work around at the forward edge of the miter gauge, and there will be a tendency for the work to move along the gauge, called *creep*. To avoid the spoilers, keep the work firmly in position as you saw and make the pass a bit more slowly than you normally would. A miter-gauge extension will assist a lot when trying to keep the work in correct position as you saw (FIG. 5-27). NOTE: Attach a strip of fine sandpaper to the extension; its abrasive surface will keep the work from sliding.

*Fig. 5-27  A miter gauge extension will help to keep the work in place as you saw.*

**Special jig for miter cuts**  One way to saw miter cuts accurately without having to worry about work movement or miter-gauge settings is to make a sliding table jig, like the one detailed in FIG. 5-28. This project consists of a plywood platform mounted on bars that slide in the table slots. A V-shaped guide, attached to the platform, positions the work exactly right for the cut. Because the work and jig move together, common problems are eliminated.

To make the jig, cut the platform first. Then form the two bars to slide in the slots. Put the bars in the slots and then place the platform so the kerf you will cut in it is centered and parallel to the platform's sides. Attach the platform to the bars with *brads* and then cut a kerf that is about 3/4 the length of the platform. Lay out the shape of the V-guide with a triangle or protractor and, after forming it, attach it to the platform with glue and nails. Be certain that the center of the V-guide and the kerf are on the same centerline.

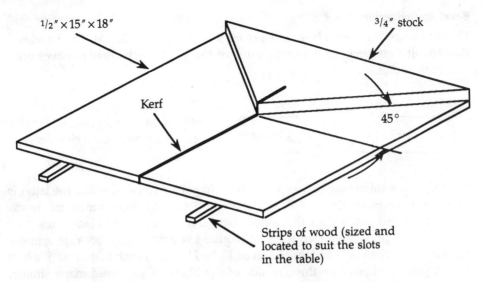

**Fig. 5-28** *How to design a sliding table mitering jig. The size of the project can be changed, if necessary, to suit your equipment.*

The jig is designed for 45-degree miter cuts. To make it more flexible, you can make guides to produce other angular cuts. If so, attach the guides only with screws so they can be interchangeable.

To use the jig, hold the work against the guide and then move the jig forward to make the cut (FIG. 5-29). Be careful, of course, to move the jig only enough to get through the work.

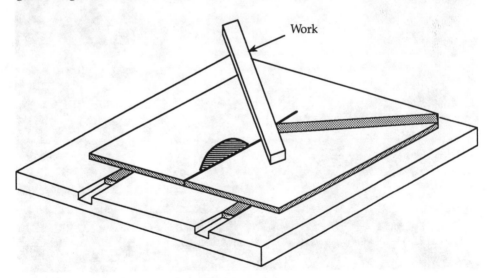

**Fig. 5-29** *The mitering jig and work move together. This guards against negative work movement that can spoil the accuracy of the cut.*

## Bevel and chamfer

The difference between a *bevel* and a *chamfer* is shown in FIG. 5-30. The bevel is a slanted cut that removes the entire edge of the stock; a chamfer removes only part of the edge.

**Fig. 5-30** *The difference between a bevel and a chamfer.*

    The major difference between a routine rip cut and a bevel is that the latter is done with the blade tilted to a specific angle (FIG. 5-31). Most times, the workpiece is the part of the stock that passes between the fence and blade. However, this can pose problems when the part required is very narrow because it might bind between the blade and fence and be kicked back. In such instances, it's best to put your workpiece on the free side of the blade. If you need many similar, small pieces and set up so the parts required will pass between the blade and fence, be sure to use a push stick and to move the work well past the blade.

**Fig. 5-31** *Bevel cuts, like the one here, are similar to rip cuts, but they are accomplished with the blade tilted to the required angle.*

A slanted cut that is made across the grain may be called a *cross-bevel* or a *cross-miter*. Such cuts are made the same way you would do a crosscut (FIG. 5-32). Since bevels are cut at an angle, the blade, being tilted, is actually cutting more wood than it does when it is vertical. Thus, beveling should be done with a slower feed, especially if the stock is thick.

***Fig. 5-32*** *Cross-bevels, or* cross-miters, *are done pretty much like simple crosscuts.*

### Special jig

When you get into constructing joints you will find it necessary to form shapes like those shown in FIG. 5-33. These are accomplished with the stock held on edge and with the rip fence used as a guide. Hand-holding the work is okay only if it is wide and thick enough to provide ample bearing down surface on the table so it won't wobble as you make the pass. That's why it's advisable to make and use a *tenoning jig* like the one shown in FIG. 5-34.

The design of the rip fence will have a bearing on the size and, maybe, the shape of the U portion of the jig. When fashioning the jig, be precise enough so it won't wobble and can be moved without having to be forced. Polishing the fence and the contact areas of the jig with paste wax will help the accessory move more easily. Be sure that the face of the jig and the bearing edge of the right angle guide form a 90-degree angle with the table.

Figure 5-35 shows how the jig is used. The work, placed so its end is flat on the table, is butted against the right angle guide and clamped in place. Jig and work are moved as a unit to make the cut. The workpiece will be secure, the cut

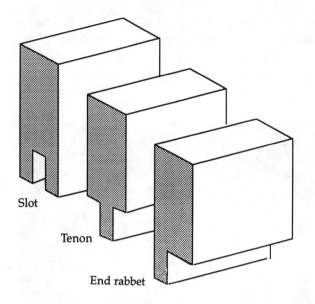

**Fig. 5-33** *Typical end cuts that should be made with a tenoning jig.*

Slot

Tenon

End rabbet

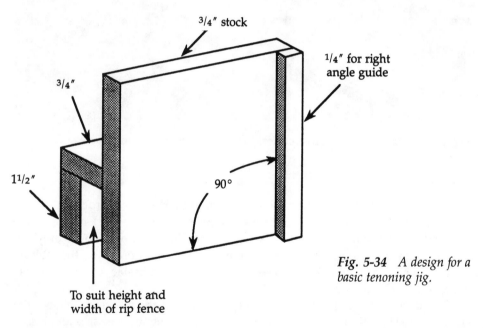

3/4" stock

1/4" for right angle guide

3/4"

11/2"

90°

**Fig. 5-34** *A design for a basic tenoning jig.*

To suit height and width of rip fence

will be accurate, and you control the operation with your hands well away from the saw blade.

## Dadoes and grooves

A *dado* is a U-shaped cut that is made *across* the grain; a *groove* is the same type of cut made *with* the grain (FIG. 5-36). *Ploughing* is another term used to identify the

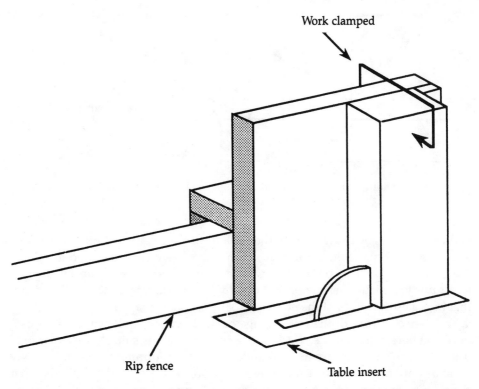

Work clamped

Rip fence

Table insert

**Fig. 5-35** *How the tenoning jig is used. The work is butted against the right angle guide and clamped to the jig's face. Jig and work move as a unit. This is the safe way to make end cuts on narrow stock.*

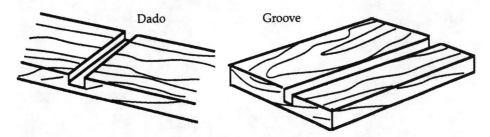

Dado

Groove

**Fig. 5-36** *Dadoes and grooves are U-shaped cuts that are often used in woodworking joints.*

cut when it is made with the grain. Regardless of the terminology and the direction of the cut, the form is always U-shaped and it is usually sized to suit the thickness of the component that will be inserted in it (FIG. 5-37).

Dadoes and grooves are used extensively as part of wood connections. For example, the installation of shelves in a bookcase presents a picture of when it makes sense to incorporate the shapes. If the ends of the shelves are set into the

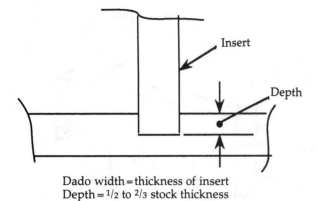

Insert

Depth

*Fig. 5-37* *Dadoes and grooves are usually sized to suit the thickness of the part that will be inserted.*

Dado width = thickness of insert
Depth = 1/2 to 2/3 stock thickness

vertical members by using a dado, they will have more stability and there will be less chance of separation in the joint, than if they were simply butted in place.

U-shaped cuts can be formed with a conventional saw blade by using a *repeat-pass* technique. Set the projection of the saw blade to a mark on the work that indicates the depth of the cut (FIG. 5-38). Then make repeat passes that overlap a bit—working with the miter gauge for dadoes, the rip fence for grooves—until you have achieved the width of the cut. The idea is suitable for occasional use, but since such cuts are needed quite often when forming joints and usually must be duplicated, it makes more sense to work with a special cutting tool that is designed for the application. Once the dadoing tool is set, it will make any number of cuts of equal width and depth and will accomplish them in a single pass.

*Fig. 5-38* *Setting the saw blade to a mark on the work that indicates how deep the cut must be. This is a good way to set cutter projection whether you form a dado with a saw blade and repeat passes or whether you use a dadoing tool.*

**Dado assembly** A common dadoing tool, called a *dado assembly*, consists of two outside cutters, which are really heavy saw blades that cut a 1/8-inch kerf, and an assortment of *chippers* which are always placed between the blades (FIG.

5-39). The units are mounted on the machine's arbor and secured as you would a single saw blade. If just the outside blades were installed, you would form a U-shape, 1/4 inch wide. By adding chippers, the cut-width can be increased in stages, usually up to a maximum of 13/16 inch.

**Fig. 5-39** *The dado assembly consists of two outside blades and a set of chippers. The chippers are always mounted between the blades. The size of the chippers you use plus the blades determines the width of the cut.*

Chippers have *swaged* edges—meaning that the edge on the blade that does the cutting is wider than the gauge of the chipper. The chippers are placed so the swaged edges fall between the gullets on the blade (FIG. 5-40). In action, the outside blades form the shoulders of the cut, while the chippers, in overlapping

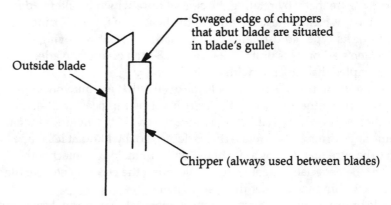

**Fig. 5-40** *Chippers that abut the blades are placed so their swaged cutting edges fall between the gullets on the blades. The chippers make overlapping cuts, resulting in total clearance of waste between the kerfs made by the outside blades.*

fashion, remove the bulk of the waste. Mount chippers so their cutting edges are not in line. Staggering them contributes to better balance of the assembly as a whole.

Not all dado assemblies are alike. In addition to differences in diameter—6- and 8-inch sizes being common—and in the number and cut-width of the chippers, the outside blades might be flat-ground, have set teeth, or be hollow-ground. More expensive units have chippers and blades that are carbide tipped. They perform with optimum results and, like carbide tipped saw blades, will stay sharp much longer than all-steel cutters.

A problem with dado assemblies is that each of the components cuts a kerf of specific width, so the concept doesn't allow adjustment for odd-sized cuts. But there is a solution. Paper washers, often supplied by the manufacturer, are used to make minor changes in cut-width. You adjust for an odd-sized cut by using one or more of the washers as part of the assembly. It doesn't matter if the washers are placed between chippers or between chippers and blades.

**Adjustable dado** If you mount a saw blade so its perimeter will oscillate from side to side, the blade will make cuts that are wider than the normal kerf. That, in essence, is the concept of adjustable, *wobble-type* dadoing tools. The major advantage of such units is that settings are infinitely variable; thus, any cut-width between minimum and maximum is possible.

The most elementary design consists of a pair or pairs of heavy collars that have a tapering cross-section. When an ordinary saw blade is mounted between the collars, it will be tilted. The blade will wobble from side to side as it rotates, making cuts that are wider than it does when used conventionally. The collars have registration marks so they can be set to tilt the blade for particular widths.

The product shown in FIG. 5-41 is representative of more sophisticated adjustable dadoing tools. For one thing, it works with its own heavy gauge blade that has a host of carbide tipped teeth so it cuts smoothly and efficiently. Cut-width adjustments are made by rotating the central hub, which is calibrated for settings from $1/8$ inch, which is the kerf-width of the blade itself, up to $7/8$ inch. Like other products of its type, adjustments can be made without removing the tool from the machine's arbor. This unit works with an 8-inch diameter blade, but there are other examples that function with a 6-inch blade.

**Dado tools in use** Dadoing tools make cuts that are much wider than a regular saw kerf, so the regular table insert must be replaced with a special dado insert that is always offered as an accessory (FIG. 5-42). Before plugging in the machine and turning it on, rotate the dadoing tool by hand at least one full revolution to be sure that it turns as it should without making contact with any part of the insert. Be especially attentive when elevating the cutter to be sure that its cutting arc is within the limits of the insert's slot.

Dado or groove cuts remove a lot more material than normal saw cuts, so it's wise to feed the work more slowly than usual. Like saw blades, the teeth on dadoing tools are designed to remove just so much wood at a given rate of feed.

**Fig. 5-41** *Example of a high quality, adjustable dadoing tool. The central hub is rotated to adjust the tool for a particular cut-width. The heavy gauge blade has carbide tipped teeth.*

Forcing is a bad practice that will harm the cutter and cause poor work. Trying to make very deep cuts in a single pass, especially when the dado or groove is quite wide, is another bad practice. It's better to make a first pass to less than the depth you need and then make a second pass after adjusting the cutter's projection. You'll discover, after some practice, how deep you can cut efficiently and with optimum results in a single pass. Important factors, when using a dado tool are: the cut-width, the density of the material, and the machine's horsepower. Work

***Fig. 5-42*** *Dadoing tools are used with special table inserts that have slots wide enough to accommodate them. Always check before turning on the power to be sure the cutter will not hit the insert.*

that chatters during the cut, having to use excessive force to make the cut, and a cutter that slows up excessively are warning signals. Usually, these signs indicate that you are cutting too deep or too fast.

# 6

# Hand planes

An experienced woodworker rates hand planes on a par with any essential tool, even though much of today's wood is surfaced on four sides (S4S). But it's a rare project that doesn't require dressing wood to specific dimensions. Planes are used to reduce the width and sometimes the thickness of lumber and to smooth rough edges left by other tools (FIG. 6-1). They can square edges, true them to a flat plane, do beveling and chamfering, and contribute to joint constructions. Planes can be adjusted to remove a lot of material, within practical limits, or to produce a shaving fine enough to be translucent. The latter thought endorses the need for a plane in any toolbox, if only because it can remove a smidgen of material from, for example, a door or drawer that doesn't operate smoothly. This function presents the plane as a maintenance tool as well as one for sizing and shaping project components.

It's interesting to note that the "equivalent" of the hand plane in the power tool category is the *jointer/planer*, like the example in FIG. 6-2. In one sense, the handtool is more flexible because it can be applied with greater freedom, for example, on a completed assembly.

## Bench planes

Hand planes—with names like *smooth*, *jack*, *jointer*, and *fore*—all belong in the bench plane category. The major physical differences are in length, weight, and sometimes in the width of the cutter (FIG. 6-3). This may suggest that particular units are more appropriate for either light or heavy-duty applications. The thought is correct, but only to a degree, because there is considerable overlap in

**Fig. 6-1** *One of the major functions of hand planes is to smooth and true the edges of boards. When the tool is set and used correctly, the waste curls out like a strand of ribbon.*

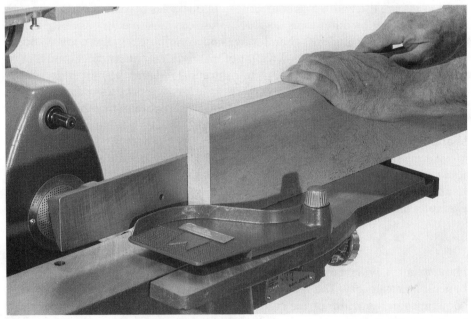

**Fig. 6-2** *The power tool that comes closest to emulating what can be done with a hand plane is the* jointer-planer.

**Fig. 6-3** *The two large units in this example are typical bench planes. The smaller tool is called a* block *plane.*

the functions of bench planes, even though one or another might be ideal for a particular purpose.

A short, light plane is a good choice for touch-ups on work that is already reasonably smooth and level. A long, heavy plane is appropriate when bringing a workpiece to acceptable smoothness requires removing a lot of material. Also, a long plane makes it easier to bring an irregular edge to true levelness because it spans high points, whereas, a very short plane might follow the dips and hollows (FIG. 6-4). The longest of the planes earns its name, *jointer*, because it can be used to smooth and true the edges of long boards precisely enough so they may be butted together to form a tight-fitting joint.

### Smooth plane

The smooth plane, which is the smallest bench plane, is probably the best "first choice." Its length ($9^1/4$ inches or $9^3/4$ inches) and comparatively light weight contribute to easy handling. Although you will probably eventually purchase other longer, heavier units, the smooth plane is a fine learner's tool. You will never obsolete the smooth plane, no matter how much equipment you garner in this

*Fig. 6-4* *Long planes span across irregularities; short planes tend to follow dips and hollows.*

tool area. Many experts rely on a smooth plane for final touches on surfaces that have been brought to a point with another type of plane.

Obviously all plane blades must be kept keen, but that on the smooth plane's blade must be constantly maintained razor-sharp and adjusted to produce an extremely thin shaving. Because the plane is short, it's important to use it with smooth, even-pressure strokes. If consistency in stroke is not maintained, it's possible for hollows to form when you are working on a long edge.

### Jack plane

The jack plane is longer and heavier than a smooth plane; an average one being about 14 inches long and with a 2-inch wide cutter. In a sense, it's a more powerful tool. While it is suitable for obtaining smooth, flat, true edges, it is especially good for doing rough, heavy work—those times when it is necessary to reduce stock to a specific size. For such applications, the work goes faster when the plane is adjusted for a relatively coarse shaving. On some jack planes, the blade ends in a gentle, convex curve, a feature that enables the tool to take deeper bites in the stock. The jack plane is the tool to select when, for example, reducing the width of a board or when doing jobs like fitting new screens or storm sashes in window frames.

### Jointer plane

Jointer planes are the longest and heaviest hand planes. Their lengths range from 18 inches to 24 inches and they can have blades as wide as $2^3/8$ inches. The extra length of the planes enables them to bridge concavities that a shorter plane might dip into. To appreciate one of its basic functions, envision having to true a board that has a scalloped edge. The long plane will ride across and gradually take down the high spots until the edge is level. Another common application is smoothing and truing boards for edge-to-edge joining. Several boards, clamped or gripped together in a vise, can be dressed simultaneously so the edges will mate perfectly.

### Fore plane

The fore plane spans the gap between jack and jointer planes. It is often referred to as either a *long-jack* plane, or a *short-jointer* plane. A typical unit would be 18 inches long and have a blade that is $2^3/8$ inches wide. Like the jack plane, the cutting edge of its blade is often shaped as a slight convex curve instead of being straight across.

## Makeup of a bench plane

All bench planes have the essential components that are shown in FIG. 6-5. The assembly that consists of the blade—or *iron*—and the blade cap is often referred to as a *double plane cutter*. While the blade does the actual cutting, the cap lifts the shaving and curls it up and away from the blade (FIG. 6-6). The cap also serves to stiffen the blade and, together with the toe of the plane, acts to prevent splitting in front of the cutting edge.

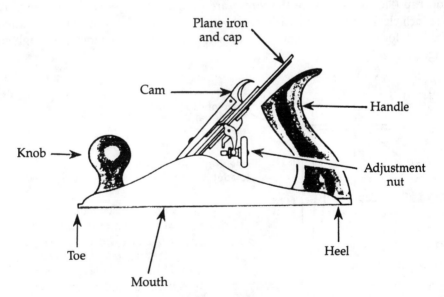

**Fig. 6-5** *The main components of a bench plane. The mouth is a rectangular opening through which the blade projects. This is a metal plane, but there are many modern planes that are made of wood. Metal or wood, they have similar adjustment features.*

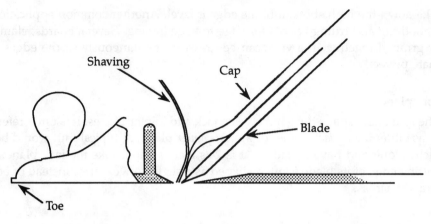

**Fig. 6-6** *When the cap is oriented correctly with the blade, it causes shaving to curl up and away.*

To make the adjustment between the cap and the blade correctly, first set the cap on the flat side of the blade so that its leading edge is away from the blade's cutting edge. Finger-tighten the screw that holds the two units together and then slide the cap forward until there is a 1/16-inch gap between the edges of the blade and cap (FIG. 6-7). Be sure the edges are parallel, then secure the screw. The 1/16-inch clearance is good for general work, but it can be reduced to as little as 1/32 inch for very fine shaving or increased to as much as 1/8 inch for rough cutting.

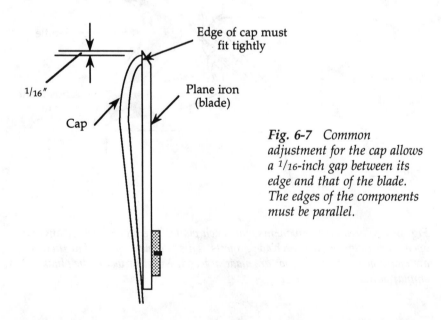

**Fig. 6-7** *Common adjustment for the cap allows a 1/16-inch gap between its edge and that of the blade. The edges of the components must be parallel.*

The final step is to add the cap, but do not tighten it until you have adjusted the lateral position and the projection of the blade. The lateral adjustment is made with a lever that is just below and behind the blade; projection is controlled with the adjustment nut.

Hold the plane in an inverted position and sight along its base as you adjust the blade's projection so it can be clearly visible. If necessary, shift the blade adjustment lever to the left or right until the edge of the blade is parallel to the base of the tool. If the blade is not parallel it will cut deeper into one edge of the work.

Sighting along the base of the plane while turning the adjustment nut is also a common method used to determine blade projection, but it does leave room for human error. A more precise way, at least to start with, is to improvise using a gauge like the one in FIG. 6-8. The shims can be various thicknesses of cardboard, veneer, plastic laminate, whatever. Set the plane on the shims and then adjust the blade so it just touches the wood. The same gauge can be used to ensure that the blade's edge is parallel to the base of the plane.

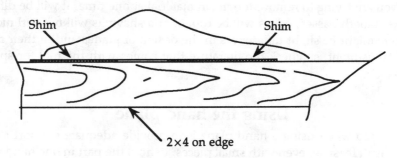

Shim          Shim

2 × 4 on edge

*Fig. 6-8* *A blade projection gauge. The thickness of the shims will determine how far the blade projects below the sole of the tool. The project will also help you adjust the blade's cutting edge parallel with the sole.*

Two other factors that affect the cut are the bevel on the cutting edge of the blade and the size of the *mouth* or *throat* through which the blade projects. The bevel, as shown in FIG. 6-9, must not be blunt or too long. As a rule, the length of the bevel should be a bit more than two times the thickness of the blade.

The rectangular throat opening may be widened or made narrower by moving the *frog*, the casting that supports the blade, toward the toe or heel of the plane. Use a narrow throat for fine planing and for when the wood is dense and close-grained. A wider throat, that results in thicker shavings, is useful when you need to remove stock quickly and when working with coarse-grained or resinous wood. Note that there is a relationship between throat width and depth of cut. Generally, a wide opening is compatible with deep cuts. Be aware though, that splitting might occur when the opening is too wide for the type of cut you need.

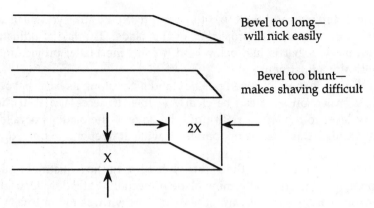

**Fig. 6-9** *As a general rule, the bevel on the blade is twice as long as the blade thickness.*

Always use the minimum of blade projection that will smoothly accomplish your task and with just reasonable effort on your part. You will quickly know when you are trying to remove too much material at one time. It will be difficult to make smooth passes, edges will be rough, and shavings will not curl nicely.

There might be slight differences in the design of planes and in their methods of adjustment, so check the literature that comes with the tool for specific information.

## Using the hand plane

The first step when using a hand plane is to provide adequate support for the work. It isn't feasible, even with small pieces, to hold the part in one hand while you apply the plane with the other hand. Most times, work can be gripped in a vise (FIG. 6-10), but there will probably be times when you will have to improvise. The type of V-block shown in FIG. 6-11 can be used to hold work on edge when planing. A similar solution is to tack-nail three narrow strips of wood to the bench so they form a closed slot that suits the thickness of the work. Very long work can be clamped across sawhorses. Whatever the method, the motive is to allow you to concentrate on using the plane, not on whether the work will stay still.

Always examine the stock to determine the direction of the grain so that you will be planing *with* the grain rather than *against* it. If you are ever in doubt, or in error, the first cuts will be educational. If your first pass is made against the grain, it will be rough and pitted and the shaving will not curl smoothly—if at all. Stroking with the grain makes for easy passes, smooth cuts, and even-curling shavings. If you are working on old or salvaged material, check it for nails, embedded debris, and defects that can damage the cutter. When you have a choice, avoid planing on a side of the wood that contains knots.

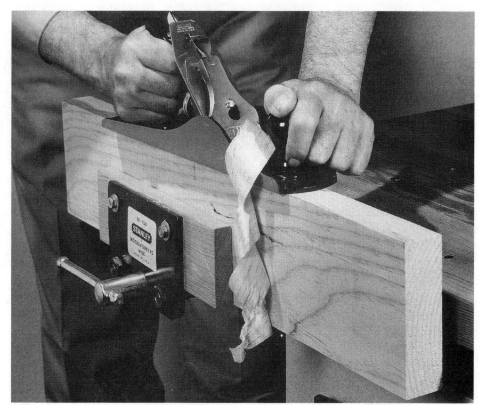

**Fig. 6-10** *A good way to provide adequate support for the work is to grip it in a vise.*

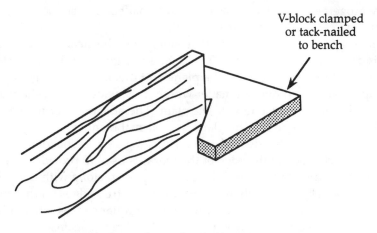

V-block clamped
or tack-nailed
to bench

**Fig. 6-11** *V-blocks can be used to hold work in correct position for planing.*

Planing proceeds most efficiently when you coordinate the swing of your arms and body, something like a planing ballet. The stance you take depends on how the work is situated and whether you will move the plane to the left or the right. If the pass direction is to the left, stand with your left foot forward. Do the reverse if you are planing toward the right. This is suggested so it will be easier to rock forward together with the movement of the plane. If you stand flat-footed with your feet together, it will be awkward to advance with the plane even when you are smoothing short pieces. Remember, be somewhat relaxed when planing and avoid moving the plane only by extending your arms.

Start the pass by placing the toe of the tool flat, and firmly on the work where the cut will start. At the beginning, apply a bit more pressure on the toe of the tool than elsewhere. Distribute pressure equally over the plane as you get into the cut. Continue your pressure until the cut is complete and you can lift the plane clear of the stock. Don't drag the plane back over the work—this contributes to faster dulling of the cutting edge.

Some people have a tendency to relax pressure and lift the plane at the heel of the stock before the cut is complete. Tapered edges result if this continues throughout your cut. Start the pass correctly, maintain uniform pressure, and the result will be straight, flat edges. Don't despair if first attempts are not ideal. Practice on a piece of pine, 2 or 3 feet long. You'll soon get the hang of it.

A common problem during an initiation period is that while the cut is smooth, the planed edge is not square to the sides of the work and more stock is removed at one or both ends of the work than at its center. Assuming that the lateral adjustment of the blade is correct, the flaw is caused by not maintaining the tool on a horizontal plane. To assist you, hold a short wooden block under the plane and against the side of the board. Hook your thumb over the knob and grasp the front side of the plane and the guide block at the same time so they can be moved together. The block provides additional bearing surface for the plane and helps to keep it flat as you make the pass.

A more advanced system, one that eliminates the need to hand-hold the guide, is demonstrated in FIG. 6-12. The right-angle guide, or jig, consists of two pieces of wood that are as long as the plane and that are nailed together to form an L-shape (FIG. 6-13). It doesn't matter whether the wide piece is shaped to conform with the profile of the tool or left plain. The advantage of the jig is that it leaves both hands free to use the plane in a normal manner.

Another idea, one that doesn't involve making a jig, is shown in FIG. 6-14. A strip of wood, clamped to the edge of the work, is used to provide extra bearing surface for the plane. In this case, the guide is planed along with the work. The method is especially useful when it is necessary to true edges on thin material.

The jig that is shown in FIG. 6-15, will ensure square edges when it is necessary to plane a small piece of wood. The work is braced against the stop as the plane is used on its side (FIG. 6-16).

**Fig. 6-12** *A right-angle guide will ensure that the planed edge will be square to the sides of the work. The guide may be used on the left or the right side of the tool.*

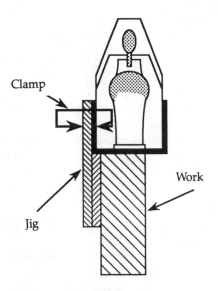

Clamp

Jig

Work

**Fig. 6-13** *The right-angle jig can be held in place with small clamps. Some operators drill and tap holes in the side of the plane so the jig can be secured with screws.*

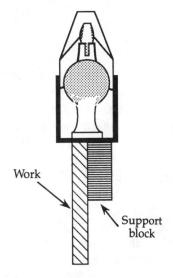

Work

Support block

**Fig. 6-14** *The support piece is planed along with the work. This is a good method to use when the work is thin.*

*Using the hand plane* **103**

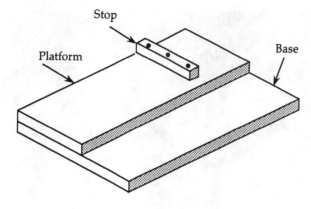

Stop

Platform

Base

*Fig. 6-15* *A squaring jig is easy to make and very helpful when small pieces must be planed.*

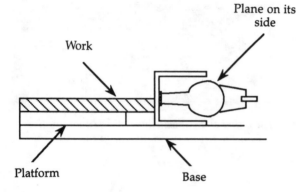

Plane on its side

Work

Platform

Base

*Fig. 6-16* *How the squaring jig is used.*

## Block planes

We haven't talked about the block plane so far simply because it is in a class by itself (FIG. 6-17). The palm-sized tool—most popular length is about 5 inches long—differs from bench planes in that its blade is set at a lower angle. This lower angle, usually 12 or 20 degrees (FIG. 6-18), makes the tool especially suitable for shearing end grain and for smoothing hardwood that has an oblique grain pattern. The beveled edge of a block plane's blade always faces upward instead of downward as on larger planes. The blade is secured by means of a lever cap that is tightened with a lever, cap screw, or thumbscrew. The top end of the cap is shaped to nestle comfortably in the palm of the hand.

Most times, the block plane is cradled in one hand with the index finger resting on the concave finger rest at the toe, and the thumb and other fingers bearing against the sides of the tool. A knurled nut at the heel is used to adjust the projection of the blade. Some models incorporate a lever for tilting the blade to left or right so its cutting edge can be adjusted parallel with the sole of the tool. When the lever is not included, the lateral blade adjustment is accomplished by loosening the lever cap and rotating the blade a bit toward one side or the other.

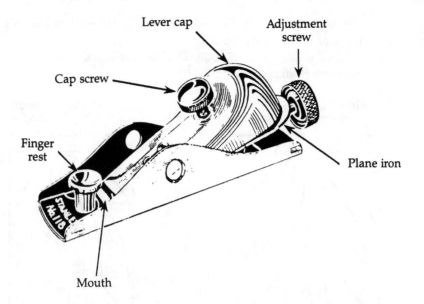

**Fig. 6-17** *A typical block plane that can be used for many routine planing chores.*

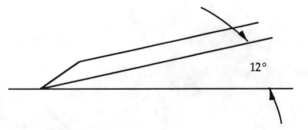

**Fig. 6-18** *The blade angle on a block plane is less than the angle used on bench planes. The blade bevel always faces upward, the opposite of bench planes.*

12°

A common error with the block plane is to have too much blade projection. Projection should be about the thickness of a hair, just enough to produce either extremely thin shaving or, when planing end grain, just sawdust.

## Planing end grain

While the block plane can be used to shave like a bench plane, its blade projection should be minimal when it is used to plane end grain. A characteristic of planing end grain is the splintering that will occur at the end of the pass. One way to counteract this is to plane from both ends of the work toward its center; however, avoid creating a high spot in the center. Another procedure to use to avoid splintering is to form a slight chamfer at one end of the board and then plane in one direction (FIG. 6-19). The edge that is chamfered can then be removed by planing or by making a rip cut.

The best method is shown in FIG. 6-20. The backing block, clamped in place, will prevent the work from splintering.

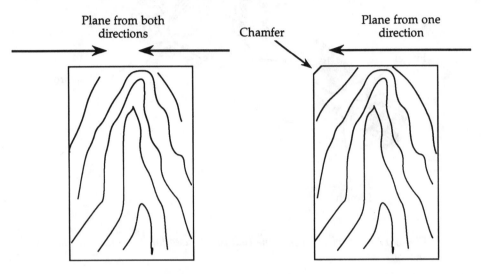

**Fig. 6-19**  *Two ways to work when planing end grain.*

**Fig. 6-20**  *The best way to avoid splintering at the finish of end-grain cuts is to mount a block to the stock's finish side.*

# Creating bevels and chamfers

You can plane bevels or chamfers freehand, but to achieve accuracy, you need to work with the type of guides shown in FIG. 6-21. In one, a strip of wood that is fitted with a V-block, is clamped to the side of the plane. The shape of the V-block determines the angle of the cut. The second method utilizes a guide that is just clamped to the work. The height of the guide above the work is what controls the cut-angle. In both cases, the size of the cut is controlled by the number of strokes you make.

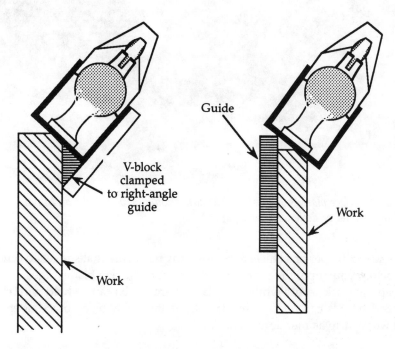

*Fig. 6-21* *Tested methods of working when you wish to plane bevels or chamfers accurately.*

# Surface planing

Surface planing, whether it's done to reduce the thickness of a board or to smooth a rough surface, requires a heavy plane that is adjusted to take a shallow bite. Start the job by making overlapping strokes obliquely across the grain (FIG. 6-22). Don't bear down excessively; you're not going to cut any deeper than the blade projection allows anyway, so why force? Finish the job by stroking with the grain, setting blade projection to practically zero. This is probably the hardest type of planing to do. Even experts don't expect to produce a finish that doesn't require further attention with sandpaper. This phase of planing is often done to true the surface of a slab that's composed of boards glued edge-to-edge. In such

**Fig. 6-22** *Surface planing is feasible, but cuts should be very light and final smoothing should be done with sandpaper.*

cases, use sandpaper or a chisel to remove any hard glue that squeezed out of the joints before you apply the plane. Hard glue can damage blade edges.

Keep the work secure while you plane. Large slabs can be held with clamps; strips and boards can be kept in place by using the V-block brace or the tack-nailed wood strip as mentioned earlier.

## Care of planes

When the plane is not being used, place it on its side so the blade's edge will not contact another object. Before putting a plane away, retract the blade inside the mouth to protect it from possible damage. There are times when shavings accumulate around the mouth of the plane. When this happens, use a splinter of wood or a sharpened dowel to clear away the debris. Never use a metal implement, like an awl or screwdriver, to do the clearing. If the tool will be stored for a long time, coat the sole with a film of light oil.

# 7

# Wood chisels

It's been said that you must be a chiseler in order to be a good woodworker. That comment contains humor here because of the disparaging connotation of the word "chiseler," but it also has considerable truth, since wood chisels can be used alone to perform many woodworking tasks or to augment and assist other tools like the plane and saw by making starting or finishing cuts, cutting away waste stock, or getting into tight places. Too often, chisels get short shrift on lists of fundamental woodworking tools, especially when suggestions are made for beginners. Of course there are more basic tools like saws, hammers, screwdrivers, and such, but it's a mistake to neglect wood chisels if for no other reason than the assist they provide for such chores as hand-forming joint shapes like dadoes, rabbets, and mortises.

The basic chisel (FIG. 7-1) can play a primary role in a woodshop. Think of the chisel as an associate or accessory tool. A common chore is forming the rectangular cavity needed for a mortise-and-tenon joint. The job is easier and goes faster if the bulk of the waste is removed by first drilling a series of overlapping holes and then using a chisel to do the final paring.

## Types and sizes of chisels

The variety of chisels that are available can be bewildering, but to make it easier, special groups like *turning chisels*, used for shaping work in a lathe; *gouges*; and other such groups whose primary function is woodcarving will not be discussed. This chapter details the common chisels shown in FIG. 7-2.

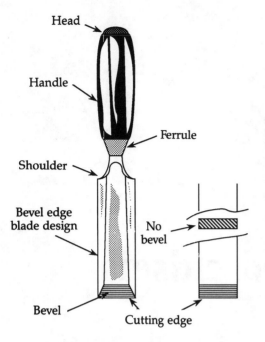

**Fig. 7-1** *Nomenclature of a modern wood chisel. Many of those that are manufactured in the United States have impact-resistant plastic handles.*

Head

Handle

Ferrule

Shoulder

Bevel edge
blade design

No
bevel

Bevel

Cutting edge

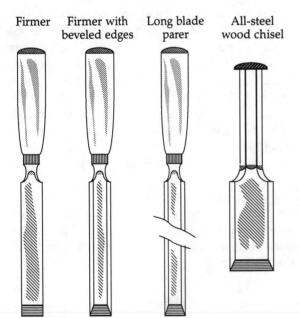

Firmer

Firmer with
beveled edges

Long blade
parer

All-steel
wood chisel

**Fig. 7-2** *Some of the chisels that are available today.*

The *firmer* chisel, usually available with a flat blade and square edges along the length of the blade, is very common and considered an all-purpose tool. The husky blade provides considerable bulk behind the cutting edge, which is usually ground at an angle of 27 or 30 degrees. While the tool can be used for finesse applications, its bulk makes it appropriate for heavy cutting, often with the driving force supplied by a mallet or even a hammer. This extra force, however, should never be extreme. Using a wood chisel as you would a wedge to split a log is not recommended.

The *beveled-edge firmer* is identical with the basic firmer design but, as the name tells, the blade is beveled on its face along all sides. This reduces the weight and the rigidity of the tool—factors that indicate it is especially suitable for light-duty applications with driving power supplied by hand or with light tapping with a mallet.

*Paring* chisels, that have blades as long as 7 or 8 inches, are available with square-edge blades, but are more commonly designed so they resemble the beveled-edge firmer. While a common use is forming or trimming the U-shaped cuts that are required for dado and groove joints, parers are suitable for many woodworking chores that require a light touch with a chisel.

The *all-steel wood chisel* is made with a short, beveled-edge blade and a husky, hexagonal handle. The end of the handle is dome-shaped so the tool can be more easily driven with a hammer. Obviously, this is a super strong chisel that is made for tough carpentry work. It's not one that is important to have in a basic tool kit.

*Butt* chisels, often called *pocket chisels*, are shorter versions of the firmer designs. Their blades can be as short as 2 or 3 inches, and they usually run full-length through the handle to a cap so it's permissible to drive them with a hammer or mallet. It's possible to find a butt chisel with a wider blade than is available in other designs. This chisel is tough but sophisticated enough for fine touch-ups. Butt chisels are a popular choice among pattern and cabinetmakers, as well as carpenters in general.

The average *mortising chisel* (FIG. 7-3), has a comparatively long, narrow, square blade—usually 1/4 inch to 1/2 inch wide—that is especially useful for removing waste material when forming the square or rectangular opening that is required for a mortise-and-tenon joint. This may be its forte but not its limitation. This chisel serves nicely in any application that involves shaping or removing wood in a tight area.

## Chisel handles

Most chisels will tolerate being struck with a mallet, a soft-faced hammer, or even a conventional hammer, but the force of the impact should be governed as much by the design of the tool's handle as it is by the job being done (FIG. 7-4). The *tang-handled* chisel, especially when made of wood, will take the least punishment and should be used mostly with hand pressure. Keep blows very light when it's necessary to use this with a striking tool. Modern versions, with impact-resistant plastic handles that terminate in a dome-shaped metal cap, enable the tool to hold up under harder use.

*Socket* handles have a round taper that fits a mating cavity at the top of the one-piece blade. Hardwood handles are still much in evidence here. Often, the

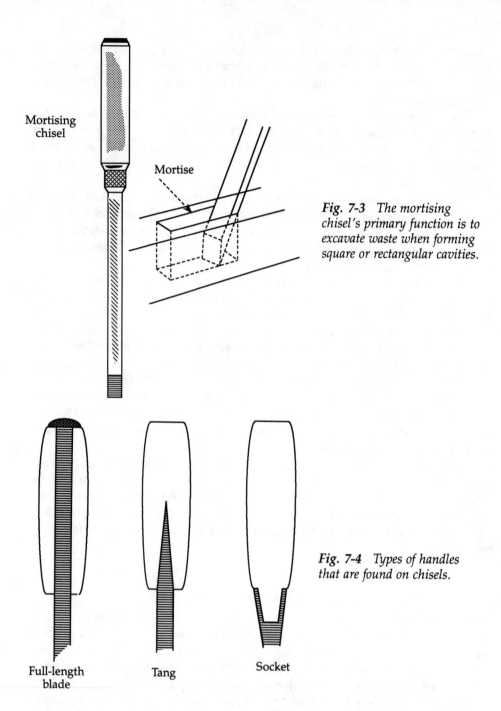

Mortising chisel

Mortise

**Fig. 7-3** *The mortising chisel's primary function is to excavate waste when forming square or rectangular cavities.*

**Fig. 7-4** *Types of handles that are found on chisels.*

Full-length blade

Tang

Socket

top of the handle is fitted with a leather butt washer that relieves the wood of some of the impact and guards against splitting. You may even find some that have a metal cap and are reinforced with a brass ring and ferrule. The socket-handled chisel is a durable tool that holds up well on jobs that require much driving with a mallet. An advantage claimed by many users is that, if ever necessary, the handle can be replaced. It's not unusual to see a socket chisel fitted with a custom designed handle made of a tough, exotic hardwood.

The heavy-duty chisel is the one with a one-piece blade and shank that passes through the handle and makes direct contact with a steel cap. It's obvious that blows on the cap travel directly through the blade to the cutting edge with minimum effect on the handle. Thus, this chisel tolerates continuous use with striking tools. Don't let the term "heavy-duty" lead you into thinking that this type of chisel is meant only for rough, tough work. They are excellent, general-purpose wood cutters that can be used with the light-fingered finesse that is appropriate with any chisel.

## Purchasing the right chisel

The overall length of a chisel is usually determined by its type, but blade *width* is a factor that, except in special cases, applies to any type. Generally, widths increase from a minimum size of $1/8$ inch up to 1 inch (size increases by $1/8$-inch increments) to larger sizes that go up to 2 inches (each step increasing by $1/4$ inch after 1 inch and by $1/2$ inch after 2 inches). It's not likely that you will find chisels wider than $1 1/2$ inches in a local store or even listed in craftsman's catalogs.

Chisels can be purchased individually, but it's more economical to buy them in sets. Although sets of chisels rarely include the full range of blade widths, a good starter set will have $1/4$, $1/2$, $3/4$, and 1 inch widths. A six-piece set will include $3/8$- and $5/8$-inch chisels. Quality sets will be offered in compartmented, heavy plastic wrappers or even in wooden boxes. In either case the package material makes it easy to store the tools neatly and safely. Don't buy chisels that are scattered with other handtools in a bargain bin. They will lack the quality that's necessary in the handles, steel, and cutting edge, and using them is not the way to get started in woodworking.

## Using a chisel

How a chisel is applied depends on the job that must be done, but a basic approach that will suit many situations is to use one hand as a control and the other hand to supply the pressure. Assuming you are right-handed, hold the blade in your left hand with your thumb on the bevel side. Have the thumb as close to the cutting edge as the work will permit. Grasp the handle with your right hand, almost as if you were holding a hammer. When extra pressure is required, the end of the handle can rest against the palm of your hand.

As is usually the case, the tyro adopts suggestions but makes changes that are right for him or her as confidence increases along with familiarity with the tool and growing adeptness. This is fine as long as overconfidence does not lead to carelessness. Remember that chisels are cutting tools and are super sharp if correctly maintained. Their edges can cut you more easily than they can cut wood. In all situations, make it standard procedure to keep both hands and your body in back of the business end of the tool.

Chisels may be used with the beveled face either up or down depending on the work being done. Generally, working with the bevel *down* is appropriate for rough cuts and when a lot of waste must be removed. Working with the bevel *up* is a good procedure for paring cuts, producing shaving as if you were using a plane. When possible, make paring cuts with the chisel held at a slight angle to the pass direction (FIG. 7-5). The result is a shearing action that produces smoother results with less effort.

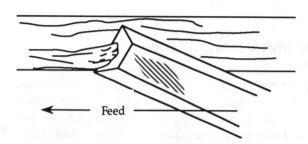

**Fig. 7-5** *Paring cuts with a chisel are made as if the tool was a hand plane. The bevel faces up; cuts should be light to produce thin shavings.*

Make cuts with the grain of the wood whenever you have a choice. There is a definite possibility of producing splinters rather than shavings when you cut against the grain. Making a series of shallow cuts rather than a single heavy one is good practice and always results in better work. Regardless of whether you are using the chisel with the bevel up or down, the angle you maintain between the tool and the work will determine the amount of material you remove. For a *paring cut*—removing a minimum shaving—hold the chisel almost flat on the work. For heavier cuts and to form depressed areas, increase the tool-to-work angle as you cut. The results will help guide you toward the most efficient angle to use.

## Typical chores

### Forming an end half lap joint

An example of how a chisel can play a practical, major role in woodworking is forming the half lap joint that is often used to connect the parts of a square or rectangular frame assembly (FIG. 7-6). While the chisel can be used vertically, tapped with a mallet, to form the shoulder of the shape, it's better to do that phase of the work with a saw (FIG. 7-7). After sawing, mark the depth of the cut on the sides and end of the workpiece and start removing the waste by cutting from both sides toward the center of the form with the bevel face of the chisel facing up. The first cuts can be on the heavy side, but reduce the amount of material you remove with each cut as you approach the bottom of the form. Remove the last pyramid-shaped waste by cutting toward the shoulder.

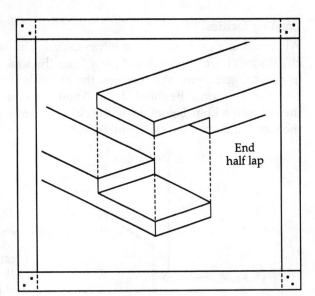

**Fig. 7-6** *End half lap joints are often used as the corner connections on square or rectangular frame assemblies.*

End half lap

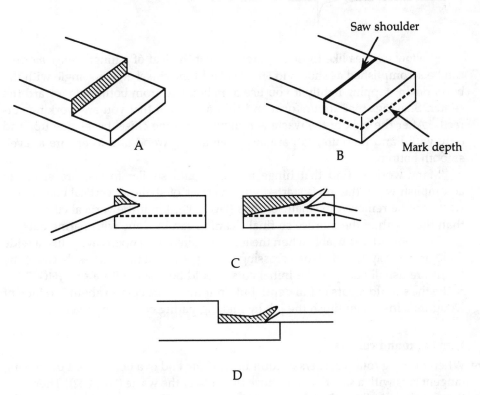

Saw shoulder

Mark depth

A

B

C

D

**Fig. 7-7** *To work with a chisel to form an end lap (A), saw the shoulder to a marked depth (B), make cuts from both sides toward the center (C), and then remove the center waste (D).*

## Creating cavities

When creating cavities, or even when making shoulder cuts, remember that the chisel's bevel compresses wood away from the back of the blade (FIG. 7-8). Thus, in order to get clean, sharp edges, the chisel is used with the bevel facing the center of the form to be chiseled out. Another technique is to incise the outline of the cut with a knife before using the chisel in order to sever the surface fibers of the wood and ensure a clean entrance.

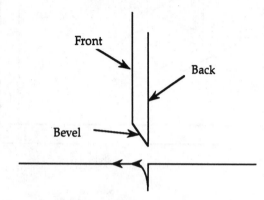

*Fig. 7-8* Keep the bevel facing away from perimeters when using a chisel to form a cavity. The bevel compresses the wood away from the back of the blade.

Shallow cavities like those required to seat the leaf of a hinge (*hinge mortise*) can be accomplished as shown in FIG. 7-9. Hold the chisel at a low angle with the bevel down, tapping lightly if you use a mallet. Cut from both ends toward the center. Shavings that are uniform and thin are a sign that you are working correctly. After the bulk of the waste is removed, use the chisel bevel-side up, and only with hand pressure, to pare away remaining wood and to ensure a level, smooth bottom.

Many workers find that hinge mortises, and similar forms, are easier to accomplish when the job is started with a series of shallow, vertical cuts so the waste can be removed in small sections (FIG. 7-10). Limit the vertical cuts to less than the depth of the mortise so final cleaning can be done with paring cuts.

The same idea is usable when the form required is an open cavity, like a wide dado or the shape needed for a crossing half lap joint. In these cases, because the forms are usually deeper, the initial cuts should be made with a saw (FIG. 7-11). Make the shoulder cuts to full depth but limit the waste cuts so about $1/32$ inch of wood remains. Then finish the job by making paring cuts with the chisel.

## Forming round corners

When forming round corners or rounding off the end of a board, start by making tangent cuts with a saw first to remove the bulk of the waste (FIG. 7-12). Then, use the chisel vertically with its bevel facing away from the arc. Small corners can be rounded by working only with the chisel, taking small bites and keeping the

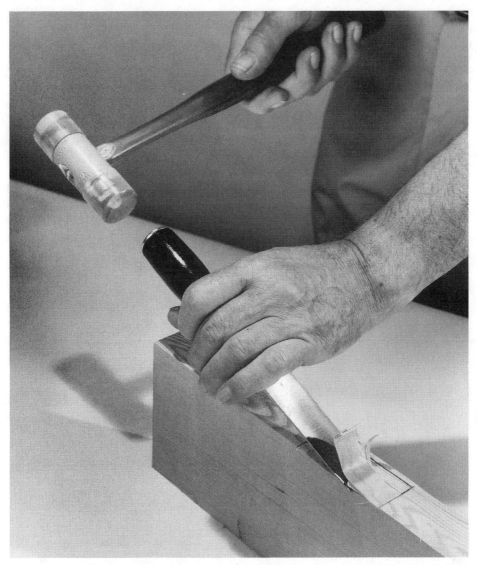

***Fig. 7-9*** *Shallow cavities can be accomplished by using the chisel with the bevel down and tapping with a mallet.*

back of the chisel tangent to the curve (FIG. 7-13). Working with the component on a piece of scrap will prevent splintering at the end of the vertical cuts.

You can do much with the chisel to create a true curve, but such forms are typically brought to final smoothness by working with sandpaper, wrapped around a block of wood.

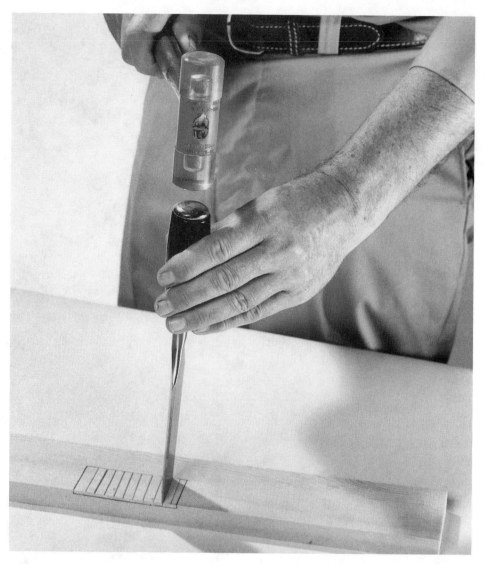

**Fig. 7-10**  *Starting with shallow, vertical cuts will make it easier to remove waste.*

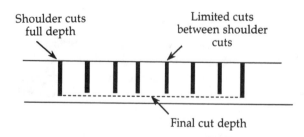

Shoulder cuts
full depth

Limited cuts
between shoulder
cuts

Final cut depth

**Fig. 7-11**  *Saw the shoulder cuts to full depth, but limit the others to a bit less than the depth required. Finish the job by making paring cuts with the chisel.*

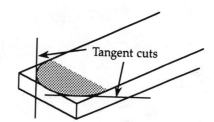

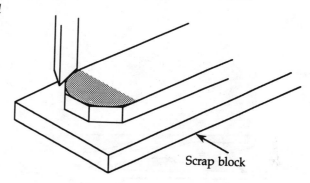

**Fig. 7-12**  *Use a saw to make tangent cuts when you wish to round off the end of a board or to form large, round corners. Finish the job with the chisel.*

Tangent cuts

Scrap block

**Fig. 7-13**  *When forming slight, round corners, keep the chisel vertical so its back is tangent to the arc. Be sure to take small bites.*

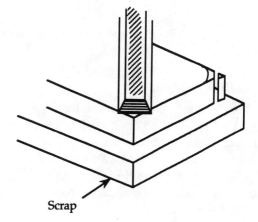

Scrap

### Fixing end curves

Use the chisel as shown in FIG. 7-14 when the curve is convex. A good deal of the waste can be removed by working with a mallet, but finish with hand pressure, rotating the chisel vertically as you cut so it will conform to the shape of the arc. Keep the bevel face away from the work.

Figure 7-15 shows how to use the chisel when the curve is concave. Note, in both cases, the bevel faces away from the arc. A technique to consider when forming end curves is to get rid of a lot of the waste by first making a bevel cut

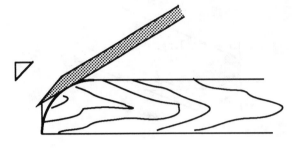

**Fig. 7-14**  *Proper use of the chisel for creating a convex end curve.*

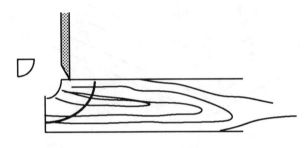

**Fig. 7-15**  *Proper use of the chisel for creating a concave end curve.*

with a saw. This will leave a minimum amount of shaving to be done with the chisel.

### Chiseling end grain

When working on *end grain*, which is essentially cross-grain cutting, hold the chisel so it forms an open angle with the direction of the cut (FIG. 7-16). Use a sliding, slicing action so you shear through the wood grain. Rotating the chisel a bit as you cut minimizes resistance and results in a smoother finish.

Splitting at the end of cuts can result if you shave end grain by making a complete pass in one direction. To avoid the possibility, do the cutting from both ends of the stock.

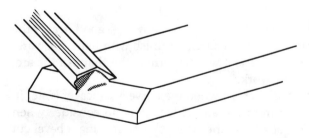

**Fig. 7-16**  *Shaving end grain is like a paring cut. Maintain a minimum angle between the blade and the work. Cutting goes faster if you sweep the cutting edge across the work as you move forward.*

# Caring for chisels

Chisels should be kept keen, with correct bevel angles (FIG. 7-17). Maintaining the edge on a chisel is no more difficult than sharpening kitchen knives. With an *oilstone* or a *whetstone*, a sharpening stone with a *coarse* and *fine* surface, you can occasionally touch up the cutting edge by *honing* on the fine side of the stone.

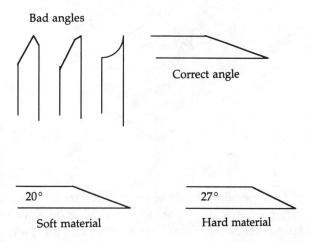

**Fig. 7-17** *Cutting angles for wood chisels. The less the angle of the bevel, the more bulk there is behind the cutting edge. Thus, an angle of 27 or 30 degrees is better for hard materials.*

The first step is to place the blade with its bevel flat on the stone. Move it to and fro and rotate it just a few times. Then place the blade on its flat side and again rotate it to remove any burrs that might be present. The last step is to repeat the honing with the bevel facing up but with the blade tilted a few degrees (FIG. 7-18). One way to ensure that the bevel will be placed correctly is to improvise a guide like the one suggested in FIG. 7-19.

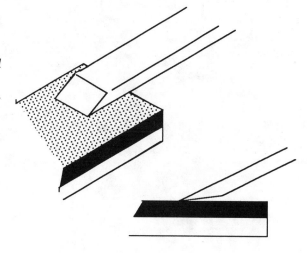

**Fig. 7-18** *The blade is honed with the back side down after the bevel has been attended to. A second honing on the bevel side with the blade at a very slight angle produces a secondary bevel that contributes to keenness. This should not be overdone.*

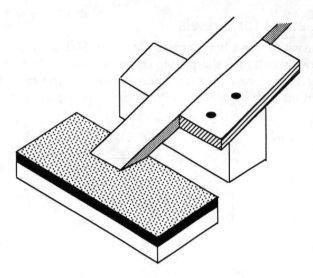

**Fig. 7-19** *There are commercial guides available for positioning chisels (and plane blades) for correct honing, but you can easily make one. The angle of the block on which the chisel rests matches the chisel's bevel. The side piece ensures that the tool will be held square.*

Remember that these procedures are just for maintaining a keen edge. They are not applicable if the tool is nicked or otherwise damaged so the cutting edge needs renewing. This chore requires a *grinding wheel* and the expertise needed to operate it. Until you acquire this special tool and learn how to use it, let a professional reshape your chisel, should it become necessary.

# 8

# Files

Many different types of *files* and *rasps* are available, and each unit was designed for its own purpose (FIGS. 8-1 and 8-2). Many files serve a special purpose, like those designed for sharpening saw teeth or for smoothing surfaces left by other tools. Others, like rasps and Stanley's Surforms, which are of major interest to woodworkers, can be used to do a considerable amount of shaping and, thus, are often used to create contours that other tools can't handle or for which special tools may be lacking. Examples of such applications include forming handles or spiral forms, contouring arms and legs for furniture projects, and creating in-the-round art or craft projects (FIGS. 8-3 and 8-4).

As accessory tools, filing implements can often right a wrong. For example, they can be used to remove a fraction of material from a tenon so it will fit a mortise just right, or enlarge a bored hole that's a little too tight for what it must receive.

## Nomenclature

The size of a file is always called out by its length from heel to point. The length of the tang, which is the tapered end on which a handle is fitted, is not included (FIG. 8-5). The shape of a file usually refers to its cross section. Those illustrated in FIG. 8-6 are not the only ones available, but are commonly accepted as being the most useful in woodworking. The shape of a file can also relate to the outline or contour that it has lengthwise. Some files, called *blunt*, are uniform in thickness and width from the heel to the point. Others, referred to as *tapered*, gradually become narrower, and sometimes thinner, as they approach the point.

**Fig. 8-1** *Typical modern files and rasps. The lower two are rasps, which are more efficient for woodworking because they cut fast and do not clog as easily as files when they are used on soft materials.* Nicholson

**Fig. 8-2** *A typical Stanley Surform file.*

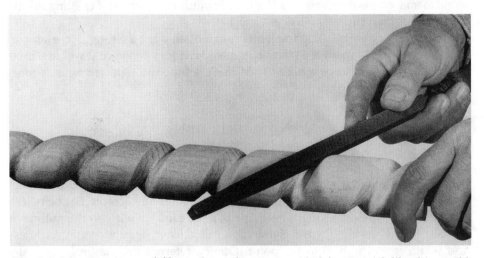

**Fig. 8-3** *A square, tapered file can be used to start a spiral form. A job like this would be finished with a half-round file or rasp.*

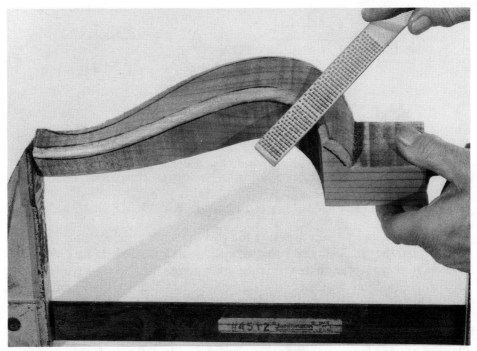

**Fig. 8-4** *A rasp is a good tool to use to do the final shaping of a cabriole leg. Work being filed should be gripped in a vise or with clamps.*

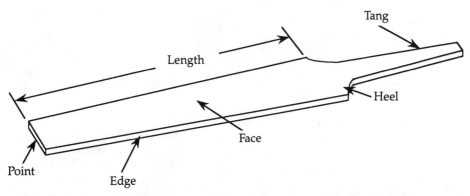

**Fig. 8-5** *Nomenclature of a file. A ''safe'' edge is one that is smooth. Many file edges are serrated so they, as well as the face, will cut.*

Tapered files are more flexible in use because they are a different "size," depending on the area of the file being used. Thus, they can get into tighter areas than a similar blunt file. For example, because the diameter of a tapered, round file varies through its length, it can be used to smooth or ream out different size holes.

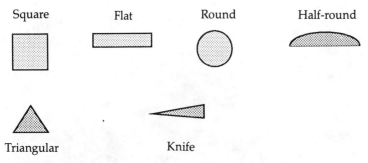

Square      Flat      Round      Half-round

Triangular      Knife

***Fig. 8-6*** *Cross-sectional shapes of some common files.*

## File teeth

The spacing of the cutting edges of a file and the angle at which they cross the face is called the *cut*. Teeth that run diagonally in a single direction are *single-cut*. When a second set of teeth that run diagonally across the first ones is added, the file is *double-cut*. Both types of cuts are generally classified in terms of roughness, such as *bastard, second cut,* and *smooth* (FIG. 8-7). The degree of roughness of a file also relates to its length, a factor that affects the spacing of the teeth. A 16-inch *coarse* file will leave a rougher surface than a 6-inch *coarse* file. Because of this, files can be used for smoothing in a progression of lesser degrees of coarseness.

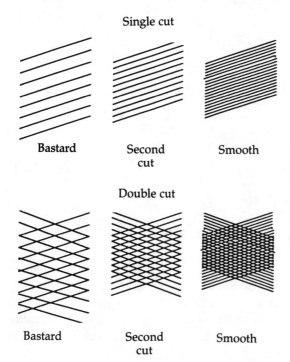

Single cut

Bastard     Second     Smooth
         cut

Double cut

Bastard     Second     Smooth
         cut

***Fig. 8-7*** *Typical file names. The spacing of the teeth determines whether the file will cut rough or smooth. A long file will cut rougher than a similar, shorter unit.*

For example, a job can be started with a 16-inch bastard file for rough shaping and brought to the point where sandpaper can take over by switching to a 10-inch, or shorter, bastard file.

*Rasps*, which are essentially wood cutters, differ radically from common files in that the teeth, instead of being parallel to each other across the face of the file, are cut individually (FIG. 8-8). They work more like miniature gouges that are arranged in rows across the face of the rasp. Alternate rows are staggered so that each tooth is situated between two teeth on abutting rows. This assures better coverage than if the teeth were in straight lines. The advantage of rasps in woodworking is that the shape and size of the teeth and their spacing allows them to be used for a considerable amount of shaping without clogging.

**Fig. 8-8** *The teeth on rasps are individual cutters. Each works like a small gouge to remove its share of the wood. Because of the shape and size of the teeth, rasps do not clog as easily as files.*

Like files, rasps are available in various sizes, ranging from 6 inches to as much as 16 inches. Also, like files, shorter units produce smoother cuts than similar, longer ones.

There are literally hundreds of types and sizes of files. Many of them, especially those designed for smoothing metal, should not be used on wood because they will easily clog. The units that prove most useful in a woodshop are various lengths of half round bastard files and rasps. A combination file/rasp, like the one in FIG. 8-9, is a good starting tool. This tool has various names, like "4-In-Hand," "4-Way Rasp," and "Shoe Rasp," the latter name being applicable because the concept is commonly used by shoemakers. Whatever the name, this tool offers, for example, a half round and a flat side, each side being part rasp and part double-cut file. Tools of this type do not have tangs but ends are smooth and rounded for safe handling.

## File handles

Files and rasps are not supplied with handles, but that doesn't mean it's okay to work without the protection they provide; tangs are sharp enough so they can

**Fig. 8-9** *A typical combination file/rasp will have a flat and a half round face, each with a rasp and file section of different coarseness.* Nicholson

easily puncture palms. A primary safety rule to establish is: don't use a file without fitting it to a handle. Handles are available in different sizes and are usually interchangeable. Always buy a handle for each file or rasp that you add to your tools. This provides safety and also convenience, since you won't have to fuss with fitting a handle each time you have use for a file or rasp.

Don't mount a handle by smacking it with a hammer. Instead, insert the tang into the handle socket and set it by rapping the handle squarely on a solid surface. The tang must fit snugly, but if you overdo the fitting, you run the risk of splitting the handle.

## Using a file

Working with a file or a rasp is essentially a two-hand operation. One hand grips the handle, the other hand acts as a control at the point (FIG. 8-10). The tool is stroked by the hand on the handle while either or both hands contribute feed pressure. Deeper cuts result when both hands bear down, but excessive pressure is not good practice, especially when using coarse files or rasps on wood. The tools cut in one direction—on the forward stroke—so you need not drag the tool back and forth. A good practice is to lift the rasp a bit when you return to start another stroke. Use the full length of the tool and make long, diagonal passes. Keep the cutter moving. Staying in one place will result in bumps and, in the case of a half round tool, will cause scallop-type depressions. When rounding off an edge, start by creating a small chamfer along the entire edge to *break* the corner. Then use strokes to follow the line of the finished arc. The handle end of the tool is "down" when you start, and "up" at the end of the stroke; something like following the contour of a wheel that is held vertically. Always stroke from the "good" side of the stock.

Form concave surfaces by working with the rounded surface of the tool (FIG. 8-11). It's a good idea to rotate the tool a bit as you stroke and to minimize cutting pressure as you approach the final shape. Use the flat side of the tool to shape convex curves, taking strokes that follow the shape that you desire. On all shaping jobs, you must see the form that is in the wood like the sculptor who envisions the shape that is encased in a block of stone.

Be careful with the hand that is used at the point of the tool. Lacerations can happen when the file moves but your hand does not. Some workers use a glove on the free hand for protection. If you do this, be sure the glove fits tightly. Any type of loose apparel that can snag is a hazard regardless of the work being done.

**Fig. 8-10** *Most filing or rasping jobs call for controlling the tool with both hands. Feed pressure can be supplied by one or both hands, but use only the hand on the handle to stroke the file forward.*

A trick used by many woodworkers is to cover the point of the tool with a short piece of garden hose.

## Caring for files

Files and rasps must be kept clean. Avoid allowing your tool to reach the stage shown in FIG. 8-12. This results when a file is dragged in saw-fashion across work and when the operator ignores cleaning the teeth as the work proceeds. Some workers rap the tool periodically on a hard surface to dislodge the waste that accumulates between teeth, but this is not the best practice. Files are tough, but they are also brittle and can chip or break. It's better to frequently stroke across the teeth with a soft wire brush to remove waste.

A special combination *file card* and *brush* designed for cleaning purposes, is available. One side of the accessory has a mat of soft-iron wire, the other side is matted with stiff bristles (FIG. 8-13). Thus, the unit can be used for stubborn or easy waste removal. When some teeth are too clogged for the file card to be effec-

**Fig. 8-11**  *Use the half round face of a rasp to form concave shapes.*

**Fig. 8-12**  *Using a file, even a coarse one, on wood will result in clogging unless you stop occasionally to clean the tool. A file that gets to this condition will be useless. Use a file card and brush frequently, as explained in the text.*

tive, you can often pick out waste with a length of stiff wire. Never use an awl, or something similar, for cleaning.

On occasion, I have cleaned wood-clogged coarse files and rasps by soaking them for a few minutes in warm water and detergent before working on them with a file card. If you try this method, be sure the tool is completely dry before you store it.

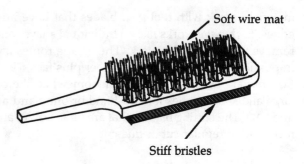

**Fig. 8-13** *A file and rasp cleaning tool, like this combination file card and brush, should be part of your equipment.*

Soft wire mat

Stiff bristles

A common technique that is often used when working on soft or resinous material, is to stroke the tool's teeth lightly with a piece of chalk before working. This technique prevents an adhesive bond from forming between waste and teeth. At times, I have dusted a tool with talcum powder. Both techniques work to minimize, if not eliminate, clogging.

Files and rasps should be kept from banging against each other and other objects that can damage them. Thus, it's not a good idea to store them in a drawer unless the compartment is partitioned for individual tools. Another storage idea that will keep the tools handy and protected is to make a simple rack like the one shown in FIG. 8-14.

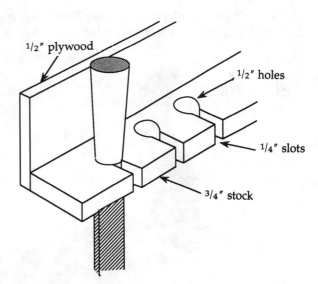

1/2″ plywood

1/2″ holes

1/4″ slots

3/4″ stock

**Fig. 8-14** *You can make a simple rack to store files and rasps safely.*

## Surforms

You can't help but think of old-fashioned cheese graters when you examine Stanley's *Surform* tools because their tooth design and cutting action are similar. But the analogy ends there. *Surform* tools, which are super cutters for wood and other materials, work with tool-steel blades that have hundreds of razor sharp cutting edges. Each edge works like an individual shaver and has its own throat to lift and remove waste from the work. The escape routes are so generous that it's almost impossible to clog the tools. Another plus factor is the number of forms in which *Surforms* are available. Some look somewhat like conventional rasps, others like large and small planes for two-hand or one-hand application (See FIGS. 8-15, 8-16, and 8-17). The cutting blades, that are replaceable, are available in flat or half-round form and in regular-cut or fine-cut.

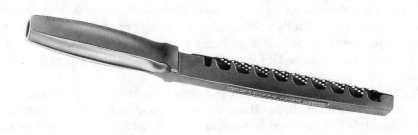

**Fig. 8-15**  *Typical Stanley* Surform *file. This variety of cutter works with replaceable, tool-steel blades that have hundreds of individual cutting teeth.*

**Fig. 8-16**  *Plane type* Surform *has an aluminum body and hardwood handles.*

*Fig. 8-17* Palm-size Surform *plane is only 5¹/₂ inches long and is fine for working in tight places and for trimming work.*

The tools can remove a lot of material or a little and can do it quickly or slowly. Much depends on the feed pressure you apply and the attitude of the cutter in relation to the wood-grain. A general approach is to stroke at an angle to the grain to remove material quickly and then gradually swing to an in-line action as you approach the form or the condition you desire (FIG. 8-18).

*Fig. 8-18* When using a Surform *plane for surfacing, take light, diagonal strokes to start with. Gradually swing the tool until you are stroking in line with the grain.*

Be cautious when working on narrow surfaces or edges because a cross-grain or even an angular stroke can cause the edges to splinter or feather. When you need to remove a lot of material from an edge, it's a good idea to first form slight bevels along both edges by taking light strokes with the tool tilted. In a sense, you are removing material that might splinter, should you work strictly with the tool held flat. Try to work, at least for final strokes, *with* the grain. Cutting will be easier and results will be smoother. Keep changing the direction of the tool as you stroke so individual cuts will overlap.

Most *Surform* tools, like files and rasps, cut on the forward stroke. An exception is the model called *Shaver* which is designed for cutting on a pull stroke (FIG. 8-19). How you grip the tool depends on how it is designed. File types, like the round one in FIG. 8-20, can be handled like a conventional file or rasp. Others, like the one that was shown earlier in FIG. 8-18, are controlled pretty much as you would a regular plane.

The tools have particular cutting characteristics. One way to become acquainted is to grip a piece of scrap, preferably a species like pine, in a vise and to

**Fig. 8-19** *The little* shaver *is one tool that cuts on the pull stroke. It can be applied with one hand, or you can press down on the toe with your other hand when greater feed pressure is required.*

use the tool to form an arbitrary shape or simply to round off the edges of the wood. By using different stroke directions and varying feed pressure, you'll soon get the right "feel" that's needed for efficient utilization.

**Fig. 8-20** *The round file Surform can be used to enlarge holes and to produce various shapes and decorative cuts. The hardened steel blade is 14¹/₂ inches long and ⁵/₈ inch in diameter. A blade that is about 10 inches long is also available.*

# 9
# Drills

Unless you deliberately plan otherwise, most woodworking projects require drilling holes for various reasons. For example, wood screws are easier to install and will hold as they should when correct-size holes are first drilled to receive them. Many wood joints gain strength when they are reinforced with dowels, which require holes to suit their size. A mortise is accomplished more quickly and easily when the bulk of the waste is removed by drilling overlapping holes. To make an internal cutout with a *keyhole* or *coping saw*, you must first drill an insertion hole for the blade. Holes, or a part of their circumference, can even contribute a decorative touch when they are planned as part of a design. The list can go on, but the point is that tools for drilling holes are essential equipment in a woodworking shop.

Holes are either *drilled* or *bored*. The distinction seems to apply to the size of the hole and the tool that is used. It's said that small holes are drilled with a *hand drill* or a *push drill*, while large holes are bored with a *brace* and *bit*. One thing is certain, the tools are used to form holes. Because size is such a relative thing and the terms are used interchangeably, it seems picayune to belabor the point.

## Types of drills

### Hand drills

The hand drill functions by means of a circular, hand-cranked gear with teeth that engage *pinions* (i.e., tapered gears) that are secured on a central shaft. At the end of the shaft is a *chuck*, the gripping device for the cutters that form the holes. This design provides the mechanical advantage that is needed for sufficient torque at the tip end and manageable *revolutions per minute* (rpm) in order to drill the hole. This may sound complicated, but all it means is that hand drills can spin their bits (FIG. 9-1).

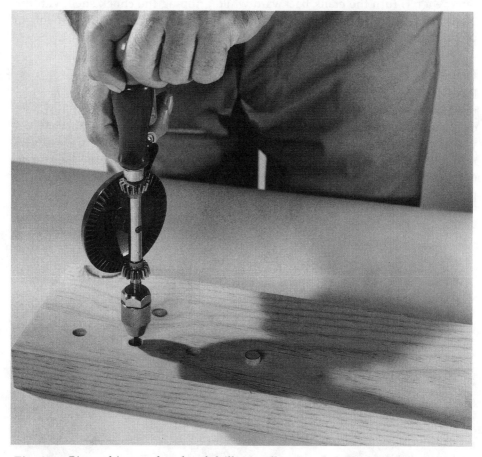

**Fig. 9-1** *Pictured is a modern hand drill. Usually, enough drilling pressure is supplied with one hand while the other hand rotates the circular gear. When more feed pressure is required, you can lean over the tool and add some body weight.*

All chucks are adjustable so they can grip various size bits or drills, but capacity can vary. An acceptable one for the average shop should be able to handle up to a 1/4-inch bit *shank* (the blank end of the bit that is gripped by the chuck). Heavy-duty versions have chuck jaws that open up to 3/8 inch. Some such models have a hi-low drive adjustable crank. The distance from the handle to the center of the speed gear can be set in an outer position for greater torque or in an inner position for more speed.

Most hand drills have a 3-jaw chuck that will center bits automatically when the correct procedure is followed. Open the jaws by turning the shell of the chuck so the opening is a bit more than the size of the bit. After inserting the bit, grip the chuck shell with one hand while turning the crank forward with the other hand. Don't ever use another tool, like pliers, to tighten the chuck. To remove a bit, turn the crank backward while gripping the chuck shell with the other hand. Handles on hand drills often have screw-on caps that are hollow to provide storage for bits.

### Push drill

Push drills are often called *automatic drills* because rotation of the bit occurs when pressure is applied downward on the handle of the tool (FIG. 9-2). Pushing down on the handle activates an internal spiral spindle that rotates the chuck. When you release the pressure, the handle returns on its own so you are ready to repeat the action. It's a very handy tool for forming small holes, especially when one hand is needed to hold the work. A typical example is keeping a hinge in place while you drill starting holes for the screws.

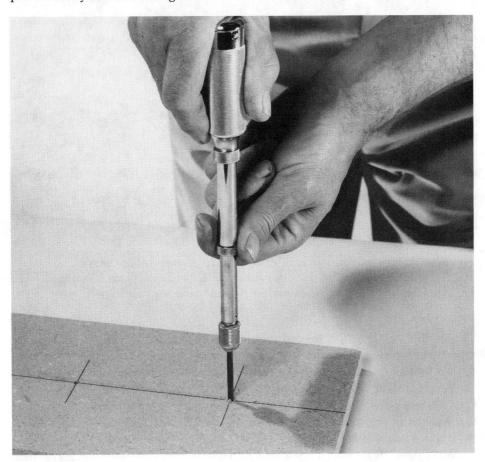

*Fig. 9-2  Pictured is a typical push drill.*

The push drill works with special bits, called *points*. The points that typically range in size from $1/16$ inch to $11/64$ inch, have a single, straight flute so they don't remove waste like a conventional, spirally fluted twist drill. Thus, when drilling a deep hole, it's good practice to occasionally remove the point from the hole to avoid clogging. Like the hand drill, the push drill also has a hollow handle for easy storage of its points.

The chuck on a push drill is special and should not be used to grip regular straight-shank bits. The blank ends of the points the tool works with end in a half circle and have a V-notch cut into them. To install a point in the chuck, grasp the chuck sleeve and move it forward, away from the handle end of the tool. Drop in the point and rotate it until you feel it mesh into place inside the chuck. Then release the sleeve. When installing a point, or removing one, always work so the sharp cutter is pointing away from you.

### Bit brace

The bit brace is considered a heavy-duty drilling tool because it can be used to form holes much larger than can be accomplished with a hand drill or push drill (FIG. 9-3). Because of the length of the bits that are used in a brace, it can be used to bore deeper holes than are possible with other tools. The brace provides a turning force to the bit by continuous full-circle rotations of its handle in a clockwise direction. The diameter of the circle, called *the sweep*, which on typical models can be 8, 10, or 12 inches, tells the size of the tool. The greater the sweep, the heavier and larger the tool and the more torque it can apply to the bit.

Good-quality bit braces have a ratchet mechanism located above the chuck that can be set to allow either a clockwise or counterclockwise turning of the handle. Convenient in normal use, it is particularly desirable working in close quarters when a full sweep of the handle isn't possible. By using the ratchet, you can turn the handle to and fro in limited arcs. Adjustment of the ratchet can differ from tool to tool, but usually, you turn a knurled *cam ring*, located on the arm just above and at a right angle to the chuck. Turning the ring to the right allows torque to be applied to the bit in normal fashion, but provides the ratchet action that allows swinging the handle in the opposite direction without turning the bit. This action is reversed when the ring is adjusted to the left.

Most bit braces have a chuck that is designed to grip *auger* bits that have tapered tangs (FIG. 9-4), but some products are available with a universal chuck that will grip conventional straight shank bits as well. Be careful when installing a bit. Even though chuck-jaws are designed to help center the bit automatically, there is room for error. A good procedure is to grip the chuck shell and turn the handle to the left until the jaws are wide open. Insert the tang of the bit in the square socket at the bottom of the chuck and, while gripping the chuck sleeve, turn the handle to the right until the bit is held firmly by the jaws in the chuck.

One of the plus features of bit braces is the availability of special accessories like the *expansive bit* (FIG. 9-5) and *screwdriver bits* (FIG. 9-6) so the tool can be used to drive or to remove heavy screws.

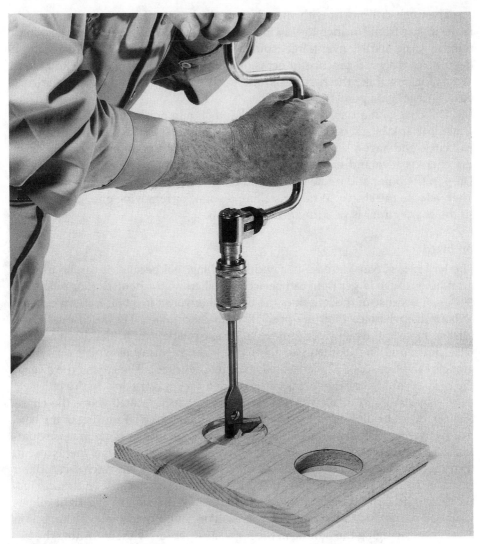

**Fig. 9-3** *The bit brace is able to drill holes that are much larger than you can accomplish with a hand drill or push drill.*

**Fig. 9-4** *Auger bits with screw points and tapered tangs are the drilling tools most often used in a brace. This bit is a "solid center" design. Its stiffness makes it a good tool for deep holes.*

*Fig. 9-5* Expansive bits with screw points are used in a bit brace. They usually are supplied with two cutting blades. Hole sizes can range from ¹/₂ inch to 3 inches.

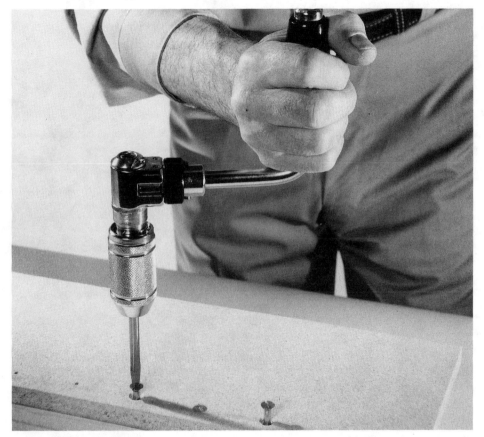

*Fig. 9-6* Screwdriver bits can be used in a bit brace. Because both hands are needed to control the brace, you must be careful about keeping the driver tip in the slot of the screw.

### Portable electric drills

If there is one power tool in addition to handtools that the beginning wood-worker should have it is a portable electric drill. Today's units really should be called something other than "drill" even though they are super tools for forming small and large holes accurately and with minimum effort. Modern innovations and a host of accessories that are available for it make this drill a lightweight, multipurpose tool you can hold in your hands. Among accessories that can be gripped in its chuck are disc and drum sanders, screwdrivers, hole saws, wire brushes, felt discs, polishing bonnets, and special bits that form exactly the right size holes for various wood screws. It can also be used as a power source to drive a specially designed, miniature lathe (FIG. 9-7) or, in a nonwoodworking application, to drive a small water pump (FIG. 9-8). Place it in a stand and it serves adequately as a small, stationary drill press (FIG. 9-9).

*Fig. 9-7* *Electric drills can be used as a power source for a miniature lathe. Here, the accessory is being used for faceplate turning.*

**Types, sizes, and speeds**  There are many types and sizes of portable electric drills, some of which are shown in FIG. 9-10, but they all work in similar fashion. A motor drives a shaft that holds the chuck that, in turn, grips a cutting tool. Encased in the tool's housing is a gearing system that suits the correct torque and speed for what the drill is designed to do. While this is a simplistic picture of the concept, there are other factors that are part of today's products. Among them, power, variable speed controls, speed range, reversing switches, double insulation, and, sometimes, electronic features.

**Fig. 9-8** *Driving a small pump is one of the offbeat uses for an electric drill. The pump can move up to 200 gallons an hour depending on the drill's rpm.*

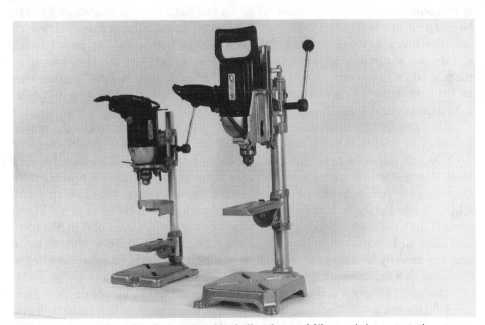

**Fig. 9-9** *Special stands allow a portable drill to be used like a miniature, stationary drill press. There are many types of stands available but they can't all be used with any drill. You must be sure the two units will work together.*

**Fig. 9-10** *Examples of modern, portable drills.*

Common electric drill sizes are $1/4$, $3/8$, and $1/2$ inch. The fraction indicates the maximum tool-shank diameter that the chuck will grip, but this is not necessarily its hole drilling capacity. There are quite a few cutting tools, like *spade bits*, which range in size from $1/8$ inch to $1 1/2$ inch that have $1/4$-inch shanks and so can be installed in the smallest drill. Many *hole saws* and similar accessories, which can form holes well over what can be accomplished with a drill bit, have $1/4$-inch shanks and so can be gripped in any of the power tools (FIG. 9-11). However, complete freedom to use any cutting tool in any drill is another matter. The unit may lack the power or the correct combination of power and speed to do a particular job efficiently and safely.

The capacity of a drill or, in a sense, its power, is always listed in the manufacturer's specifications. For example, a $1/4$-inch unit with a speed range of $0-2000$ rpm might be rated at $1/2$-inch holes in hardwood and $1/4$-inch holes in steel. Along with an increase in drill size there is an increase in power and a decrease in speed. A $3/8$-inch drill might have a speed range of $0-1200$ rpm and might be rated at $3/4$-inch holes in hardwood and $3/8$-inch holes in steel. When you get up to a $1/2$-inch product with a speed range in the area of 0 to 850 rpm, you can drill 1-inch holes in hardwood and $1/2$-inch holes in steel. Note that the drill size usually indicates the maximum size hole it should be asked to form in steel, but that the capacity doubles in hardwood.

The fact that speed decreases as power increases tells a lot about good practice with electric drills. Trying to drill a $1/2$-inch hole in steel with a small drill and at high speed will never work. That kind of job calls for good power and low rpm. There is always some overlap in function, even among tools of different size. For example, a small drill can occasionally be used beyond its rated capacity

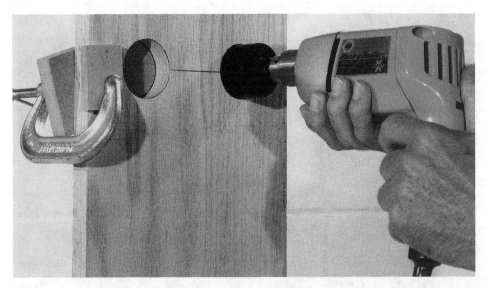

***Fig. 9-11*** *Pictured is a portable drill driving a hole saw. Grip the drill firmly and start the operation at slow speed. Always use a backup block to minimize the feathering that can occur when the saw breaks through.*

for a hole in steel by forming progressively larger holes. Start with a small bit and gradually increase bit-size—a technique that is generally good practice with any drill. On the other hand, there is no reason why a large drill can't form small holes. Some signs of poor practice are: the tool gets too warm, it stalls, or there is a drastic decrease in speed.

The trigger-controlled variable speed feature that is pretty standard on modern units eliminates the single speed limitation that the tools once had and makes any drill a more versatile tool. Fairly standard good practice is to start work at a slow speed, gradually increasing rpm until the cutter and the tool are performing without strain. The variable speed feature also makes any drill usable as an electric screwdriver, since the right speed for such work is critical. Add a reversing feature, also fairly standard today, and you can retract screws as well as drive them.

### Cordless drills

The option of working anywhere without needing electricity and without the nuisance of a dangling cord has made battery operated drills very popular (FIG. 9-12). I find myself using a cordless drill even in the shop, if only for the convenience it provides. The concept was introduced a few years ago and since then, much progress has been made in their features, power, and the length of time needed to recharge batteries. Power of today's concepts (in volts) can range from about 7.2 to as much as 12; recharge times can range from as little as 15 minutes to a more average 60 minutes.

**Fig. 9-12** *Typical cordless drills. Today's products have the power and the features to compete with most any plug-in type.*

Like conventional electric drills, cordless units have features like variable speeds and reversing switches. Quite a few products have a *clutch* that, for example, provides control for such tasks as driving screws. The clutch is set by the operator to slip at a particular torque level so the screw will be driven just so far.

### Choosing the right drill

You can go overboard when making a choice in terms of power, especially since cost goes up along with voltage. I have found that the 7.2-volt tool has more than enough power for most woodworking chores.

Statistics indicate that a 1/4-inch drill is a popular first choice, but it may not always be the best one. This drill-size may not have the power that is needed for some relatively heavy-duty tasks, like driving hole saws or for out-of-the-shop jobs like drilling a hole in concrete. A 3/8-inch drill might be the best first selection because it's huskier and can also do most of the lighter work ordinarily done with a smaller tool. Actually, because the price of each drill is not too extreme, you might want to equip yourself with one of each.

# Hole cutters

Call them drills, points, bits, or whatever—all are designed to cut holes. Each product works in its own fashion to form a circular cavity by removing a core of wood. A factor to remember when choosing a cutter has to do with whether it will be driven by hand or with power. Tools with brad-type points are okay to use in an electric drill, but cutters with screw tips, like those on auger bits, are not (FIG. 9-13). The screw tip is designed to pull the bit into the work, which is fine when using a hand brace, but would require specific rpm to match the pitch of the screw if driven by power—a factor that's not feasible when working with an electric drill.

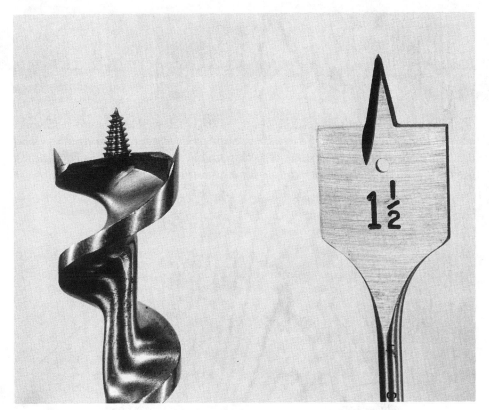

**Fig. 9-13**  *Pictured is an auger bit with a screw tip and a spade bit with a plain point.*

### Twist drills

*Twist drills* are most likely the most frequently used hole-forming tools (FIG. 9-14). This is due to the fact that they can be driven by hand or with power and because size-availability is so extreme. Actually, the common twist drill, with an 118-degree cutting angle, is designed for drilling metal. Technically, they do not offer

*Fig. 9-14  Twist drills are probably the most commonly used hole-forming tools. They can be used with handtools or with a power drill.*

offer the most efficient way to drill wood, but they are usable. Many woodworkers will grind the cutting angle to a more applicable 90 degrees for drilling wood (FIG. 9-15). However, because they do a respectable job when used as is, grinding the cutting angle seems a bit extreme for a home shop.

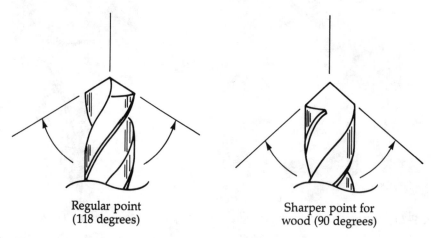

Regular point
(118 degrees)

Sharper point for
wood (90 degrees)

*Fig. 9-15  Most twist drills are offered with a* regular *point. A sharper point makes them more suitable for wood drilling.*

Twist drills are available in number, letter, and fractional sizes (TABLE 9-1). They may be purchased individually, but buying them in sets is more economical and provides you with bit-sizes for various jobs. Woodworkers will be amply

## Table 9-1. Fractional, Letter, and Number Sizes of Twist Drills

| Size (inches) | Decimal equivalent | Number or letter | Size (inches) | Decimal equivalent | Number or letter |
|---|---|---|---|---|---|
| 1/64 | 0.0156 | 78 | 17/64 | 0.2656 | G |
| 1/32 | 0.0312 | 67 | 9/32 | 0.2812 | L |
| 3/64 | 0.0468 | 56 | 19/64 | 0.2968 | M |
| 1/16 | 0.0625 | 53 | 5/16 | 0.3125 | N |
| 5/64 | 0.0781 | 48 | 21/64 | 0.3281 | Q |
| 3/32 | 0.0937 | 41 | 11/32 | 0.3437 | R |
| 7/64 | 0.1093 | 36 | 23/64 | 0.3593 | U |
| 1/8 | 0.125 | 31 | 3/8 | 0.375 | V |
| 9/64 | 0.140 | 28 | 25/64 | 0.3906 | W |
| 5/32 | 0.156 | 23 | 13/32 | 0.4062 | Z |
| 11/64 | 0.1719 | 18 | 27/64 | 0.4218 | — |
| 3/16 | 0.1875 | 13 | 7/16 | 0.4375 | — |
| 13/64 | 0.2031 | 6 | 29/64 | 0.4531 | — |
| 7/32 | 0.2187 | 3 | 15/32 | 0.4687 | — |
| 15/64 | 0.2344 | A | 31/64 | 0.4813 | — |
| 1/4 | 0.250 | D | 1/2 | 0.5 | — |

equipped with a fractional-size set that usually contains 29 units starting at 1/16 inch and increasing in 1/64-inch increments to 1/2 inch.

### Auger bits

*Auger bits*, meant for use in a bit brace, cut clean holes and help you do so with minimum effort because of screw points that pull the bit into the wood (see FIG. 9-13). The bits have perimeter spurs that contact the wood immediately after the screw is seated to score the edge of the hole before cutting actually starts (FIG. 9-16). This action cuts the surface fibers of the wood and ensures a clean entry. The circle formed by the spurs can also serve as a guide. If it is complete and of uniform depth, you'll know that you are applying the brace correctly; the bit will be square to the work.

Theoretically, the hole-depth cut by each revolution of the bit is controlled by the pitch of the lead screw. A medium screw is best for general woodworking. A screw with a steep pitch (fast screw) produces thicker waste chips and makes the bit brace harder to turn. A slow pitch (fine screw) allows easier turning of the brace because it produces thin chips, but it might try your patience.

Bit sizes are graded by 1/16 inch and by number. The number stamped on the bit indicates the number of 1/16. Thus, a number nine bit bores a 9/16-inch diameter hole. A typical 13-piece set runs in sizes from 1/4 inch to 1 inch. A 6-piece set might start at 1/4 inch and increase to 3/4 inch.

### Expansive bits

*Expansive bits*, sometimes called *expansion bits*, of the type shown in FIG. 9-17, are made for use in a bit brace. They can be used to form holes larger than what can

**Fig. 9-16** *The spurs on auger bits contact the wood before cutting starts. The spurs sever surface fibers and ensure a clean entry. When the circle is complete and uniform in depth, you'll know that the bit is in vertical position.*

**Fig. 9-17** *Expansive bits can be used for large holes, but they have another advantage. The cutting blades can be adjusted for hole sizes that can't be accomplished with fixed diameter bits.*

be accomplished with conventional bits, but because the tool has adjustable cutters, *you* have control over the diameter of the hole as well. Thus, you can organize the cutter for holes that are a fraction less or more than you can form with a fixed-diameter tool. Viewed this way, the bit takes on another dimension.

Most types are offered with two interchangeable cutters that overlap in the size holes for which they can be used. One two-cutter product can be used for holes from ⁵/₈ inch to 1³/₄ inch. Another example, also with two cutters, has a minimum hole-size of ⁷/₈ inch and a maximum size of 3 inches. Three inches, a fairly substantial capacity, seems to be the largest size hole the tools can form.

NOTE: The cutters are graduated so you can preset for the hole you need, but some caution is in order. Use the graduations to start with, but do a test on scrap stock so you can check for accuracy before you work on the project material.

### Spade bits

*Spade bits* (FIG. 9-18), sometimes called *wing* or *flat* bits, are available with various cutting-end configurations, but all are meant for wood drilling with power.

**Fig. 9-18**  *An example of a spade bit, which must be used in a power drill.*

Although they do more scraping than shearing, they form clean, accurate holes when kept sharp and used correctly. The long point, which is a feature on all types, helps provide accuracy when starting a hole and makes it a lot easier to get started when you must drill a hole at an angle. The point, which you can embed a bit by applying a little pressure and hand-turning the chuck, will set the cutter firmly before the hole starts to form.

Contrary to the wise, general rule that advises using low speeds for large-hole drilling, spade bits work most efficiently at higher rpm than you would use with another cutter of comparable size. Working at about 1500 rpm, even when drilling a 1¹/₂-inch hole is not out of line.

Spade bits are available individually or in sets that start at ¹/₈ inch or ¹/₄ inch and range up to 1¹/₂ inch, usually increasing in increments of ¹/₈ inch.

### Hole saws

*Hole saws*, which should be used with power, are essentially cup-like units with saw teeth and a central pilot drill (FIG. 9-19). Their primary purpose is to form holes that are larger than you can accomplish with a conventional set of wood bits. That's why, individually or in sets, they range from about ³/₄ inch up to 2¹/₂ or 3 inches. Cup-type hole saws come in specific sizes. Another type has a holder, or *mandrel*, to which can be affixed various band-type blades of different diameters (FIG. 9-20). A third concept works with several, individual, straight,

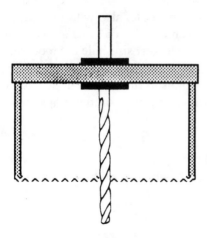

**Fig. 9-19** *Fixed diameter hole saws are shaped like cups that have perimeter saw teeth. They mount on a mandrel that holds a pilot drill.*

**Fig. 9-20** *Another type of hole saw works with bandsaw-type blades that lock in circular grooves in the mandrel.*

metal or wood-cutting blades. The blade diameter settings are infinite, so the tool can be used for any size hole within its capacity.

These cutters work hard and should be applied with only enough pressure to keep them cutting. However, if you try to be too gentle, you will do more burnishing than sawing. Always start the cutter at a slow speed. Increase speed gradually to the point where the teeth are working efficiently. Although the tools cut cleanly and with minimum feathering when they break through the stock, it's usually a good idea to back up the work with a scrap block.

Think of hole saws as dual-purpose cutters. They form holes by removing discs, but the discs can be the part you want; usable for, among other things, wheels for toys. Since the saws have a pilot drill, the axle hole is already formed, accurately centered. If, in other cases, the pilot hole is a problem, it can be plugged with a matching or, for a decorative detail, a contrasting dowel.

# Drilling techniques

Some drilling jobs require more feed pressure than others, but it should never be necessary to force the bit into the work. When this action is necessary, it's usually because you are using a dull cutter, employing the wrong cutter for the material, or trying to drill a large hole in a single step. Except for auger bits and other cutters like spade bits, it's often good procedure to start with a small hole and increase its size in steps. Efficient drilling occurs when you coordinate the rotation speed of the tool with the cutting action of the bit. You control this manually with a handtool and by adjusting the speed control when using an electric drill. The cutter must work constantly. Being too gentle with feed pressure so that the cutting lips of the bit just rub, won't form holes and will lead to untimely dulling of the cutter.

The work being drilled must be secure for the sake of accuracy and safety. You don't want a small piece spinning about like a top, which can happen, especially with power drills, should the cutter snag. Grip the work in a vise or secure it to a bench with clamps. Use both hands to control the tool.

A certain amount of splintering or feathering will occur at the breakout point when you drill through stock. The amount will vary depending on the cutter, but regardless of the tool in use, it is good procedure to back up the work with a piece of scrap. Keep drilling until you are sure the cutting lips of the bit have penetrated into the backup stock.

# Hole cutter accessories

## Accurate alignment and drill guides

Although accurate alignment is not an actual accessory, it must be achieved before you drill a hole. An accurate way to mark a hole's location is to draw intersecting lines that cross where the center of the hole must be. This method leaves little room for error. Use a hard, sharp pencil and lightly draw the lines. Don't use a knife or scriber for this kind of layout or you will have problems when applying a finish.

All holes, even those that will be drilled with a lead-screw bit, should be started by forming an indent with an awl or punch. When you use the indenting tool, hold it at a slight angle as you put the point directly on the intersection of the lines (FIG. 9-21). This provides a clear view of where the point must be before you bring the tool to vertical position and apply pressure to form the indent.

Applying the tool also requires accuracy and alignment. First, hold the tool at a right angle to the work's surface so that the hole will be square. Determining a hole's accuracy is something you can eventually tell by sight, but when learn-

**Fig. 9-21** *Spot hole locations by drawing intersecting lines. Start the job, regardless of the drilling tool, by first forming a slight indent with an awl or punch.*

ing, it's a good idea to align the drill accurately by placing a square on the work, butted against the tool.

The simple drilling guide that is sketched in FIG. 9-22 and shown being used with an electric drill in FIG. 9-23 will guide you toward holding the drill vertically and will also help you drill accurately. The guide block should be marked as shown so it can be aligned with intersecting marks on the workpiece. Because the block should be available for various jobs, the hole through it should not be more than 1/16 or 1/8 inch. The idea is to use it for pilot holes that can later be enlarged to the right size. Once you have a true pilot hole, it's not likely that you will go off line when using a larger bit.

A practical accessory that guarantees drilling at a 90-degree angle when using an electric drill is the Portalign *DRILL-GUIDE* shown in FIG. 9-24. The drill

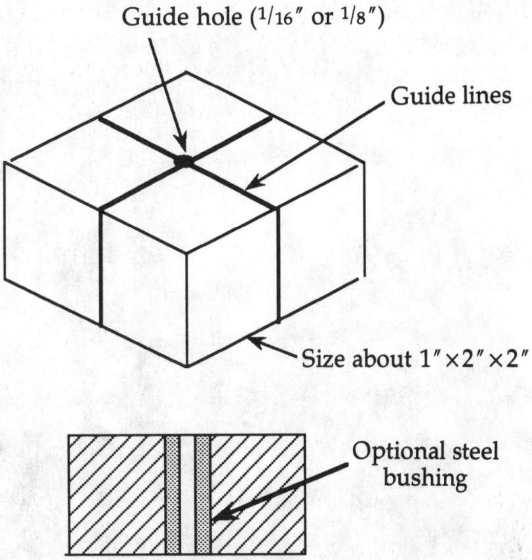

Guide hole ($^1/_{16}$" or $^1/_8$")

Guide lines

**Fig. 9-22** *A simple block that serves to hold bits vertically so holes will be square to the work's surface.*

Size about 1"×2"×2"

Optional steel bushing

**Fig. 9-23** *The lines on the block are aligned with the layout lines on the work. Thus, the guide block increases accuracy and helps you drill vertically.*

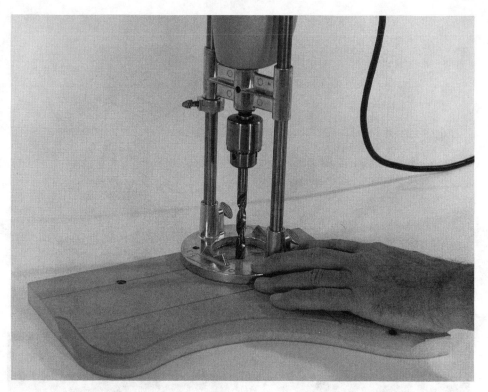

***Fig. 9-24*** *The* DRILL-GUIDE *is a commercial accessory that ensures drilling holes that are square to the work's surface.*

is mounted on a bracket that slides on twin, vertical bars that assure a vertical posture. An adjustable stop ring on one of the bars allows control over how far the bit will extend. Thus, the accessory can be used for holes that pass through the stock, or *stopped* holes, those that penetrate a preset distance.

Homemade guide blocks can be designed to suit various drilling jobs. The one shown in FIG. 9-25, makes it easy to drill holes accurately and squarely into the edges of stock. This is a good way to drill holes for dowels when they are used to reinforce an edge-to-edge joint.

### Angular drill guides

Trying to judge a particular angle by eye is asking a lot. It's best to use a protractor or a T-bevel to set the tilt of the drill. If you lack such tools, you can make a layout on a piece of still cardboard and cut it so it can be used as a gauge. It's often a good idea to start an angular hole by starting with the tool in a vertical position, then tilting the cutter to the angle described by the gauge. This is especially true of auger bits because, when held at an angle, the spurs of the bit will contact the work before the screw is seated. You will be cutting on one side of the hole and it will be very easy to move off the mark if you try to force the entry.

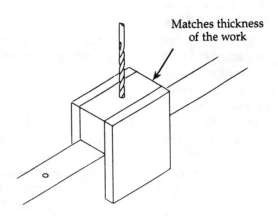

*Fig. 9-25*  *A guide of this type ensures accurate center holes in stock edges. The thickness of the center piece can be designed so the guide will also act as a stop to control hole depth.*

Matches thickness
of the work

Another way to go, especially when you need many similar holes, is to make a guide block similar to the one that was shown for straight drilling (FIG. 9-26). First step is to drill a hole through a block of wood that has parallel sides. Then saw off one end so the block will tilt to the angle you need. If you make the block so its thickness is to a particular dimension, it can also serve to limit the bit's penetration.

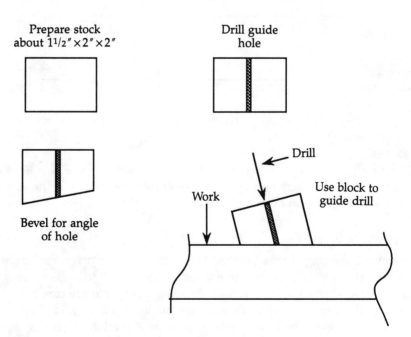

Prepare stock
about 1¹/₂″ × 2″ × 2″

Drill guide
hole

Bevel for angle
of hole

Drill

Work

Use block to
guide drill

*Fig. 9-26*  *This sketch shows how to make a guide for angular drilling. The guide can be tack-nailed or clamped to the work.*

### Stops and stopped holes

*Stopped* or *blind* holes are just cavities that penetrate the stock a specific distance. Preparing holes for dowels, drilling for screws, and drilling to remove waste when forming a mortise are all good examples of when to use stopped holes.

Trying to drill to the depth that is needed can be difficult without some sort of gauge. The simplest method of all is just to wrap several layers of masking tape around the bit so you'll know when to stop feeding. Another way is to drill a hole through a small block of wood of suitable width, then mounting it on the bit before you drill.

Commercially available adjustable *drill stops*, like those shown in FIG. 9-27, are available as accessories. A set of two units will fit bit sizes from $1/16$ inch to $1/2$ inch. The stops function almost like chucks. Turning the top collar reduces the inside diameter so the unit grips the bit it is mounted on very tightly.

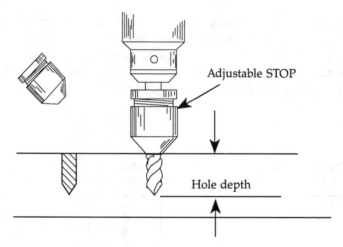

**Fig. 9-27**  *These adjustable drill stops are simple but practical and efficient.*

Another type of stop, shown mounted on an auger bit in FIG. 9-28, is just a fancy collar that locks to the bit by means of a screw. Because it is the screw that supplies security, this unit can be used on various diameter bits.

### Center drilling jig

The center drilling jig that is detailed in FIG. 9-29 will help you drill accurately while eliminating tedious layout time when it's necessary to drill centered holes along the edge of a board. It's a simple design but does require care in construction. Make the bar, using a hardwood like maple or birch, and then drill the guide hole and the two holes needed for the nails. Be certain the holes are on the bar's centerline. The additional holes in the bar will provide more flexibility in the jig's placement. Frequent use of the jig may cause enlargement of the guide

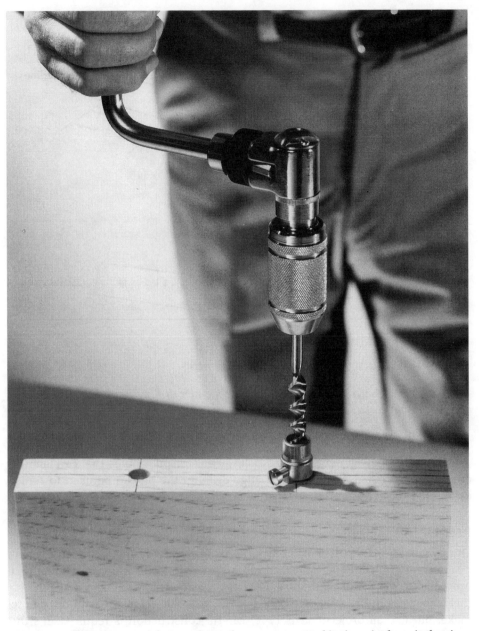

***Fig. 9-28*** *This commercial stop, shown here on an auger bit, is a single unit that is secured with a screw. The one stop can be used on various diameter bits.*

hole, so it's a good idea to install a steel bushing that has a $1/16$- or $1/8$-inch center hole. The bushing can be forced into a slightly undersize hole or installed with an epoxy.

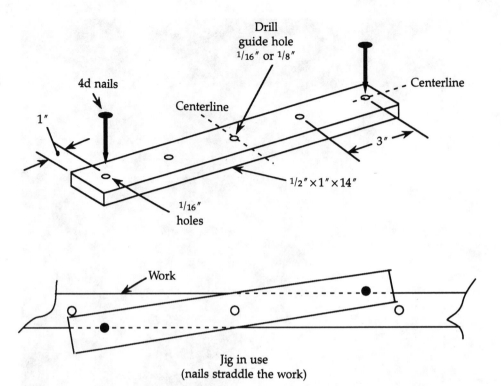

**Fig. 9-29** *This sketch shows you how to make a center drilling jig. It can be used to center-drill into surfaces as well as edges.*

The guide hole is deliberately small; meant for pilot holes that can later be enlarged to any size. In addition to edge-drilling, the jig can be used to center drill in the surface of any board that it can straddle.

### Radial hole-drilling jig

One of the more difficult chores encountered in woodworking is drilling diametrically through cylinders. It's practically impossible to do it accurately without providing some sort of mechanical guidance. A good solution is to make the jig that is pictured in FIG.9-30 and detailed in FIG. 9-31. The accessory isn't difficult to make, but like all projects of its type, careful construction is required. It's the kind of work where taking 10 minutes to do a 5-minute job makes sense.

Marking the work when a series of holes is required on the same centerline can be accomplished as shown in FIG. 9-32. The position of the cylinder in relation to the strip of wood on which the pencil rides is not crucial.

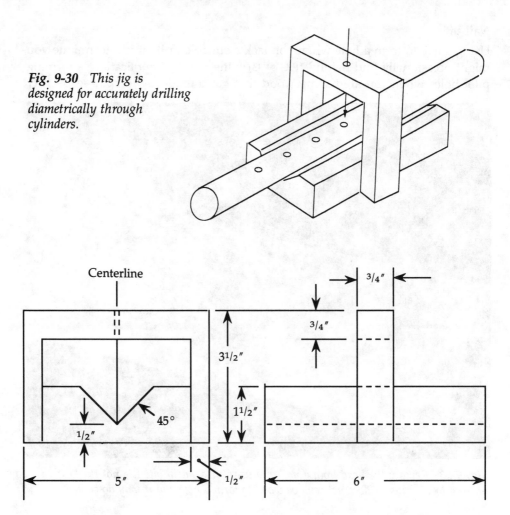

**Fig. 9-30** *This jig is designed for accurately drilling diametrically through cylinders.*

Centerline

3½"

¾"

¾"

45°

½"

1½"

5"

½"

6"

**Fig. 9-31** *Construction details for the radial hole drilling jig.*

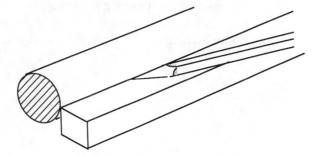

**Fig. 9-32** *One way to accurately mark a longitudinal centerline on a cylinder is to hold a strip of wood to the cylinder's side. A pencil can then be used to mark the accurate line.*

## Nail bit

Using a nail to form a hole when you lack a suitable drill bit is a technique you might occasionally find helpful (FIG. 9-33). One practical application is forming pilot holes when you are nailing wood that has a tendency to split—especially

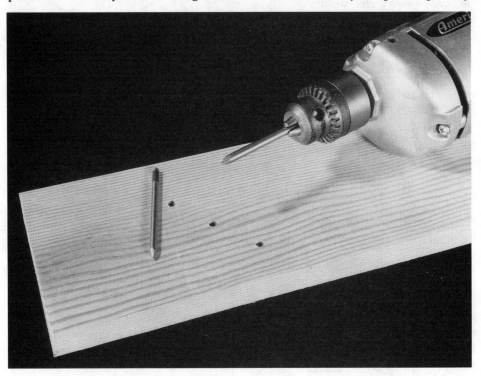

**Fig. 9-33** *Remove the head from a nail and use it like a drill bit. It's not the best drilling tool because it does not remove wood to form a hole and it may do some burning.*

when nailing near edges. In this instance, drill pilot holes with a nail that is smaller than those you will use for fastening.

Nails used this way compress the wood fibers instead of cutting them away, and thus, some burning might occur, but the idea is functional.

# 10
# Hammers and nails

Like many tools, the basic concept of the hammer hasn't changed substantially, even though it has matured to a super product with specific designs available for particular applications. The *nail hammer* is not an all-purpose tool. It must not be used to hammer metal or to split a piece of masonry. Likewise, a light hammer, like one that is suitable for shop work, is not appropriate for driving house-framing nails and is not tempered for striking hardened masonry nails or cold chisels. The nail hammer, or *claw hammer*, the design that's most useful for furniture and cabinetmaking and for general in-the-shop use, is not designed for such work. In addition to being inefficient, such use can present a hazard because of the possibility of chipping, which would lead to eye injury. The eye injury factor, generally, deserves consideration. Reach for safety goggles every time you hammer.

A quality hammer contributes to professional work. It's tough, durable, and has poise, balance, and beauty. Don't even consider the cast blobs, often attached to rough and improperly shaped handles, that are offered in bargain bins. Today's hammers may be equipped with wood, steel, even fiberglass or graphite handles. Technical pros and cons have to do mostly with the shock absorbing qualities and wear-resistance of these various materials. For example fiberglass won't chip like wood or rust like steel. Steel can rust, but one with a forged head/handle assembly won't loosen at the head and it's not likely that the handle will ever break. A wooden handle is replaceable, and so on. There are many construction workers who won't change from wooden handles because "they don't feel as cold as steel, especially in inclement weather"—a pretty sensible argument!

In the final analysis, choosing a hammer is a more personal thing than it is with just about any other tool. How the tool feels in your hand may be the deciding factor. A good thought is that you don't just go out and buy a hammer, you shop for one.

# Types of hammers

### The claw hammer

Claw hammers, like other designs, are available in different weights and with curved or straight claws. For general woodworking, the 16-ounce, curved-claw design is the most valuable first choice. A close look at the claws will, or should reveal, that they are ground at the end so they can fit narrow spaces between nails and between nail heads and wood surfaces. The sides of the slot between the claws should be beveled so there will be sharp edges to allow gripping a nail anyplace along the shank, not just under the head of the nail.

The face of the poll always has some curvature but there is variation in the degree of convexity. Professionals who do interior trim prefer a hammer with a pronounced *crown*, or bell-faced tip, because it makes it easier for them to drive a nail flush or even a bit below the surface of the wood without denting it. Such a design, however, requires some expertise that can only be acquired through use. For the kind of work ordinarily done in the shop, it's best to acquire hammering know-how by starting with a unit that has minimum crown (FIG. 10-1).

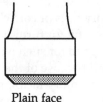

Plain face          Bell face

*Fig. 10-1  Plain face hammer is a good choice, at least to start with. The curvature of the bell face makes it easier to slip off a nail, so the design requires some experience for efficient use.*

Claw hammers are available with two styles of claws. On the curved-claw hammer in (FIG. 10-2), the claw follows a pronounced arc and is especially suited to removing nails. On the second concept, the claws have a heavier cross section and are almost straight. While they can be used to remove nails, they are particularly suitable for prying apart nailed assemblies (FIG. 10-3). For this reason, they are preferred by construction workers for such work as ripping off siding or roof boards.

### Tack hammer

The tack hammer, (FIG. 10-4), is usful in any woodshop, even if it's never used to drive a tack. These are the drivers to use for light constructions and fasteners like

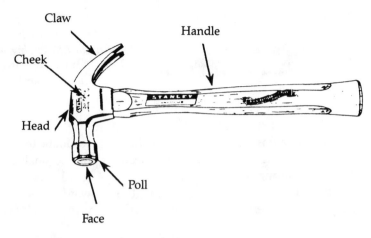

Fig. 10-2  *Nomenclature of a hammer.*

*Fig. 10-3*  *Straight claw hammer is useful for prying apart nailed assemblies. It can be started with a mallet. Never strike the head of a hammer with another hard tool.*

**Fig. 10-4** *A tack hammer is not limited to driving just tack. It can also be used to drive brads and small wire nails.*

small nails and *brads*, situations where your regular hammer would be too cumbersome. The most practical design has a magnetized head, or pole, so small fasteners can be started without having to use fingers (FIG. 10-5). A good procedure is to attach the nail to the hammer and then exert enough downward pressure to seat the nail where it must be driven. Then tap the fastener home in routine fashion.

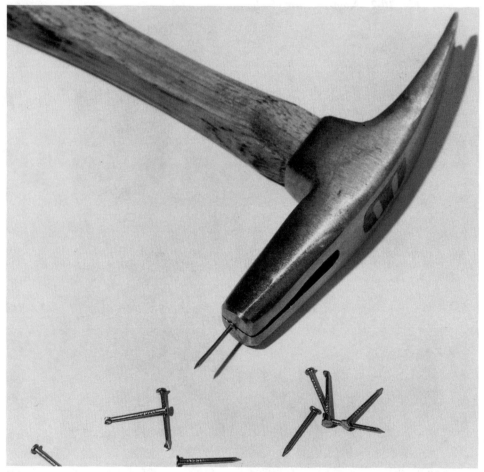

**Fig. 10-5** *A tack hammer with a magnetized head is a good choice to use with small fasteners.*

**Mallets**

Regardless of the type, mallets have soft faces so they can't damage the tool or the material being struck. Two of the most common applications in a woodshop are driving wood chisels and tapping together tight-fitting wood connections. At one time, "mallet" was a synonym for wooden hammer. While wooden ones are still available and popular, other concepts that may have faces of hard rubber, rawhide, or plastic have been introduced.

Actually, some modern ones are called "soft-face hammers" rather than mallets. The example in FIG. 10-6 has replaceable, plastic heads and is available in sizes that range from 1½ to 32 ounces.

*Fig. 10-6  Mallets come in different materials and sizes but they all have "soft" faces so they can't damage tools or materials. This example has replaceable plastic heads.*

Whatever the choice, remember that they are adapted to striking other objects, like tools or finished surfaces without danger of marring or chipping. They are not intended for jobs like driving nails.

# Types of nails

There are hundreds of different types of nails, many of them with names that tell you what they should be used for—wallboard nails, roofing nails, flooring nails, and a host of others. To avoid confusion, only those that are of major use in a woodworking shop are discussed (FIG. 10-7).

*Common* and *box* nails are similar in length (TABLE 10-1), but have different applications. Common nails are general-purpose, heavy-duty fasteners that are generally used for house framing and similar constructions. They are also suitable for outside projects like fences and decks, but unless they are especially coated to prevent rust, they will, in time, leave ugly stains. The solution is to use galvanized nails—common steel nails that have been coated with zinc. The coating is applied by dipping the nails in molten zinc or by electroplating. Dipped nails are rough and may have some sharp edges. Electroplated ones are smoother but have a thin coat that is less durable than dipped ones.

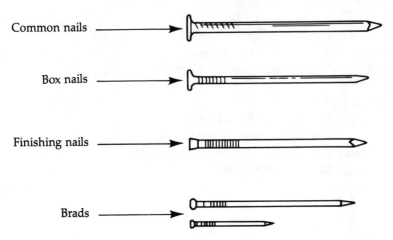

**Fig. 10-7** *These are the nails that are most useful in a woodworking shop.*

### Table 10-1. Sizes of Common and Box Nails

| Penny (d) size | Length (inches) | Penny (d) size | Length (inches) |
|---|---|---|---|
| 2 | 1 | 10 | 3 |
| 3 | $1^{1}/4$ | 12 | $3^{1}/4$ |
| 4 | $1^{1}/2$ | 16 | $3^{1}/2$ |
| 5 | $1^{3}/4$ | 20 | 4 |
| 6 | 2 | 30 | $4^{1}/2$ |
| 7 | $2^{1}/4$ | 40 | 5 |
| 8 | $2^{1}/2$ | 50 | $5^{1}/2$ |
| 9 | $2^{3}/4$ | 60 | 6 |

Box nails have large heads like common nails but have smaller shank diameters. Thus, in addition to being easier to drive, they are more adapted to delicate work because they are less likely to cause splitting.

*Finishing nails* are the fasteners to use for in-house or shop work when hiding the nail is important. They are manufactured of lighter-gauge wire than common or box nails and have smaller, specially-shaped heads that are only about one-third larger than the nail's shank. Thus, finishing nails are easily driven below the surface of the wood so they can be concealed. Most times, the top surface of the head is cupped so that a *nail set*, a tool used to finish driving them below the wood's surface (FIG. 10-8), will seat firmly. Finishing nails are available in lengths that range from 1 inch to 3 inches or even more (TABLE 10-2).

*Wire brads* are actually small finishing nails that are available in lengths ranging from $3/16$ inch to $1^{1}/2$ inch, with each length made in several gauges (TABLE 10-3). These are the fasteners for small assemblies involving thin components. Nails that are similar in size to brads but with conventional flat heads are called *wire nails*.

**Fig. 10-8** *Nail sets are used to drive finishing nails or brads below the surface of the wood so they can be concealed. It's best to buy the tools in sets so you will have units to suit the size of the nail head.*

### Table 10-2. Sizes of Finishing Nails

| | Size d = penny | Gauge | Length (inches) |
|---|---|---|---|
| | 2 | 16 1/2 | 1 |
| | 3 | 15 1/2 | 1 1/4 |
| | 4 | 15 | 1 1/2 |
| | 6 | 13 | 2 |
| | 8 | 12 1/2 | 2 1/2 |
| | 10 | 11 1/2 | 3 |

### Table 10-3. Sizes of Wire Brads

| | Length (inches) | Gauges | | Length (inches) | Gauges |
|---|---|---|---|---|---|
| | 3/16 | 20 – 24 | | 1/4 | 13 – 21 |
| | 1/4 | 19 – 24 | | 7/8 | 13 – 20 |
| | 3/8 | 18 – 24 | | 1 | 12 – 20 |
| | 1/2 | 14 – 23 | | 1 1/8 | 12 – 20 |
| | 5/8 | 13 – 22 | | | |

### What does penny mean?

The size of most nails is designated by the word *penny* a term indicated by the small letter d. This system of measuring probably originated in England and was based on the price of 100 nails. For example, 100 4d nails would have cost 4 pennies. Today, d tells the length of a nail. For instance, a 2d nail is 1 inch long, a 60d nail is 6 inches long, and so forth (see TABLE 10-1). Actually, when you buy today either in bulk from a bin or by the box, both the d size and the length of the nail will be listed.

### Nail substitutes

*Corrugated* and *Skotch* nails are special fasteners that have practical applications (FIG. 10-9). Corrugated nails are ribbed lengths of metal that are sharp along one edge. Generally, they are used as reinforcements when appearance is not important or when they will not be visible. An example application is using them at the back on all four corners of a picture frame. The nails will add considerable strength to the miter joints and will not be visible when the frame is on the wall.

Corrugated nails                    Skotch nails

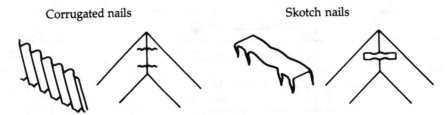

**Fig. 10-9**  *Corrugated and Skotch nails can be used to reinforce many types of wood connections. They are especially useful on miter joints.*

These nails should be driven very carefully, across the grain whenever possible. Driving them with the grain, especially near ends or edges can cause splitting.

The Skotch nails are used in similar applications but are less hazardous than corrugated nails because they penetrate the wood with individual, sharp prongs so there is less chance of splitting.

## Using a nail hammer

When using a nail hammer, grip the hammer near the end of the handle so you will have maximum leverage. This provides the most power and drive. Hold the handle firmly so the tool won't twist when you strike. Caution though, if the grip is too tight it could contribute to fatigue. Normally, your thumb will curl around the handle in natural fashion (FIG. 10-10), but when you want more control you can extend your thumb along the handle. This is often done when starting a nail or when using a light hammer.

You can swing a hammer with your wrist, elbow, shoulder, or all three. Much depends on the force that's needed to drive the nail. Small nails can be the impact point of an arc that has your wrist as its center. At the other extreme, with very large nails, your shoulder joint might be the center of the swing-arc. Any-

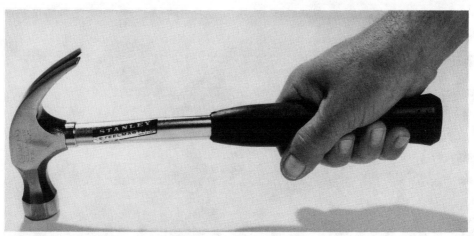

**Fig. 10-10**  *Pictured is the correct way to hold a hammer.*

time you feel that you should start the swing from somewhere behind your spine, it would be wiser to reach for a different striking tool.

A most important consideration is the squareness of the hammerhead to the nail at the moment of impact. If you did a drawing of the procedure, it would show that the entire action occurs within the confines of a quarter circle. The length of the arc decreases in proportion to the lightness of the blow that is needed. Sometimes to get a nail started, it's convenient to grip the handle closer to the head, but this is not a normal procedure because it substitutes your forearm for the handle.

Other examples of misuse are striking with the cheek of the hammer instead of the face, and using the claws of the hammer for work best done with a wrecking bar. The cheek of a hammer is not hard or thick enough for use as a striking surface, and a wrecking bar is the tool to use for removing very large nails or rusted spikes or for disassembling heavy constructions.

## Driving nails

Driving nails is not a contest. It should not be your intention to do the job with the least number of blows. That course will lead to missing the nail or to striking inaccurately so you cause damage to the work or to yourself. Also, nails that are driven home calmly will hold better because they cause minimum distortion in the wood fibers. Bent fibers spring back more easily to grip the nail than those that are split apart.

Blunt nails are less likely to cause splitting than sharp ones. That's why you will often see a professional, in some situations, deliberately blunt the point of the nail before installing it (FIG. 10-11). There are situations where even this precaution won't prevent splitting. Then the solution is to drill pilot holes for the nails before you drive them. The pilot-hole size shouldn't be more than about

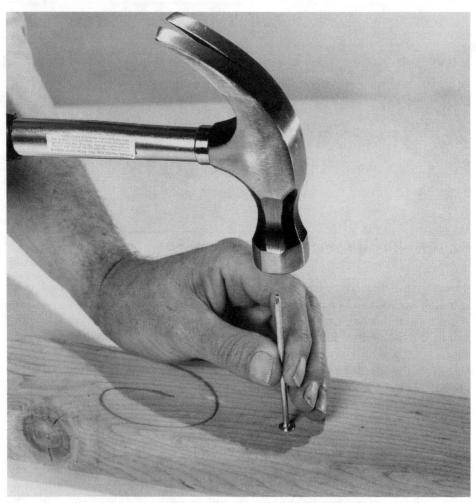

***Fig. 10-11*** *Carpenters will often blunt a nail when there is a danger of splitting the wood. Blunt points bend wood fibers; sharp ones separate them.*

75% of the nail-shank diameter. Its depth can match the length of the nail, but minimizing it will allow the nail to grip some solid wood.

To start a nail and to determine your aim with the hammer, rest the face of the hammer on the nail head and then draw back a bit so you can deliver a light blow. Then strike the nail squarely. Striking squarely is the key to avoiding marring the project, bending the nail, or striking your thumb. Most workers start by holding the nail near the head between thumb and forefinger. Others claim that it's better to invert the fingers so they will be well away from the nail head (FIG. 10-12). The important factor is that the nail should be struck, not your fingers. The safest procedure, regardless of finger position, is to tap the nail lightly to get it started. Then you can move your hand out of the danger zone.

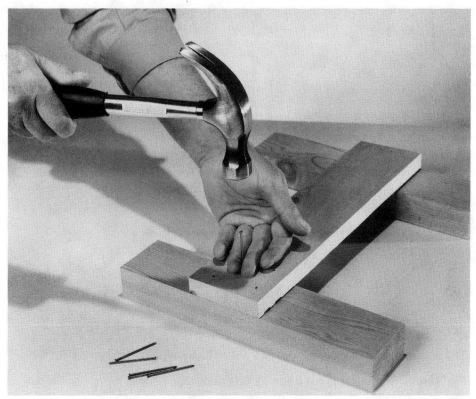

**Fig. 10-12** *Pictured is a commonly used method for holding a nail so that your fingers do not get struck.*

There are ways to start nails without placing your fingers near the impact area. They can be adopted as standard procedure or employed when the situation and nail-size suggest using them. Small brads can be held in place for starting by pressing them through a slim strip of cardboard. The gadget that is shown in FIG. 10-13, can be a permanent accessory, useful anytime you have a small brad or nail to install.

When face-nailing two pieces of wood (i.e., when the parts are surface to surface), use a nail that is about 3/16 inch less than the combined thickness of the parts. A standard rule for edge-nailing is to choose a nail-length that is three times the thickness of the piece being secured. This isn't always possible due to the possible length or width of the mating piece; however, when the standard rule doesn't apply, just figure that about two thirds of the nail should penetrate the second piece.

Whenever possible, use a staggered pattern for nail placement. Driving them on a common centerline can cause the wood to split. Splitting can also occur when nails must be driven near the ends of components. The solution is to first

**Fig. 10-13** *This holder is just a slim strip of wood with a short, narrow slot at one end, used when you wish to avoid striking your fingers when hammering.*

drill pilot holes that are smaller than the shank diameter of the nails through the part being fastened (FIG. 10-14).

Nails that are driven at a slight angle provide a better grip than nails driven straight (FIG. 10-15). Be careful when the nail head nears the surface of the stock because the face of the hammer will be at an angle and can dent the surface of the wood. When appearance is important, finish driving the nail with a nail set. On rough work, where appearance usually is not critical, you can increase the holding power by using nails that are longer than necessary and then *clinching* (bending over) the projecting end at right angles to the wood grain (FIG. 10-16).

## Concealing nails

The routine method, used with finishing nails and brads, is to drive the fastener only until the head is still exposed. Final driving, until the head is below the surface of the stock by 1/8 inch or so, is done with a nail set. The hole that remains is filled with a matching wood dough or putty. This method is standard procedure, but be aware that nail sets come in different sizes. Using a nail set that matches or comes close to the nail size does the job while leaving a minimum hole size to be filled. Tip sizes on typical nail sets are 1/32, 1/16, 3/32, 1/8, and 5/32 inch. The tools

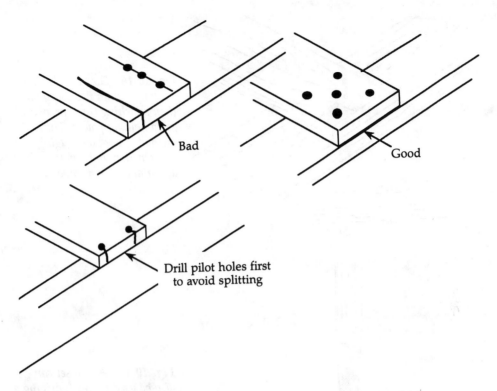

**Fig. 10-14**  *A staggered nail pattern provides good strength and is less likely to cause splitting. Providing pilot holes is good practice when nails must be driven close to an edge.*

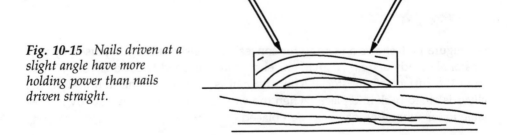

**Fig. 10-15**  *Nails driven at a slight angle have more holding power than nails driven straight.*

can be purchased individually, but it's more economical to obtain them as a group. Also, having an assortment equips you for various nailing situations. While this method is typically used with finishing nails, there is no reason why it can't be adopted for small nails with regular heads (FIG. 10-17).

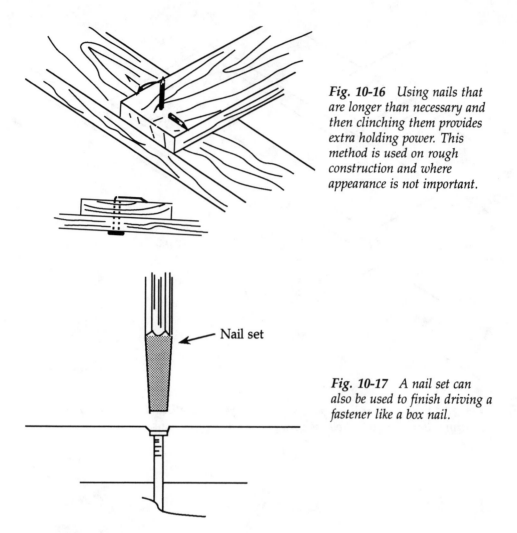

*Fig. 10-16* *Using nails that are longer than necessary and then clinching them provides extra holding power. This method is used on rough construction and where appearance is not important.*

Nail set

*Fig. 10-17* *A nail set can also be used to finish driving a fastener like a box nail.*

Figure 10-18 shows a method for concealing nails that is widely used by professional woodworkers. A small chisel or gouge is used to lift a sliver of wood from the surface of the stock. After the nail is driven into the depression, the sliver is glued back into place. When the work is done neatly, it's nearly impossible to tell where the nail has been placed.

## Removing nails

If you use a curved claw hammer correctly to remove a nail, the nail will emerge straight. If the nail head projects just a bit, set the claws so the nail head is as close to the end of the slot as possible. Pull back on the handle until the nail is partly drawn. Then slip a small block of wood under the hammer head to increase leverage and to relieve unnecessary strain on the handle (FIG. 10-19).

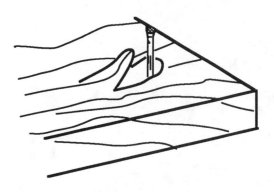

**Fig. 10-18** *A truly professional way to conceal a nail is to lift a sliver from the surface of the stock, drive the nail, and then glue back the sliver.*

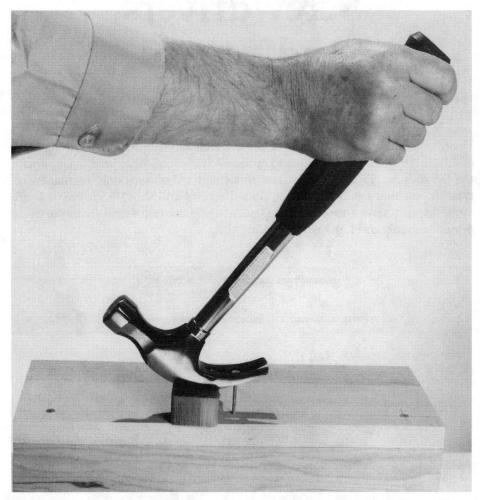

**Fig. 10-19** *A block of wood under the hammer head increases leverage when pulling nails and reduces strain on the handle.*

# 11

# Screwdrivers and screws

The many styles of screw heads that are available has caused a bewildering array of different types of screwdrivers to appear—*clutch head, Allen head, square drives,* the list goes on. To avoid confusion, this chapter discusses only regular wing-type drivers that are designed for slotted screws and those with tips that are formed to fit screws with cross slots (FIG. 11-1). These two screw styles are those most commonly used in a woodworking shop.

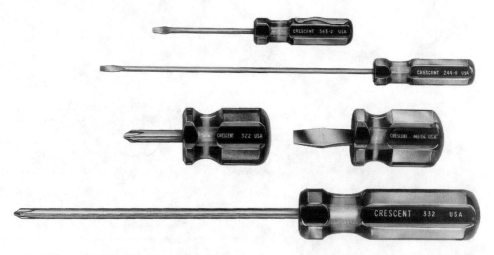

**Fig. 11-1** *Examples of screwdrivers with standard wing-blade tips and special blades designed for screws with cross-slot heads.*

# Screwdrivers

All hand-turned screwdrivers consist of the parts that are shown in FIG. 11-2. The driving force that turns a screw is a twisting action, or *torque*, that is supplied through the handle and down to the tool's tip, which is seated in the screw's head slot. The larger the screwdriver, the more power you can apply. You can assume that the size of the screwdriver is in direct relationship to the size of the screw it is designed to drive.

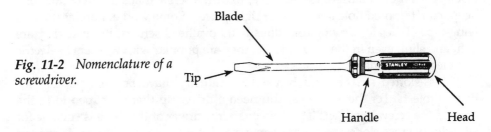

**Fig. 11-2** *Nomenclature of a screwdriver.*

Screwdriver sizes are generally determined by the length of the blade. The longer the blade, the broader and thicker its tip will be, and the larger the screws that it can drive efficiently. The tools can be purchased individually, but it's more economical and practical to acquire a set. A typical assortment of six units will have blade lengths running from 3 inches to 9 inches and will include several sizes that are designed for cross-slot screws.

There are so many top brands of screwdrivers available that the only way to make a bad choice is to select for price rather than quality. Because even professional drivers are not expensive, it's foolish not to purchase the best. Handles might be hardwood, but most units have tough, plastic handles that stand up to punishment better than wood. Handles have rounded ends to fit in the palm and, whether round or octagonal, the sides of the handle are usually fluted so the tool won't slip in your hand as you turn it.

### Basic driver-tips

The drive-tip on the most common screwdrivers has a wing-type shape and is designed to turn flathead, roundhead, and ovalhead screws that have slotted heads. The end of the blade flares out and is tapered by grinding on both edges (FIG. 11-3). The width and thickness of the tip varies with the length of the blade so a selection is based in relation to the size of the screw. This type of driver is probably the most abused and misused tool. It's almost common practice to use it as a pry, a lever, a punch, even as an ice pick or can opener. It's admitted that its style suggests such off-beat applications, but such uses can spoil it for its intended purpose.

A similar drive-tip, usually called *cabinet tip*, is tapered and ground square at its end, but it does not flare out; the width of the tip equals the diameter of the

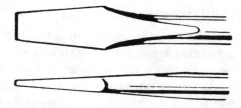

*Fig. 11-3* *The wing-type drive-tip will turn most frequently used screws—flathead, roundhead, and ovalhead.*

blade. Thus it can be used, for example, to turn a screw that's at the bottom of a deep, counterbored hole and in other tight places. Some workers prefer them to wing-type blades for driving roundhead and ovalhead screws. Because they are light and slim, even in the long lengths, they are popular with workers in electric and electronic fields.

Cross-slotted screws, widely used in industry, have become popular for home projects. For these screws, you need a driver-tip that is shaped to fit the cross in the screw head (FIG. 11-4). No one screwdriver of this type is suitable for all styles of cross-slot screws. One screw may have cross slots that are U-shaped and of uniform width; another will have V-shaped slots with tapered sides. Actually, there is no reason to be confused because any set of screwdrivers offered for woodworking will have one or two sizes of *Phillips head* drivers—and the cross-slot screws that you are most likely to find in local stores will be the Phillips head design.

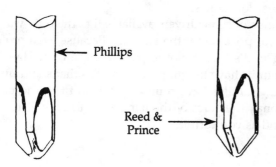

← Phillips

Reed & Prince →

*Fig. 11-4* *Two types of tips for screw heads with cross-slots.*

## Wood screws

It's pretty rare to find a piece of furniture that doesn't have screws somewhere in its assembly, if only to secure reinforcement pieces or to attach the backs of cabinets. Screws can strengthen joints, even when glue is used, and, of course, they are the fasteners to use for hinges, drawer pulls, and the like.

Common wood screws, together with washers that can be used with them are shown in FIG. 11-5. Flathead screws are driven flush with the surface of the wood in a *countersunk* hole, or below the surface in a *counterbored* hole when you wish to conceal them. Roundhead screws, often used with flat washers, are prac-

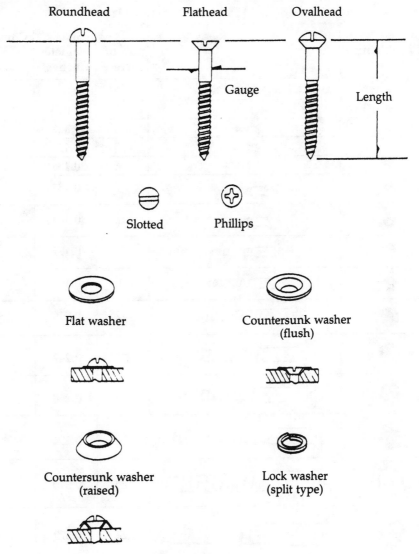

**Fig. 11-5** *Common wood screws and the washers that can be used with them.*

tical fasteners when the part being attached is thin wood, plastic, or something like sheet metal. Ovalhead screws, which may be used with *raised* or *flush countersunk washers*, are often used for easy disassembly of a component or for decorative purposes.

Sizes of wood screws include their length and diameter, but a number system makes ordering easy (TABLE 11-1). You can, for example, ask for a #12 screw in any length from 7/8 inch to 2½ inches, knowing that its shank diameter will be 0.216.

## Table 11-1. Screw Sizes

| Real Shank size | | # of screw | Shank diameter (inches) | Commonly available lengths (inches) |
|:---:|:---:|:---:|:---:|:---:|
| ● | | 2 | 0.086 | 1/4 – 1/2 |
| ● | | 3 | 0.099 | 1/4 – 5/8 |
| ● | | 4 | 0.112 | 3/8 – 3/4 |
| ● | | 5 | 0.125 | |
| ● | | 6 | 0.138 | 3/8 – 11/2 |
| ● | | 7 | 0.151 | |
| ● | | 8 | 0.164 | 1/2 – 2 |
| ● | | 9 | 0.177 | 5/8 – 21/4 |
| ● | | 10 | 0.190 | |
| ● | | 12 | 0.216 | 7/8 – 21/2 |
| ● | | 14 | 0.242 | 1 – 23/4 |
| ● | | 16 | 0.268 | 11/4 – 3 |
| ● | | 18 | 0.294 | 11/2 – 4 |
| ● | | 20 | 0.320 | 13/4 – 4 |
| ● | | 24 | 0.372 | 31/2 – 4 |

*Screw lengths increase by 1/8″ up to 1″; by 1/4″ from 1″ to 3″; by 1/2″ from 3″ to 5″.

When joining boards of equal thickness, select a screw-length that is about 1/8 inch less than the combined thickness of the parts. The general rule when components differ in size is that about two-thirds of the screw's length should penetrate the thicker piece.

# Holes for screws

When the screw is quite small and you are driving it into soft wood, you can often form a starting hole for the fastener by using an awl. Most times though, if the screw is to hold as it should and be drivable with minimum effort, the correct procedure is to drill a *body hole* and *lead hole* and, when necessary a countersink or counterbore (FIG. 11-6). Countersinking is done with the type of cutter shown in FIG. 11-7. A counterbore, whose diameter should match or be a bit larger than the diameter of the screw head, can be formed with a twist drill, an auger bit, or a special counterboring tool.

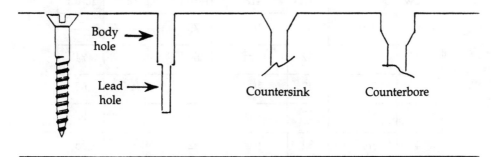

Body hole →

Lead → hole

Countersink            Counterbore

***Fig. 11-6*** *To drive screws efficiently and so they will hold with maximum strength, you must drill suitable body and lead holes. Flathead screws are set flush in a countersink. A counterbore is added when the screw will be hidden with a wooden plug.*

***Fig. 11-7*** *These are examples of countersink bits. The one on the right is often called a* rose head. *Those made for flathead wood screws have an 82-degree cutting edge. They are available for use in an electric drill or a handtool, like a bit brace.*

The sizes of the holes are not arbitrary. If the lead hole, sometimes called *pilot hole*, is too small, the screw will be hard to drive, especially in hardwoods, or cause splitting. If it is too large, the threaded portion of the screw won't *bite*, or hold the screw in place.

The correct sizes of drills to use for the holes are listed in TABLE 11-2. Generally, the body hole should be about the same as the shank diameter of the screw; its depth can match the thickness of the part being secured. The depth of the lead hole should be about half the length of the threaded part of the screw.

**Table 11-2. Drill Sizes for Flathead Wood Screws**

| Size of screw | Body hole | | Lead hole | | | |
|---|---|---|---|---|---|---|
| | | | Hardwood | | Softwood | |
| | Fractional size | # or letter | Fractional size | # or letter | Fractional size | # or letter |
| 0 | 1/16 | 52 | 1/32 | 70 | — | — |
| 1 | 5/64 | 47 | 1/32 | 66 | 1/32 | 71 |
| 2 | 3/32 | 42 | 3/64 | 56 | 1/32 | 65 |
| 3 | 7/64 | 37 | 1/16 | 54 | 3/64 | 58 |
| 4 | 7/64 | 32 | 1/16 | 52 | 3/64 | 55 |
| 5 | 1/8 | 30 | 5/64 | 49 | 1/16 | 53 |
| 6 | 9/64 | 27 | 5/64 | 47 | 1/16 | 52 |
| 7 | 5/32 | 22 | 3/32 | 44 | 1/16 | 51 |
| 8 | 11/64 | 18 | 3/32 | 40 | 5/64 | 48 |
| 9 | 3/16 | 14 | 7/64 | 37 | 5/64 | 45 |
| 10 | 3/16 | 10 | 7/64 | 33 | 3/32 | 43 |
| 11 | 13/64 | 4 | 1/8 | 31 | 3/32 | 40 |
| 12 | 7/32 | 2 | 1/8 | 30 | 7/64 | 38 |
| 14 | 1/4 | D | 9/64 | 25 | 7/64 | 32 |
| 16 | 17/64 | I | 5/32 | 18 | 9/64 | 29 |
| 18 | 19/64 | N | 3/16 | 13 | 9/64 | 26 |
| 20 | 21/64 | P | 13/64 | 4 | 11/64 | 19 |
| 24 | 3/8 | V | 7/32 | 1 | 3/16 | 15 |

*Fractional drill sizes are close, but letter and number sizes are more accurate.

It's often desirable to conceal flathead screws. The usual procedure is to counterbore the holes for the screws. A good procedure is to first form a counterbore 1/4 to 3/8 inch deep. The hole will have its center marked because of the point on the bit that was used. Next, drill the lead hole and then enlarge its top area to shank size.

The counterbore is then filled by gluing in a *plug* that you can supply by cutting short lengths of dowel or by using readymade ones that are available in various sizes. Plain plugs are sanded flush after the glue dries; *button*-types are used when you wish to provide a decorative detail (FIG. 11-8).

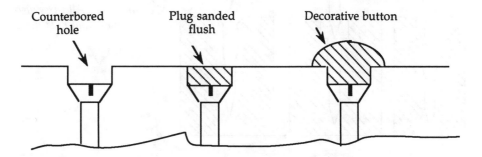

**Fig. 11-8** *Plain plugs are sanded flush after the glue dries. Buttons are used to add a decorative detail to the project. Both types are available commercially in various wood species. Usual sizes are 1/4, 3/8, 1/2, and 5/8 inches.*

Working with conventional drill bits to form the holes that are required can be tedious, but there are some modern cutters that make the job easier and even more accurate because they eliminate the possibility of human error (FIG. 11-9). These are available under trade names like *Screw-Mate* and *Screw Sink*. Their value is in being able to form whatever configuration that is required for the screw in a single operation. No single one of the products is suitable for all screw sizes, so it's best to buy them in sets. A typical five-piece assortment will be suitable for screw sizes from #6 to #12. Also, these unique cutters function most efficiently when they are used in an electric drill.

## How to drive a screw

You will have more turning power when you choose the largest blade that will fit the slot in the screw head. The tip should fit snugly in the slot, but it must not be wider than the head diameter or radically narrower. A tip that is too wide will mar the wood around the screw head. A tip that is too narrow makes the screw harder to turn, and it might break or twist out of shape or distort the slot in the screw head. The too-wide width rule is less crucial when roundhead or ovalhead screws are used because the tip will not make contact with the wood.

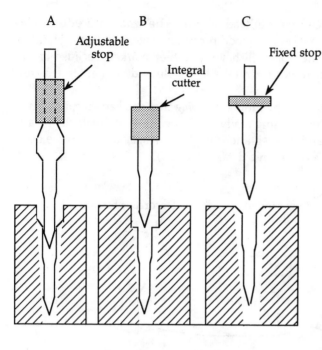

**Fig. 11-9** *Special cutters make it easy to form the right size holes for wood screws. Cutter A forms countersink and counterbore holes; B forms counterbore; C forms countersink. All three also form shank and pilot holes.*

When correct-size holes have been prepared, screws can be started simply by hand-turning them until they catch. Once the screw is placed correctly, shift your free hand to the blade, somewhere near the screw, so your fingers can serve as guides to keep the driver seated correctly. One way to start the driver correctly is to hold it at a very slight angle as you place the tip in the screw head. Then bring the driver to a vertical position before you start turning (FIG. 11-10). It's important throughout the procedure to keep the driver and the screw in true vertical position.

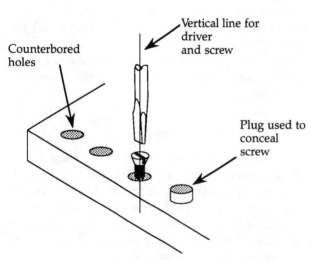

**Fig. 11-10** *Hold the driver at a very slight angle and then bring it to vertical position. The idea is to work so the driver and the screw have a common, vertical centerline. This screw is being installed in a counterbored hole.*

Another way to start a screw—a fairly common method—is to place it on the tip of the driver and hold screw and tip together with the fingers of one hand, while you hold the driver handle with the other. Put the screw point in the starting hole while retaining the same grip, allowing the hand that is holding the screw to rest on the work. Advocates of this system claim it's an easier way to be sure the screw will be started in vertical position. Whatever the starting system, apply minimum turning power until the screw is firmly engaged. Then increase torque but, always, only enough to get the job done.

There can be times, especially when working with a dense material, when screws will be difficult to drive, even when you have provided correct-size holes. Don't enlarge the holes or encourage the screw by hitting it with a hammer. Lubricating the threads, which does not reduce holding power, helps reduce friction. Rub the threads against a bar of paraffin. Soap is often used but there is a chance that moisture in the soap can cause rusting. Don't use oil.

A technique used by many professionals is to make a *threading screw* by filing off, lengthwise, about half the threaded portion of one of the screws. The threading screw is turned into each of the holes before the permanent fasteners are installed. Used so, it performs like a tap to preform threads so the permanent screws will be easier to drive. It's an excellent solution when many similar screws are needed.

## Mechanical aids

Pushing down on the handle of a *spiral ratchet* screwdriver automatically provides turning action for the screw (FIG. 11-11). The tool can be adjusted for retracting as well as driving, and it may be locked in a neutral position and used as a regular driver. The chuck of the spiral ratchet will grip regular or Phillips-type screwdriver blades and, with an adapter, may be used with points for drilling holes.

The automatic screwdriver contains a spring to return the tool to the extended position unless it is secured by turning a locking ring. Be sure to point the tool away from you whenever you release the ring. It's best to hold the chuck in one hand and allow the tool to extend gradually. This type of driver is available in light-duty and heavy-duty versions; overall lengths in extended position running from about 10 to 28 inches. Most units are supplied with one or two driver blades but others, in various sizes and styles, are available individually or in sets. Some versions have hollow handles with screw-on caps for storing blades and points.

A recently introduced ratchet screwdriver (FIG. 11-12), differs from the spiral ratchet design in that it is turned like a standard driver, not by pushing down on the handle. The new product's ratchet switch allows three drive-actions—a ratcheting action when installing a screw, a reverse action to remove screws, and a neutral position for using the tool in normal screwdriver fashion.

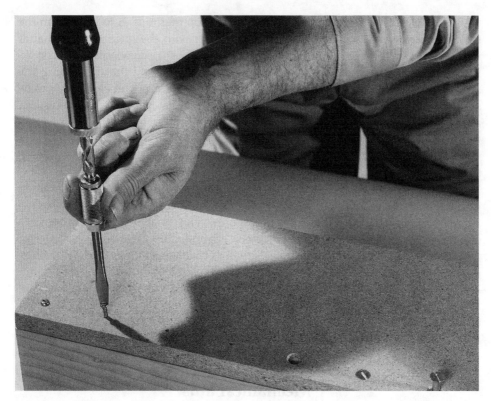

*Fig. 11-11* *An example of how to use a* **spiral-ratchet** *screwdriver.*

*Fig. 11-12* *The new* Workmaster *ratchet screwdriver is operated by turning the handle, not by pushing down on it as with a spiral ratchet design. It can be set to drive or remove screws or for use as a conventional screwdriver. Various sizes and styles of drive-tips can be inserted in its socket-type* chuck.

A factor that makes the tool very versatile is that, instead of a chuck, it holds bits in a hex socket, enabling users to quickly change bits for various screw heads. An adapter is available so the tool can be used with metric units. The product is offered with five sizes of bits for slotted and Phillips-head screws, but accessory sets that contain 14 or 26 pieces offer more variety and include adapters for metric units as well as a drive adapter for gripping bits of various shank size.

Special screwdriver blades are available that allow a bit brace to be used for installing or removing large screws (FIGS. 11-13 and 11-14). Because the brace can supply a tremendous amount of leverage, it's very important to choose a blade that is suitable for the screw and to start with adequate body and lead holes. The torque you can apply is enough to break screws that you are driving if you don't follow correct procedures. This also applies when you are removing a tight screw. Apply only as much leverage as is needed; keep the tip of the blade snug in the screw head.

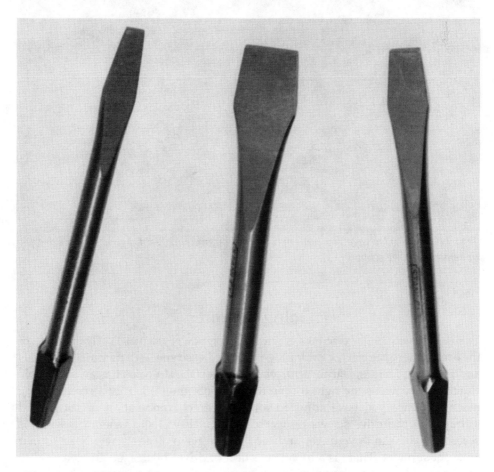

*Fig. 11-13*  *Blades of this type are available for use in a bit brace.*

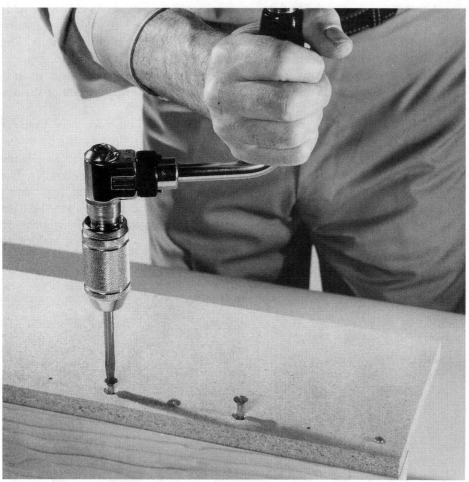

**Fig. 11-14** *The leverage you can apply with a bit brace makes it a good tool for driving or removing large screws.*

## Going to power

The easiest way to drive screws is with electric power (FIG. 11-15). This is one of the areas where the electric drill, plug-in or cordless-type with its variable speeds and reversing feature, is truly appreciated. When the drill also has an adjustable clutch that provides the right torque for each job, then it's truly a screwdriving machine. Once you have adjusted for the correct combination of speed and torque, you can drive screws perfectly. The clutch will slip when the screw is seated, so you can't overdrive, and the bit won't slip off the screw head to mar adjacent surfaces. There is a broad selection of driver blades, so an electric drill can be used to turn various sizes of screws with slotted or other style heads.

**Fig. 11-15** *The electric drill, with variable speeds and a reversing mechanism, is a super screwdriver. There are many sizes and styles of straight-shank blades that can be used in a plug-in or cordless-type drill. Be sure to use the chuck key to secure the blade.*

# 12

# Miscellaneous hardware

Many different items used in woodworking haven't been mentioned yet. They are discussed in detail in this chapter.

## Heavy-duty fasteners

Nuts and bolts don't have a prominent role in furniture and small project assemblies, but they can be appropriate, sometimes even necessary, for heavy, utility-type constructions because they can supply more holding power than wood screws (FIG. 12-1). They are often a good choice for outdoor furniture and are especially suitable for projects you may wish to disassemble for storage.

*Lag screws*, sometimes called *lag bolts*, are like oversize wood screws that have square or hexagonal heads so that they must be driven with a wrench. Installing them requires the same procedure needed for conventional screws; you supply a body hole and lead hole so they can be driven with minimum fuss while holding with maximum power. Usually, they are used with a flat washer to keep the head from marring the wood and to provide more bearing surface against the part being secured. Diameter sizes that are most applicable in a woodworking shop start at $1/4$ inch and increase to $1/2$ inch in increments of $1/16$ inch. Lengths start at 1 inch and range up to as much as 12 inches.

*Carriage bolts*, which may have oval or round heads, are a good choice for wood assemblies. A feature of the carriage bolts, is the square shoulder under the attractive head. The shoulder bites into the wood to prevent the bolt from turning as you tighten the nut. Thus, the fastener can be secured with a single wrench.

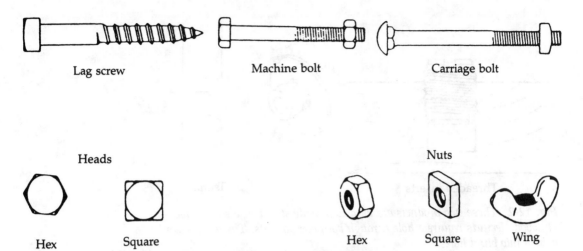

**Fig. 12-1** *Pictured are three fasteners that can be used for heavy wood constructions. A wing nut is suitable for making adjustments or for removable components. A lag screw is often used with a washer under the head, a carriage bolt with one under the nut. The machine bolt can take one at each end.*

*Machine bolts*, which may have square or hexagonal heads, range in size from 1/4 inch to 1/2 inch in diameter, and from 1 inch to 6 inches in length. The terms *National Fine* (NF) and *National Coarse* (NC) refer to the bolt's number of threads per inch. For example, a 1/4-inch NF bolt will have 28 threads per inch. The same size bolt in NC will have 20 threads per inch. For woodworking purposes you don't have to think beyond NC.

Carriage and machine bolts require you to drill shank-size holes completely through both of the parts being joined.

## Metal threads in wood

*Teenuts* and *threaded inserts* (FIG. 12-2) make it possible to provide metal threads in lumber or plywood so you can pull parts together with a machine screw or provide a means of making a particular component removable. Both items are installed in the part to which the mating piece will be secured.

Teenuts are installed in holes that match the outside diameter of the barrel. The prongs on the flange grip the wood when the item is pressed into place. Most times, they are *surface-mounted* (i.e., the flange remains above the surface of the wood). Setting them flush is a matter of counterboring a shallow hole whose diameter matches that of the flange.

The inserts have exterior as well as internal threads and can be driven into blind holes so they will not be visible. Since the external threads on the units are designed as *knife threads* that easily cut into wood, they may be installed with a screwdriver whose blade fits the slot in the insert. Some units are available with

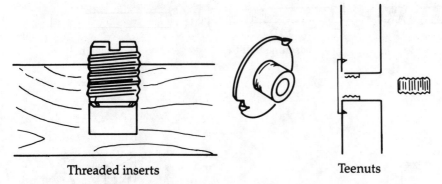

Threaded inserts                    Teenuts

**Fig. 12-2** *These two products are used to provide steel threads in lumber or plywood. Teenuts require a hole through both components. The inserts can be driven into blind holes.*

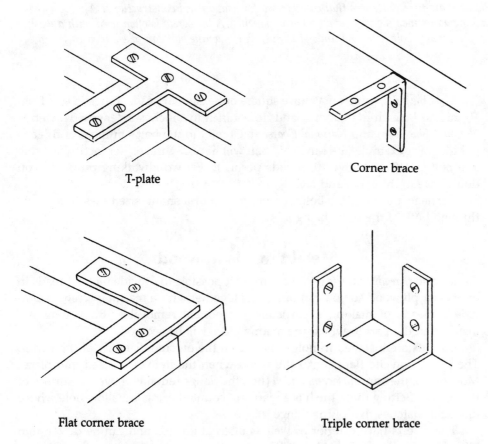

T-plate                    Corner brace

Flat corner brace                    Triple corner brace

**Fig. 12-3** *Pictured are typical products that can be used to reinforce joints. Some are available in brass as well as steel. All of them have countersunk holes to receive flathead screws.*

a hex-type socket so they can be driven with an Allen wrench. I find that this design makes the units easier to screw into place.

Both products are available in various sizes to suit standard machine screws or bolts, with NF or NC threads.

## Reinforcement irons

Reinforcement irons are called *irons*, *braces*, or *plates*. These products shown in FIG. 12-3 are typical of the many pieces of hardware that are specially designed to strengthen simple joints. Most times they are used in hidden areas, but they can also be used creatively. For example, units like the T-plate and the flat corner brace can be painted black before installation and left exposed to provide a decorative wrought-iron touch to a project.

These products are often available in packages, which include the required flathead screws for installation.

# 13
# Wood joints

Woodworking projects depend on joints for durability and appearance—relative to their location. For instance, shelves erected in a garage to hold paint cans and garden tools have to be strong, but they don't have to be as attractive as book-shelves made for use in the house. Similarly, a desk drawer made to store stamps and pens doesn't have to be as strong as one that will be used to hold shop tools.

Some workers are enamored of joints, to the point of using a complex one when a simpler one will do. That's fine, but a more practical approach, especially for the beginner who should take things in stride, is to adopt the easiest-to-make joint that is adequate for the project. Some substance is added to this thought by the super adhesives available today. Glue from a bottle can often make a bond that is stronger than the material being joined. But don't misunderstand. Glue is an aid, not a cure-all; it will not compensate for sloppy fits. The parts of any joint, including the basic ones shown in FIG. 13-1, should be formed with care.

Accuracy is crucial with all joints. For example, a butt joint will soon fail if the mating edges of the components are not true to each other; an oversize tenon can split a mortise, an undersize one is prone to wiggle; holes for dowels must not be too large or too small, and so on. Workers who use clamps to force parts together are missing the point that they are intended to keep components in contact until the glue dries. Actually, you should be able to join pieces with only hand pressure.

## Butt joints

The word *butt* tells what the joint is like; the end or edge of one part is joined to similar areas of another. A negative aspect of the joint is that there is minimum

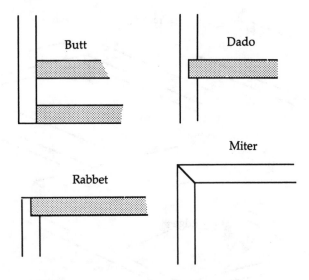

*Fig. 13-1* *The basic woodworking joints.*

contact surface and that often, end grain contacts edge or surface grain, which does not make the strongest connection (FIG. 13-2). In appearance, the joint is very neat because it exposes the least amount of joint line. This is apparent when it is compared with other basic joints like the dado or rabbet. Even the miter, which is an excellent corner joint for concealing end grain, has a longer joint line.

Often, to improve appearance, home workers and even manufacturers will treat an end butt as shown in FIG. 13-3. For best results, the end grain must be sanded and sealed enough so it will have a slick look when stained and polished. The kerf (groove) must be shallow so that contact area will not be seriously reduced. The drawing shows that a rabbet joint can be treated the same way.

### Grain direction

The grain direction of components of any joint affects strength and appearance. Dimensional changes in a board's length, that is, *with the grain*, are not serious enough to cause problems, but changes in a board's width, *across the grain*, can actually be measured. That's why the grain direction of joint components should be planned whenever possible as suggested by the end butt in FIG. 13-4. Hopefully, any change that does happen will be the same in both parts. When a dimensional change occurs in only one piece, the joint will be weakened, gaps will appear, even splitting can happen.

### Reinforcement

Butt joints take on another dimension when they are suitably reinforced in addition to being glued. Reinforcements can be obvious or subtle, much depending

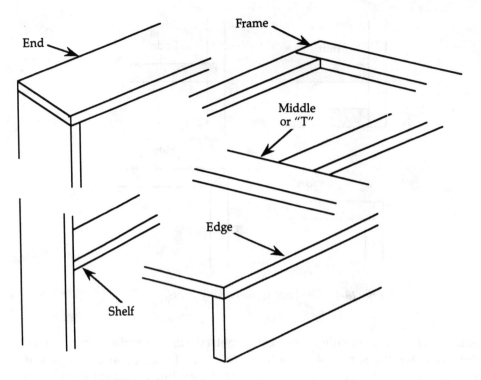

**Fig. 13-2** *Typical butt joints.*

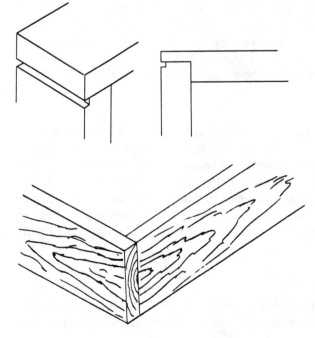

**Fig. 13-3** *A shallow kerf contributes to the appearance of a simple butt joint (left), but it should not be wider or deeper than about 1/8 inch. Note that it can also be used with a rabbet joint (right).*

**Fig. 13-4** *Planning for compatible grain directions adds to the appearance of a joint and helps to ensure that any dimensional changes will be the same in both parts.*

on the type of project (FIGS. 13-5 and 13-6). Nails and screws are, of course, obvious fasteners. Nails in end grain will hold parts together better if they are driven at a slight angle rather than straight in. Drill a pilot hole for the nail in at least the piece being attached if there is a danger of splitting.

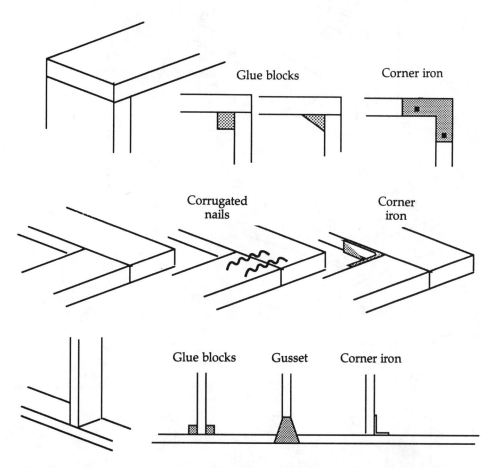

*Fig. 13-5* *Pictured are common methods of reinforcing butt joints. You should choose the one that is most appropriate for the appearance and strength of your project.*

Screws do not grip as well in end grain as they do in cross grain, so use a longer screw than you would ordinarily select and work with a smaller lead hole than is technically correct. A method to use when strength is crucial is shown in FIG. 13-7. The screws will bite into the cross grain of the dowel, thereby adding considerably to their gripping power.

Dowels can be used when other types of reinforcement are not acceptable (FIG. 13-8). The dowels can be sanded flush or allowed to project a bit so they can be rounded off to provide a decorative detail. Alignment of the holes for the dowels will be correct if the parts are held together so both will be drilled at the same

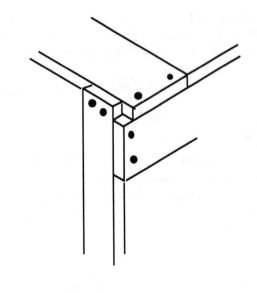

*Fig. 13-6* Butt joints arranged this way make a strong interlocking connection. This design is good for heavy-duty applications.

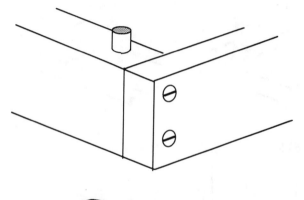

*Fig. 13-7* Screws will hold with more power if they penetrate a dowel that is inserted in one of the components.

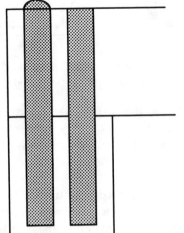

*Fig. 13-8* Using dowels to reinforce a butt joint. Drill the dowel holes while the parts are held together. Sand flush, or round off to provide a decorative detail.

time. If you drill the holes together as suggested, be sure to take the pieces apart after drilling to clean out the waste before applying glue and doing the final assembly.

End grain can absorb glue more so than surface or edge grain, which doesn't add strength to the joint. A common technique is to apply a first, light coat of glue as you would a sizing or sealer. Wait a bit for the end grain to soak up the glue before applying a full coat for the final assembly.

## Edge-to-edge joints

Edge-to-edge joints are used when a large slab is required for a project, say, a table or bench top, and plywood won't do. The chore is not complicated, but warping, that occurs across the grain, is a factor to consider. Often, even in a standard 12 inch wide board, there will be a slight concave configuration across its width. That's why, when a board of that particular width is needed for a project, the common technique is to rip the board into thirds and then reunite the pieces with the center one inverted. Even when constructing a slab by using precut, narrow boards, alternate ones are inverted so the annual rings seen at the end of the boards will not have a uniform direction (FIG. 13-9). Working this way places stresses together that are opposed to each other instead of letting them contribute to a cumulative warp.

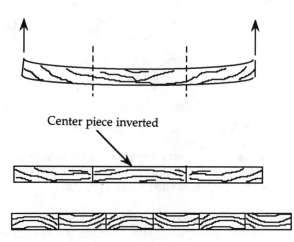

*Fig. 13-9* *It's a good idea when using a wide board to rip it into thirds and reunite the parts with the center one inverted. Narrow boards should be joined as shown, with annual rings pointing in opposite directions.*

Center piece inverted

Check the overall grain pattern that the assembly will have. Place the parts loosely, then move them about, shifting them longitudinally to achieve the most attractive results. Draw a light pencil line across them and number each piece so you will know the positions you have established when you are ready for final assembly.

## Reinforcement

Dowels, or pegs, are a good way to reinforce edge-to-edge joints, especially when working with handtools. The number of dowels used is not as crucial as the accuracy needed for the installation. If you are not precise you will be pretty frustrated at assembly time.

Some general rules for dowel location are suggested in FIG. 13-10, but don't see them as the only way to go. Many workers skip dowels at the end of parts and increase spacing considerably. The theory is that a good glue job is sufficient for an edge-to-edge joint, but a few dowels will ensure correct alignment of the components. Others go to the opposite extreme, staggering closely-spaced dowels over the entire slab. This approach might be acceptable for a heavy-duty construction subjected to a lot of abuse, but it's a bit much for anything like a table or desktop.

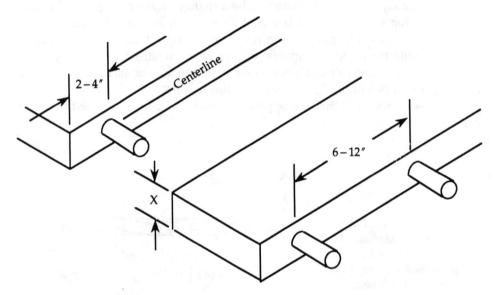

**Fig. 13-10** *How to plan when dowels are used in an edge-to-edge joint. Standard guidelines recommend the dowel diameter be half the thickness (X) of the wood; the minimum length of the dowel should be 2X.*

You could supply your own pegs by cutting pieces from the 3-or 4-foot-long dowels that are typically available, but it's not a good approach. Dowel pegs used in joints should have chamfered ends and striated or spirally cut shanks so glue can move freely. To avoid the nuisance of having to design them yourself, it's better to buy them ready-made. These ready-made pegs are available in various diameters and lengths (TABLE 13-1) from craftsman supply houses and local do-it-yourself centers.

The best way to establish hole position is to mark the location on one piece, then, with parts clamped together, use it as a guide to carry the mark across all

## Table 13-1. Good Pairs for Dowel Joints

| Diameter | Length |
|----------|--------|
| 1/4″ | 2″ |
| 3/8″ | 3″ |
| 1/2″ | 3¹/2″ |

edges (FIG. 13-11). Establish the centerline of the holes by setting the blade of a square to the correct distance, then using it as a gauge to mark from the *same* surface of each part. This way, even if the marks are not exactly centered, they will have a consistent edge distance and the dowel holes will be in alignment.

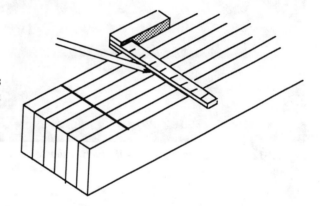

*Fig. 13-11* *One part that is marked for hole locations can be used as a guide to mark other pieces.*

Drilling the holes requires great care and patience. That's why in this area of woodworking, it's strongly recommended that you buy a *doweling jig* (FIG. 13-12). The jigs are not all alike. This one has a turret that is rotated to suit the size of the drill bit being used. Others work with various size steel bushings that are installed in the jig in a particular way. All of them make it easy to drill perpendicular holes on a common centerline.

### Splines

*Splines* are often used in edge-to-edge joints, but it's a method that's most feasible if you own a table saw. Matching grooves, that don't have to be wider than the saw kerf, usually ¹/8 inch, are cut into the edges of the parts so strips of material can be inserted as shown in FIG. 13-13. To assure alignment, mark one side of each piece and cut the grooves with that surface riding against the rip fence. Thus, even if the cuts are not exactly centered, the parts will mate as they should because the grooves will have the same edge distance.

***Fig. 13-12*** *This special jig makes it much easier to accurately drill holes for dowels.*

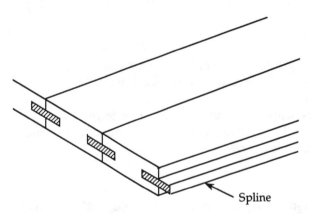

***Fig. 13-13*** *Splines are often used in edge-to-edge joints.*

Spline

Plywood and materials like hardboard, both of which are available in 1/8 inch thickness, are excellent for splines. Because wood splits more easily with the grain, splines cut from lumber will be strongest when the grain direction is across the small dimension. Sometimes, the material chosen for splines contrasts with the project parts so exposed ends will provide a decorative detail.

The width of the spline should at least match the thickness of the parts. It can be just a fraction narrower than the combined depth of the grooves, but be sure it isn't greater or the joint edges will not come together.

## Dadoes and grooves

The difference between *dadoes* and *grooves* has mostly to do with terminology. Both are U-shaped cuts, one made *across* the grain, the other *with* the grain (FIG. 13-14). The advantage of the joints, when compared with a simple butt joint, is the increase in glue area and the fact that the part that is inserted rests between shoulders. When you consider a horizontal insert, as in a bookcase, you can see that a shelf will resist vertical stresses because of the *ledge* it rests on FIG. 13-15). A vertical insert, such as a partition, will not move out of place because its end is trapped in the dado.

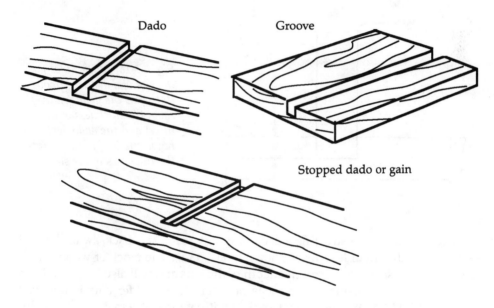

**Fig. 13-14** *A groove is cut with the grain, a dado across it. Both are U-shaped cuts.*

The width of the cut matches the thickness of the insert; its depth is usually about half the stock's thickness (FIG. 13-16). The depth can be less, but making it too deep will cause a weakness in the area. The insert should slide snugly into position. Having to force it will create stresses and will present a problem at assembly time. Actually, it's better to be a fraction on the skimpy side because you can adjust by wrapping a piece of fine sandpaper around a block of wood of suitable thickness and running it back and forth through the cut. A cut that is too wide can be a problem because you can't add wood. In a pinch, you can compensate by including a wood shaving in the joint.

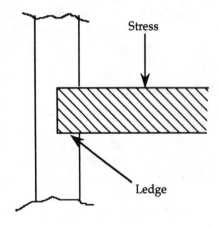

Stress

Ledge

*Fig. 13-15*   *The U-shape of a dado offers a lot of contact area for glue. The "ledge" provides good support for horizontal inserts.*

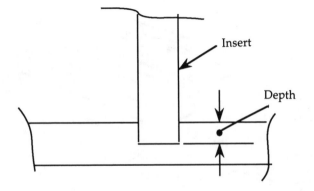

Insert

Depth

*Fig. 13-16*   *Basic rules for the size of a dado or groove state that the dado width equal the thickness of the insert and the dado depth range one-half to two-thirds the thickness of the stock.*

The first step in constructing a dado or groove is to use a backsaw or dovetail saw to make the shoulder cuts as shown in FIG. 13-17. The block of wood that is clamped to the saw will control the depth of the cuts and will also help you keep the saw in vertical position. The waste between the shoulder cuts is removed with a chisel (FIG. 13-18). It's nice when the width of the chisel matches the width of the cut. Finish smoothing the bottom of the dado by using sandpaper wrapped around a block of wood. Making U-shaped cuts is easier and faster when a table saw is handy and special dado cutters can be used (see chapter 5).

A disadvantage of the joint is that the U-shaped lines are not attractive when viewed from the front. It's not crucial when the project is something like a cabinet where facing is used for appearance and to provide a means of hinging doors (FIG. 13-19). When constructing a bookshelf, a common solution for the dado's appearance is to form a *stopped* dado (FIG. 13-20). There are two ways to accomplish the cut. First, work with a chisel to form the square end of the dado, then make shoulder cuts and remove the remaining waste by chiseling. The second method calls for slanted saw cuts running the length of the joint—full depth at

**Fig. 13-17**  *Using a backsaw to make the shoulder cuts for a dado. The clamped-on strip of wood will control the depth of the cut and will help to maintain the vertical position of the saw.*

the free end, zero at the stopped end. Then a chisel is used to remove waste. Incidentally, the stopped end does not have to be perfect since the notch in the insert can be sized to span over little flaws.

## Rabbets

Rabbets are L-shaped cuts formed on ends or edges of one of the components in the joint (FIG. 13-21). The width of the cut normally equals the thickness of the insert; its depth can be $1/2$ to $3/4$ the thickness of the part in which it is made, but there are variations. A good technique is to cut the rabbet a bit wider than necessary. Then, after the parts are joined and the glue is dry, the excess is sanded off so the edge will be perfectly flush with the mating piece (see FIG. 13-21).

When plywood is the project material, the rabbet is often cut deep enough so only the surface veneer of the insert is left exposed. It's a way to conceal unattrac-

**Fig. 13-18** *The waste between the shoulder cuts of a dado or groove is removed with a chisel. Choose a chisel that matches or comes close to the width of the dado.*

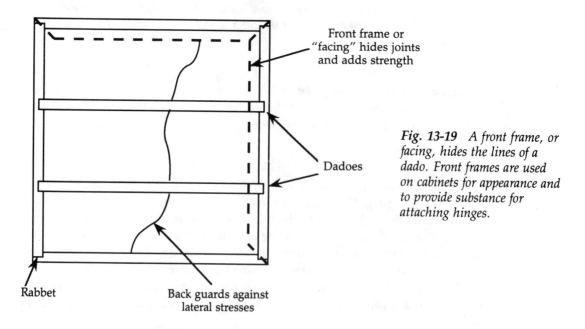

Front frame or "facing" hides joints and adds strength

Dadoes

Rabbet

Back guards against lateral stresses

**Fig. 13-19** *A front frame, or facing, hides the lines of a dado. Front frames are used on cabinets for appearance and to provide substance for attaching hinges.*

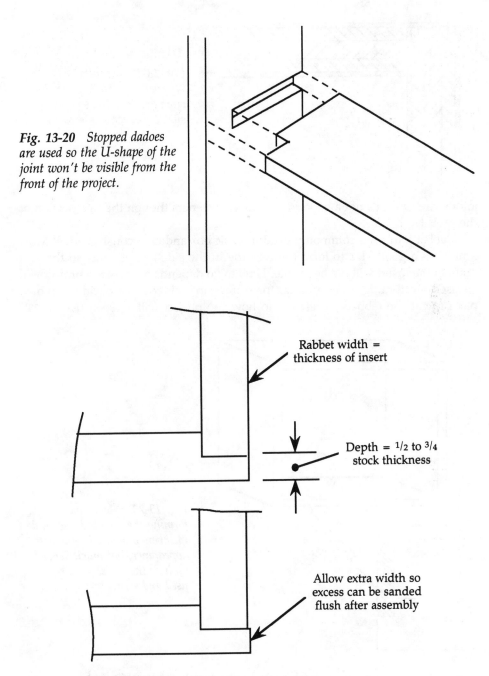

**Fig. 13-20** *Stopped dadoes are used so the U-shape of the joint won't be visible from the front of the project.*

Rabbet width = thickness of insert

Depth = $1/2$ to $3/4$ stock thickness

Allow extra width so excess can be sanded flush after assembly

**Fig. 13-21** *Sizing a rabbet cut.*

tive plywood edges but there will be a weak point at the base of the shoulder (FIG. 13-22). When this method is used, it's important for the project as a whole to be strong. Often, glue blocks or other reinforcements are used to increase the

*Fig. 13-22*  *Rabbets for plywood constructions are often deep enough so only the surface veneer can be seen.*

joint's strength. It's not a good idea to drive fasteners though the thin section of the rabbet.

Rabbet joints are commonly used in basic box and case constructions. Most times, it's a good idea to form the L-shape in the side components so the end grain of the insert will not be visible. How to go depends on how the project will be used—wall-hung, freestanding, for storage in a closet. Just decide in which parts to cut the rabbets in relation to how the project will be seen (FIG. 13-23).

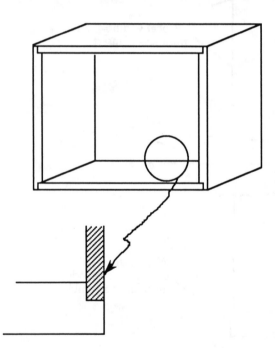

*Fig. 13-23*  *Most times, forming the rabbets in vertical members provides for the best appearance, but much depends on how the project will be used and seen.*

Most case constructions are back-sealed with panels that seat in rabbets cut into the back edges of the components. The panels can be flush as shown in FIG. 13-23, but when the project will be wall-hung, as in the case of a kitchen cabinet, it's wise to cut the rabbet wider than necessary so you can trim the back edges of the project to suit any irregularities that might be on the wall.

Rabbet joints are often used as the connection between the front and sides of a drawer. The rabbet can be cut so the sides will be flush with the ends of the front or, as shown in FIG. 13-24, they can be wider so the drawer front will have a lip. This is not the strongest joint if only glue is used; therefore, reinforce the joint with nails, screws, or even dowel pegs to add strength. The fasteners are driven through the side into the shoulder of the rabbet.

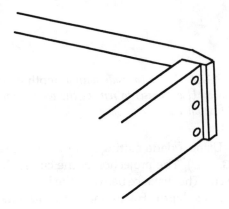

*Fig. 13-24  Drawer fronts are often rabbeted to receive side members. Nails, screws, or dowels that are driven through the sides into the shoulder of the rabbet are used in addition to glue.*

A method that has many applications is to use long or short lengths of rabbeted stock as corner posts, or blocks (FIG. 13-25). The design provides a lot of contact area for glue, and minimum joint lines when viewed from the front.

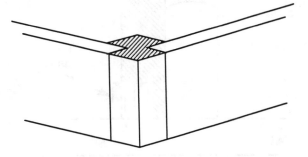

*Fig. 13-25  Rabbeted lengths of stock can be used as corner posts or blocks. They provide a good amount of contact area for glue and leave clean lines.*

### Forming rabbets

To form rabbets, the shoulder cut is made with a backsaw that has a strip of wood clamped to it to serve as a depth gauge (FIG. 13-26). The job can be finished by using a chisel to remove the waste, or by securing the stock on edge and making a second saw cut at right angles to the first one. With this second method, a strip of wood can be attached to the saw as a depth gauge.

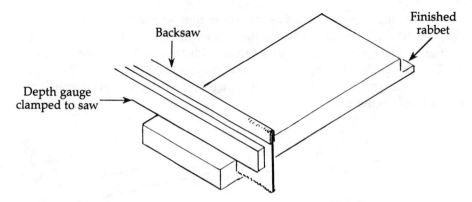

*Fig. 13-26* *Use a backsaw with a depth gauge attached to make the shoulder cut for a rabbet. Use a chisel to remove the waste or make a second saw cut at right angles to the first one.*

Using a dado cutting tool on a table saw is the fastest way to form a rabbet (FIG. 13-27). The projection of the cutter above the table determines the width of the cut. The distance between the inside face of the cutter and the rip fence establishes its depth. For example, for a 1/2-inch deep rabbet on 3/4-inch stock, the space between cutter and rip fence would be 1/4 inch.

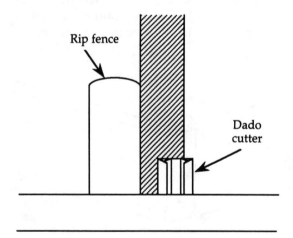

*Fig. 13-27* *Rabbets are easily cut on a table saw by using a dadoing tool.*

## Lap joints

The term *lap joint* covers the category of connections that are shown in FIG. 13-28. They are used when components cross each other or meet at a midpoint or end. *Surface laps* are the easiest to do but are also the weakest because strength depends entirely on the area of contact. Unless mechanical fasteners in addition

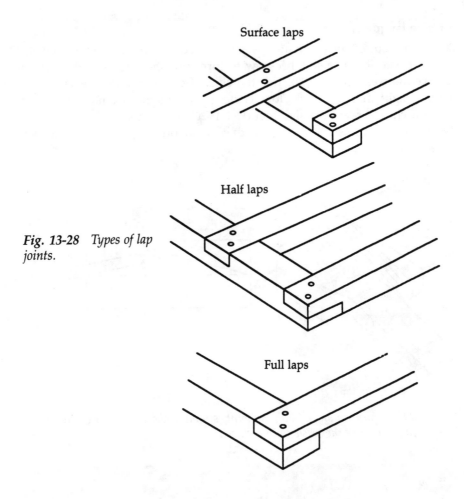

Surface laps

Half laps

**Fig. 13-28** *Types of lap joints.*

Full laps

to glue are used, the joint might not be able to withstand lateral and twisting stresses. However, it should not be shunned for light construction like garden trellises, grids, and the like, and for heavier projects, such as a compost bin or a utility fence. Fasteners can be nails, screws, or bolts, depending on the heaviness of the materials. You should use several fasteners because a single fastener will act as a pivot point for the connected part.

*Half-laps*, usually used when components have equal thickness, gain in strength because the parts interlock. The thickness of each part in the contact area is reduced by one-half so when the parts are joined, surfaces will be flush. Half-laps can be used at midpoints or to join parts at corners when a square or rectangular frame is needed.

*Full-laps* are practical when one component is thinner than the other. The seat cut, formed in the thicker piece, is essentially a wide rabbet or dado that is sized to suit the width and thickness of the mating piece. In all cases, use one of the components to mark the width of the cut and a gauge to indicate its depth.

## Forming lap joints

The form required for end half-laps is L-shaped, essentially a wide rabbet. One way to create it is to use a backsaw to form the shoulder and then chisels to remove the waste (FIG. 13-29). Use the chisel from both ends, bevel side up, to remove slight shavings until a low, center peak remains. Then finish by shaving with the chisel toward the shoulder (FIG. 13-30). The last step allows cutting with the grain, which results in a finish that is smoother than you can achieve by working strictly across the grain.

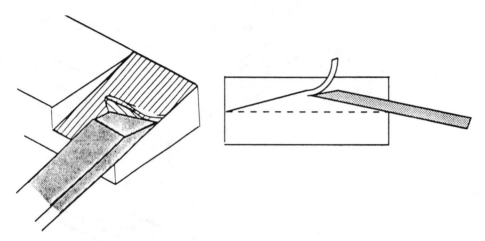

**Fig. 13-29**  *To form an an end half-lap joint, simply make a shoulder cut with a backsaw, then remove the waste with a chisel.*

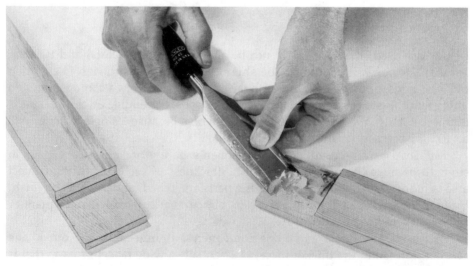

**Fig. 13-30**  *Finish an end half-lap joint by shaving the shoulder cut with a wide chisel in line with the grain.*

Another method is to produce the shape by using just a backsaw. Make the cheek cut, then the shoulder cut and the waste will be removed in one piece, or vice versa (FIG. 13-31). It is important that the cuts be vertical to the surfaces they enter. When the parts are narrow enough, they can be clamped edge to edge so the sawing can be done in both in one operation.

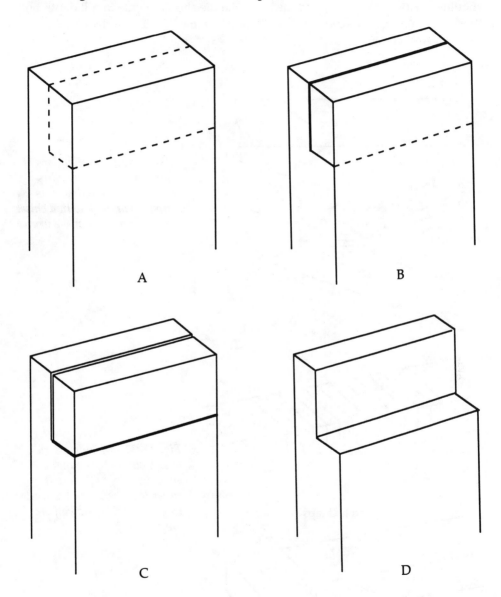

**Fig. 13-31** *Making cheek cuts and shoulder cuts with a backsaw is another way to form an end half-lap. (A) Mark cut lines with a gauge; (B) saw the cheek first; (C) then the shoulder.*

Half-laps used at midpoints or when parts cross require the form that is shown in FIG. 13-32. As you can see, it's essential that the cut matches the width of the stock and is half its thickness. Forming this joint is like that required for end half-laps, except that you start by sawing *two* shoulders. Using a chisel to remove the waste will be a lot easier if you make a series of saw cuts between the shoulders (FIG. 13-33). It's a good idea to make the shoulder cuts to full depth but those between just a fraction shorter. This will allow you to use the chisel to do the final smoothing.

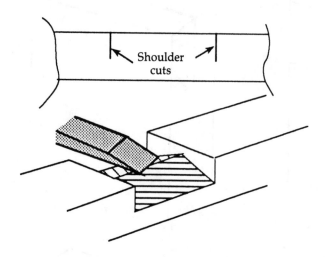

*Fig. 13-32* *For half-laps at midpoints or where parts cross, make shoulder cuts first, then work with a chisel from both edges of the wood.*

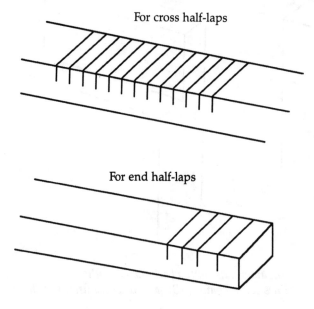

*Fig. 13-33* *Making a series of saw cuts between the shoulder cuts will make it easier to chisel away the waste as you complete the half-lap joint.*

Being able to use a dado cutting tool on a table saw will, of course, make forming end or middle half-laps easier. The cutting tool is set up for its widest cut and organized so its projection above the saw table is half the thickness of the stock. Form the shoulders first, then remove the remaining waste by making additional cuts (FIG. 13-34). Keep the work firmly against the miter gauge and, since you will be removing a lot of material, make the passes slowly enough so the dadoing tool can cut at its own pace.

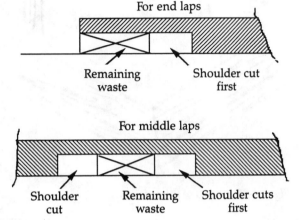

**Fig. 13-34** *The cuts for lap joints are easy to do when the work can be done on a table saw with a dadoing tool.*

## Miter joints

Miter joints are among the most popular wood connections. They will hide unattractive plies when plywood is the project material, and when relationship of components is planned for the purpose, they can present a smooth flow of surface grain pattern as is evident on the *rip miter*, shown in FIG. 13-35. The miter also serves to conceal end grain when it is the connection between components of solid wood.

The joint can even be used on frame assemblies, with parts of different width, by cutting complementary miter angles. The work can be done accurately regardless of the width of the parts by using the method shown in FIG. 13-36. Align the narrow piece with the end of its mate and make a mark to indicate its width. A line drawn from the mark to the opposite corner tells where to saw. The sawed piece is then used as a pattern to mark the cutline on the second part.

### Accuracy when forming miter joints

When two pieces are united with a miter joint to turn a 90-degree corner, each cut must be 45 degrees; there is no compromise. Parts cut inaccurately may join, but the corner will not be square. When four parts are involved, as with a frame

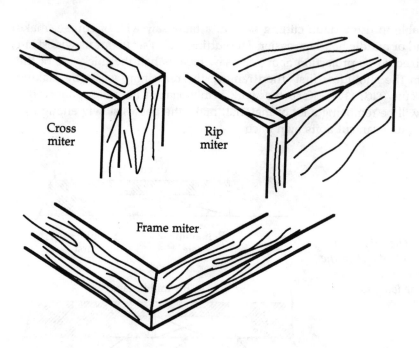

Cross
miter

Rip
miter

Frame miter

*Fig. 13-35* Types of miter joints.

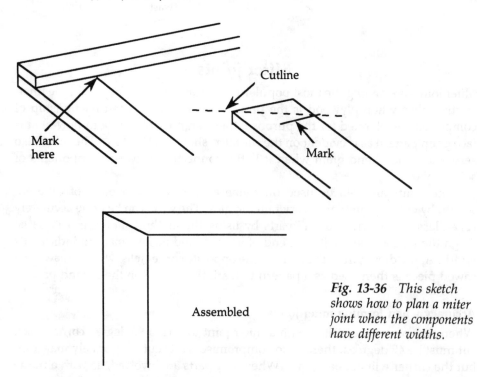

Mark
here

Cutline

Mark

Assembled

*Fig. 13-36* This sketch
shows how to plan a miter
joint when the components
have different widths.

or case, an error can be multiplied by eight. This leads to unhappy woodworking at assembly time. Since it's just as easy to be accurate as not, take your time and do it right.

Mark cutlines accurately by using a square. On work that is too wide for the blade of the tool, mark along the length of the blade and then extend the line with a straight strip of wood. Also, because the diagonal of a square forms 45-degree angles with adjacent lines, you can establish the cutline by layout. For example, assuming a piece of plywood is x inches wide, mark a line parallel to the end and x inches away. By marking a line from opposite corners of the square you created, you will establish a 45-degree cutline.

Sawing will be more successful when a guide is used to keep the saw on line and in vertical position so sawed edges will be square to surfaces. The guide doesn't have to be any more than a block of wood clamped to the work. To achieve greater accuracy use a miter box.

Miter cuts along edges like those needed for the *cross* and *rip miters*, sketched in FIG. 13-35, are a little more difficult to do by hand than *frame* miters. The method shown in FIG. 13-37 requires careful planning and sawing, but it's a reasonable approach. The guide block, which is positioned as shown in FIG. 13-38, establishes the angle for the saw.

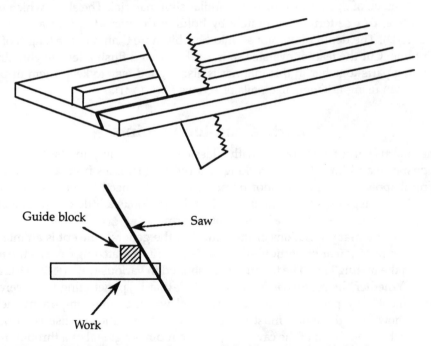

**Fig. 13-37** *A rip miter can be accomplished by using a guide block to set the angle of the saw. Saw slowly and be sure to keep the face of the blade against the top corner of the guide.*

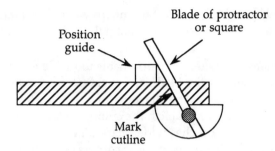

Position guide

Blade of protractor or square

Mark cutline

**Fig. 13-38** *Use this method to establish the position of the guide. Mark the cutline on the edge of the stock and butt the top corner of the guide against the tool's blade. Be sure to clamp the guide so it is parallel with the front edge of the work.*

**Strength of a miter joint**

When you consider the amount of contact area for glue, you can see that while the miter has a better appearance than a butt joint, it isn't much stronger. That's why, especially in frame constructions that don't get support from other components, reinforcements are added. The item and the method of installation depend on the strength and appearance that is required for the project (FIG. 13-39). Corner braces are usable inside projects; surface-mounted units, like gussets, flat corner irons, and corrugated nails, can be mounted on back surfaces so they can't be seen. A nice approach when appearance is important is to install a *feather*, made of thick veneer or some similar slim material. The slots, which *must* be in line, can be formed accurately by holding the parts together as you saw (FIG. 13-40). The depth of the slot should be a bit more than half the length of the joint line. Cut the feather oversize so it can be sanded flush after the glue dries. Holding parts together in this manner is also a good way to keep them in position when using fasteners like nails or screws (FIG. 13-41).

## Mortise-and-tenon joints

The mortise-and-tenon ranks with classic woodworking joints because of appearance and how it resists racking and twisting stresses from any direction. Typical applications include door frames, and the connection between rails and stretchers to legs on tables and chairs. The design looks a little complicated but the parts required are not really difficult to form.

There are many variations of the joint, but the general concept is an integral square or rectangular projection—the *tenon*—that fits a matching cavity—the *mortise*—in the mating part. The tenon can be shaped in various ways (FIGS. 13-42 and 13-43). Whether the mortise is *blind* or *stopped*, that is, penetrating the receiving component only partway or through the full width of the component, determines how long the tenon must be. The tenon for a blind mortise is cut a bit shorter than the depth of the cavity to provide room for glue. For a through mortise, the tenon is longer than necessary so it can be sanded flush after the glue dries.

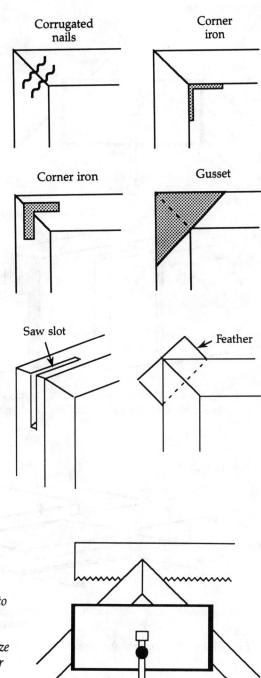

**Fig. 13-39** *Methods that can be used to reinforce a miter joint. The* **feather** *is obviously the more sophisticated design.*

Corrugated nails

Corner iron

Corner iron

Gusset

Saw slot

Feather

**Fig. 13-40** *A good way to form the slot for a feather is to saw while the parts are gripped together in a vise. Insert a feather that is oversize so it can be sanded flush after the glue dries.*

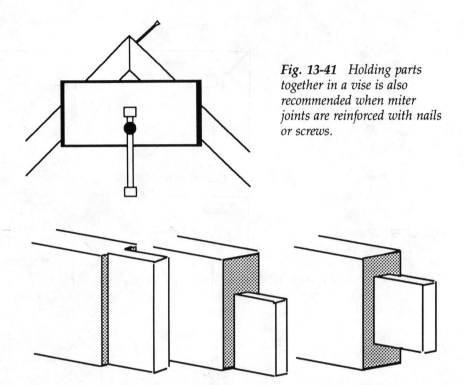

*Fig. 13-41* *Holding parts together in a vise is also recommended when miter joints are reinforced with nails or screws.*

*Fig. 13-42* *A tenon can have two, three, or four shoulders. The tenon should be one-third to one-half the thickness of the stock.*

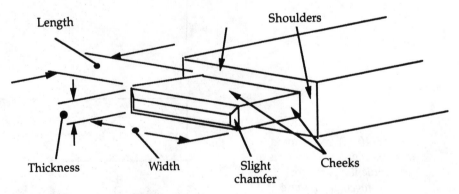

Length

Shoulders

Thickness

Width

Slight chamfer

Cheeks

*Fig. 13-43* *Nomenclature of the tenon.*

## Forming the mortise

Use a square to mark the end points of the mortise and a marking gauge to draw lines parallel to edges that will indicate its width. Use a knife to score the lines deeply enough to sever surface fibers, then work with a drilling tool (e.g., brace and bit, electric drill) to form overlapping holes that will remove the bulk of the waste. An alternate method of layout is to mark a common centerline for the overlapping holes, then clean out the remaining waste by using a chisel, as shown in FIG. 13-44. It isn't necessary to square off the ends of the mortise since the tenon can be shaped to conform to the half-circle ends of the cavity (FIG. 13-45).

**Fig. 13-44** *The mortise is formed by drilling overlapping holes that remove the bulk of the waste. Use a chisel to do the final touch-ups.*

When drilling a mortise, plan its width so a standard size bit can be used. This is not very limiting because sizes of drill bits of various types change in small increments. Use a stop on the drill bit to limit the depth of the holes when forming a blind mortise. When drilling through, have a scrap piece under the work to minimize the splintering or feathering that can occur when the bit breaks through. Another, possibly better method, is for the work to be a bit wider than necessary. After drilling, a plane can be used to remove any blemish.

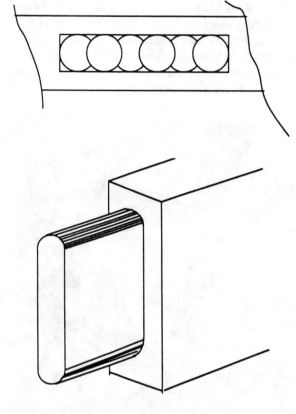

*Fig. 13-45* *Tenons for a drilled mortise are rounded off to suit the semicircular ends of the cavity.*

### Forming tenons

Use a square to mark the length of the tenon and a marking gauge to indicate its width. Secure the stock vertically and use a backsaw to make the cheek cuts. Then place the stock flat and saw the shoulders (FIG. 13-46). For both cuts, clamp a strip of wood to the saw as a control for the depth of the cuts. If the tenon will have four shoulders, the sawing operation is repeated on the edges of the stock. Be sure to make saw cuts on the waste side of the guide lines.

Tenons are easily cut on a table saw by using a dadoing tool or with a tenoning jig. Check Chapter 5 for information on these procedures.

### Open mortise-and-tenon

The tenon for the joint shown in FIG. 13-47 can be formed using the procedures already described. The slot, as shown in FIG. 13-48, is shaped by first making shoulder cuts, then removing the material that's between them. This can be accomplished by using only a chisel, but work will be easier and go faster if you remove the bulk of the waste with a coping saw.

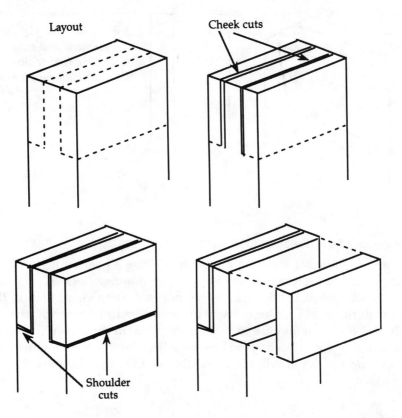

Layout      Cheek cuts

Shoulder
cuts

**Fig. 13-46** *The tenon is produced by making the series of saw cuts that are shown here. When parts are small enough, they may be ''ganged'' so several of them can be sawed in one operation.*

**Fig. 13-47** *An open mortise-and-tenon joint is a fairly straightforward design that is a good choice for frame constructions.*

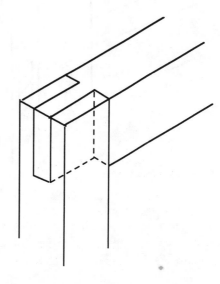

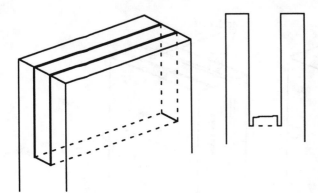

**Fig. 13-48** *The slot for the open mortise-and-tenon is formed by making the shoulder cuts with a saw, removing the bulk waste with a coping saw, and finishing with a chisel.*

## Reinforcement of mortise-and-tenon joints

Mortise-and-tenon joints are often pinned by drilling a hole through the parts while they are held together and then inserting a dowel (FIG. 13-49). To pull the shoulders of the tenon tightly against the mortised component, first, drill the hole through the mortise. Then, insert the tenon and use a pencil or an awl through the hole in the mortise to mark its location on the tenon. Remove the tenon and drill through, locating the hole a fraction closer to the shoulders of the tenon. Driving the dowel will then pull the tenoned component tightly into place.

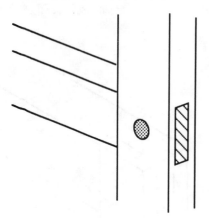

**Fig. 13-49**
*Mortise-and-tenon joints are often locked by passing a dowel through both components.*

# 14
# Adhesives

Joints that have correctly fitted components will mate nicely and will stay united indefinitely when they are properly glued. Essentially, glue is a liquid adhesive dispersed in a solvent, usually water, so it can easily be spread. The glue adheres to wood fibers and acquires strength as the solvent evaporates. This occurs while the parts are held together with fasteners or with clamps. How long clamps should hold will depend on the setting time of the glue. Read the label on the container for this information.

## Applying the adhesive

Glue will not compensate for poor woodworking. Parts to be joined should mesh precisely and be clean, dry, and smooth. Being too generous with glue is a common error. It is more economical and the cleaning chore of removing excess glue will be reduced when the squeeze-out that should occur when parts are clamped is minimal. Excess glue is often removed with a lint-free cloth dampened with warm water. Be careful not to spread a thin film of glue to other areas of your project when using this method. If you feel this would be too messy, wait until the glue is dry and then remove the excess with a scraper, used in line with the grain of the wood.

A lot of the glue used today is squeezed from a plastic bottle. It's poor practice to apply the glue in a wavy bead, feeling that it will spread adequately under clamp pressure. It's better to use something like a stiff-bristle brush to broadcast the glue evenly over all contact surfaces.

Plywood edges and end grain on lumber absorb more glue than other areas, so it's wise to apply a thin amount like you would a sealer and, after a bit, add a second, full-strength coat. A visual check will reveal if the application is uniform.

Don't use a *water resistant* glue on projects that require a *waterproof* product (e.g., picnic tables, patio benches). Inside projects (e.g., cabinets, built-ins), are okay to assemble with a water resistant adhesive. Why not just stay with a water-proof type? Well, for one thing, the other variety is cheaper.

## Types of adhesives

There are many types of adhesives available, but an adequate choice for various types of projects can be made from the following assortment, which are readily available from local woodworking supply centers. Always read the label on the container. It will supply critical mixing and application information and any safety precautions that might be necessary.

*Animal (liquid hide) glue*, made from animal bones and hides, is a perennial favorite for general woodworking assemblies. It is available in convenient, ready-to-use liquid form or as flakes that are mixed with water and heated. It is strong and doesn't become brittle, but it is not waterproof. This glue works best when its temperature is about 70 degrees. When necessary, it can be heated a bit by placing the container in warm water. The fact that it needs more set time than other glues can be an asset when the assembly involves many parts. Average clamp time is about 3 to 4 hours for softwoods and about an hour less for hard-woods.

*Polyvinyl resin* is a popular white glue for general woodworking that is widely available in plastic squeeze bottles. It stands ready to use, and will set best and most quickly at temperatures of 60 degrees or higher. Project components should be ready for clamping as soon as the glue is applied. It's not noted for resistance to moisture or very high temperatures. Clamping time averages from 1 to 2 hours, with softwoods requiring the longer periods.

*Casein* comes as a brownish powder that is mixed with water to form a glue with cream-like consistency. It's a good idea to let the glue sit for about 10 minutes after initial mixing and then to stir it again before use. A mixed quantity has a short shelf life, so prepare only as much as you can use for the job on hand. It is tolerant of most temperatures except freezing, but, like most glues, it is easier to use when it is warm. Casein glue is a good choice for oily woods, like teak or yew, but it's not recommended for species like redwood, maple, or oak because it causes stains. The glue is moisture resistant, but not waterproof. Clamping time is about the same as required for animal glue.

*Aliphatic resin* is a good all-purpose glue for furniture and case goods, face gluing, edge-to-edge joints, and so on. It is similar to polyvinyl and is purchased in ready-to-use form. This glue resists heat, is easy to spread, but is not particu-larly water resistant. Favorable factors are that it sets quickly and is usable at any temperature above about 50 degrees. Be prepared to apply clamps as soon as the glue is spread. Clamping time is between 1 or 2 hours.

*Plastic resin glue* is a urea-formaldehyde material, available as a powder that is mixed with water. It's not recommended for use on oily woods, and because its shelf life is relatively short, it's wise to prepare quantities that can be used quickly. While it has considerable moisture resistance, it is not considered waterproof. It is an acceptable adhesive for general woodworking, but glue lines will be brittle unless components come together tightly. It's best used at 70 degrees or higher. Clamping times can be quite long—as much as 16 hours for softwoods or hardwoods.

*Resorcinol resin glue* is completely waterproof and very strong. It's a fine adhesive for furniture that will be exposed to the weather, even for projects like wooden water containers and boats. This product has components consisting of a resin and a catalyst. A chemical reaction that causes the glue to set occurs when the parts are mixed. Joints will be weak if the proportions are not correct, so be sure to follow the instructions that are provided. Temperature should be at least 70 degrees, but the higher, the better. The glue leaves a dark line and sets slowly. Clamping time can run from 14 to 16 hours.

*Epoxy cement* comes as separate resin and hardener that should be joined exactly as instructed on the product's label. It's not really a woodworking glue, but handy for bonding dissimilar materials. This type of product must be used carefully and in well ventilated areas, so read and obey all safety precautions. The epoxy can be used at any temperature, but will set faster with heat. Many jobs can be accomplished without clamping, but the nature of the work and the product itself are factors to consider. The epoxy does not swell or shrink and is waterproof. Some types can be used to fill gaps or holes. Once the epoxy sets, it can be drilled, filed, or sanded.

*Contact cement* is a special adhesive that is used primarily to bond plastic laminates or veneers to a substrate. The product is applied by brush or roller to both surfaces. Accept the word *contact* literally. Once the coated surfaces touch, they can't be separated. This calls for exact uniting of parts. A common procedure is to place brown wrapping paper between sheets when the cement is dry and to pull the paper away slowly as the parts are pressed together. Be careful about the time span required between the application of the cement and the bonding of the components. The product label will suggest a simple test to determine readiness. Most times, the adhesive is ready if a piece of wrapping paper pressed against the coated surfaces doesn't stick.

NOTE: Original products, some of which are still available, were volatile and flammable. Newer, water-based types are neither toxic or flammable. In any case, follow instructions so the product will be used efficiently and safely.

# 15

# Vises
# and clamps

No woodworking shop would be complete without a variety of vises and clamps. These tools provide you with the holding power when your hands won't do.

## Types and features of vises

The primary function of a *vise* is to hold parts securely as you work on them. There are different versions of vises—some for woodworking, others for gripping metal. The *woodworker's vise*, aptly named, has features that make it especially suitable in a woodshop (FIG. 15-1). For one thing, its deep, wide jaws apply pressure over a considerable area. Quality units will have a *retractable dog* centered in the top edge of the front jaw. This dog might be raised and locked above the surface of the bench so pressure can be applied to work that is backed-up by a stop on the benchtop. It's a way to increase grip-span beyond the maximum capacity of the vise itself. It's a handy feature for securing long or wide pieces for planing or sanding. It might even serve, at times, as a clamp for edge-to-edge joints (FIG. 15-2).

Another good feature of the woodworker's vise is a half-thread on the screw bar that moves the front jaw. This allows the jaw to be adjusted in or out without having to turn the handle. With the work in place, you just slide the jaw forward to make contact and then a half-turn or so of the handle applies the pressure. This feature is convenient and allows you to avoid the nuisance of having to rotate the handle x number of times.

How the vise is secured to the workbench depends on its design. Chances are you will have to cut a notch in the bench for the stationary jaw and drive

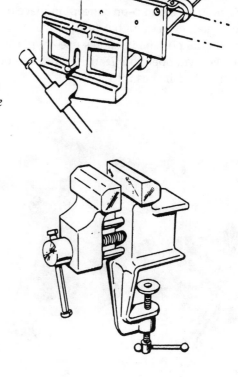

**Fig. 15-1** *A permanently mounted* woodworker's vise *(top) has wooden jaws that are supplied by the buyer and considered to be replaceable. The top edge of the jaws should be flush with the surface of the bench. The* clamp-on vise *(bottom) is suitable for metalworking. Its jaws may be corrugated or otherwise embossed so they can grip hard objects firmly.*

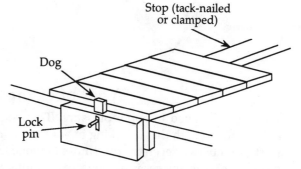

**Fig. 15-2** *Pictured is one way to make use of the* dog *on a woodworker's vise. The parts of this edge-to-edge joint have to be short because the clamp pressure is only at the central area.*

Stop (tack-nailed or clamped)

Dog

Lock pin

heavy-duty fasteners like lag screws from underneath. Manufacturer's instructions will supply the answers. The jaws will have tapped holes so you can attach hardwood facings with flathead screws. Make two sets of facings so you will have a spare on hand when the original ones have become worn.

A common location for a vise is at the left, front corner of the bench, but there can be other preferences. An important factor is that there should be standing room, and clearance for work at the front and at both ends of the unit. Be sure that the top edges of the jaws and facings are flush with the surface of the bench.

Opting for a clamp-on concept in place of or in addition to a stationary vise is not unusual, even though it won't have all the desirable features. Installation is a snap, and its portability allows use anyplace in or out of the shop. The example in FIG. 15-3 will open to 3¹/₂ inches and can be attached to any surface that is not more than 2¹/₂ inches thick.

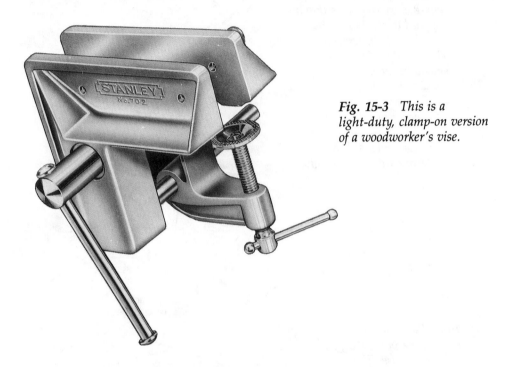

*Fig. 15-3*  This is a light-duty, clamp-on version of a woodworker's vise.

## Types of clamps

Clamps are designed to apply pressure. They supply you with an extra set of hands, with strength that is lacking in your own. You can apply enough force to distort assemblies or even to crush areas of wood. When should you stop applying pressure? The answer is obvious and simple. Stop applying pressure when mating parts are snugly joined. A visual check of the joint lines will advise when enough-is-enough. Certainly, clamps can't compensate for poorly-fitting joint-parts. For example, it's easy to split a mortise by forcing in an oversize tenon. It's even possible to pressure excess glue so it travels through the pores of the wood to emerge on a surface.

Most times it's wise to place blocks of wood between clamp faces and the work. The block protects the work from the face of the clamp and distributes clamp pressure over a wider area.

Clamps are a necessity in any woodworking shop, but the thought that you can never have enough or a sufficient variety is a little farfetched. There are clamp designs you may never have use for, and using four clamps when two will do doesn't make sense. The selection of clamps that follows doesn't include all possibilities, but they will make a good collection with which to start. As always, select and buy in quantities that suit the scope of your work.

## Handscrews

Handscrews (FIG. 15-4) are traditional favorites with woodworkers because their hardwood jaws are easily adjusted to apply equal pressure over broad areas without marring the work. There are two types: *standard* versions, which have jaws that, in addition to working in parallel fashion, can be set at angles to accommodate odd-shaped pieces of work (FIG. 15-5); and *nonadjustable* versions, which have jaws that are constantly parallel.

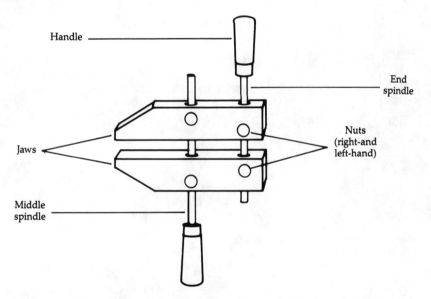

**Fig. 15-4** *Nomenclature of a handscrew. Its reach, how much of the work it can grip, is the distance from the end of the jaws to the middle spindle.*

The clamps can be set pretty quickly if you adopt the practice that is demonstrated in FIG. 15-6—right hand on end spindle, left hand on middle spindle. Rotate your hands as if they were on the pedals of a bicycle, forward to close the jaws, backward to separate them, until the opening is approximately correct. Hold the handles firmly, with your arms extended enough to keep the clamp away from your face.

Place the clamp so the center spindle is close to the work and then turn the handles lightly and alternately until you have the necessary pressure. A common procedure, after the jaws are pretty well set, is to tighten the end spindle and

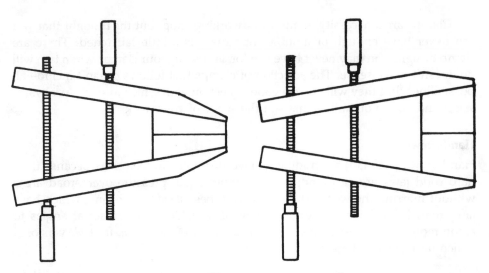

*Fig. 15-5  Standard handscrews have jaws that can be adjusted to suit various angles.*

*Fig. 15-6  Place your hands on the handles in this fashion; then rotate them as if pedaling a bicycle—forward to close the jaws, backward to open them.*

then the middle one. What to aim for are jaws that are parallel and flat on the work over their entire bearing surfaces. As shown in FIG. 15-7, the parts may be held together, but pressure will not be uniform unless the clamp is adjusted correctly.

wrong way       right way

*Fig. 15-7*   *The jaws of a handscrew must be flat on the work's surface throughout their bearing area.*

The depth of a handscrew's throat, its gripping area, is one half the length of the jaws. Sizes are called out by jaw-length, and they range from 4 inches to as much as 24 inches. A couple of small ones and several in the 10- or 12-inch range make a nice assortment for beginners.

## C-clamps

C-clamps (FIG. 15-8), are available in many shapes and sizes, and are handy for applications that range from simple clamping to auxiliary uses like that in FIG. 15-9. While they all fit the one category of clamps, they may have round or square frames, shallow or deep throats, and handles that might be levers, thumbscrews, or knurled knobs. The handle reveals something about how the tool should be applied. For example, you can't exert as much pressure with a thumbscrew or knob as you can with a lever. Certain designs might even be identified by special

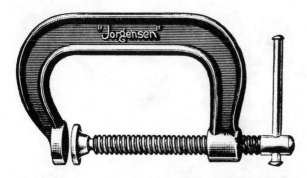

*Fig. 15-8* The category of C-clamps covers shapes like this and others that might be round or square. They cover a full range of light-duty to heavy-duty varieties.

*Fig. 15-9* In addition to holding project components together, C-clamps can be cast in auxiliary roles. Here, one is used to secure a miter box to a sawhorse.

names like the heavy-duty *carriage clamps* being used in FIG.15-10. Tiny units can have an opening (*grip area*) of ⁵/₈ inch and a throat depth of ⁷/₈ inch. Then there are size offerings ranging up to a 12-inch opening with a 6-inch throat. The way to start is to obtain several in small sizes so you can judge how the clamp style will fit into your woodworking program.

**Fig. 15-10** *These heavy-duty C-clamps are identified as* carriage *clamps. Note the use of protective pads between the clamps and the work.*

Always use a pad, at least under the swivel end of the screw. The pad will prevent the swivel from marring the work, and it will increase the clamp's bearing area (FIG. 15-11).

### Three-way edging clamp

A newcomer in the clamp field is the *three-way edging clamp* (FIG. 15-12). It looks like a C-clamp, but its design allows applying right-angle pressure to the side or edge of a workpiece. It's particularly useful for jobs like installing border strips on slabs, and attaching edge trim or moldings (FIG. 15-13). Because the three screws are independently adjustable, the right-angle screw can supply pressure off-center. It can also be used like a conventional C-clamp by threading the right-angle screw out of the way.

### Spring clamps

Spring clamps (FIG. 15-14) are like tireless, extra-strong fingers that can be used to hold work temporarily, to keep parts together while glue dries, or to stabilize

*Fig. 15-11* Using a pad avoids the kind of marring that can be caused by the swivel end of the screw. The pad also spreads pressure over a broader area.

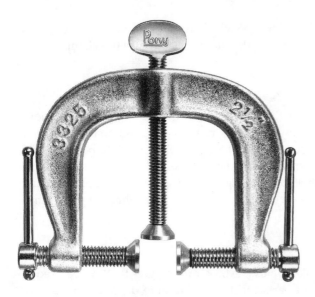

*Fig. 15-12* The 3-way edging clamp is a newcomer that will find wide acceptance.

Adjustable Clamp Company

**Fig. 15-13** *Typical applications for the 3-way edging clamp.*

**Fig. 15-14** *Spring clamps supply gripping power at the end of the jaws, but it can be increased by using pads. Small ones can be opened with fingers. Heavy-duty types require a two-hand grip.*

your project as you work on it. Jaw openings range from less than 1 inch to 4 inches. Power and *reach*, which is the distance from the jaw-tips to the spring, increase in proportion to the length of the product. Small ones can be considered light-duty units, but the larger ones are powerful enough so you need two hands to spread the jaws. Clamp pressure is always at the tip of the jaws so you can locate the grip-point anywhere within the tool's reach. Using pads under the jaws will spread pressure over a broader area. The clamps are usable on any job where the spring pressure is adequate, but they are especially nice to have when quick application and removal is an advantage.

Example uses in addition to conventional gluing chores include, holding moldings in place while you drive fasteners, securing a template as you trace around it, and keeping parts in place as you drill through them.

## Bar clamps

Bar clamps are what you might call long-span grippers. Their clamping capacity goes far beyond the maximum opening of C-clamps or handscrews. For example, the steel, I-beam concept, shown in FIG. 15-15, is available in lengths of 2 feet up to 8 feet. However, the gripping capacity is not a set factor. On clamps of this type, a *tail-stop* can be moved and locked at any point on the beam. Thus, the opening can range from maximum to zero. In practice, the tail-stop is adjusted to suit the width of the work and the screw is turned to apply or release pressure.

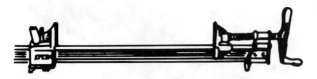

*Fig. 15-15  A bar clamp that has the tail-stop riding an I-beam. Other versions have bars with a simple, rectangular cross section.*

Another bar clamp design (FIG. 15-16) has a fixed tail, a sliding head, and greater *reach*, distance from screw to bar, than other types. Available lengths range from 6 inches to 3 feet. The smaller units are often used in place of conventional C-clamps.

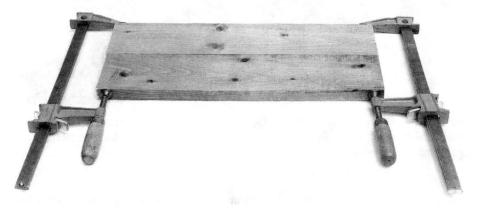

*Fig. 15-16  This type of bar clamp has a fixed tail and a sliding head. The shape of its handle tells you that it is applicable for light-duty and medium-duty chores.*

As with all clamps, protective wooden blocks should be used between the work and the clamp jaws. Special nonmarring pads are available for some types of bar clamps. They are easily slipped on or off the clamp jaws so you can do without makeshift blocks that are often a nuisance to place in correct position.

## Clamp fixtures

*Clamp fixtures* should be explored by every woodworker. The fixtures (FIG. 15-17) are actually unmounted tail-stops and clamp heads that can be used on any

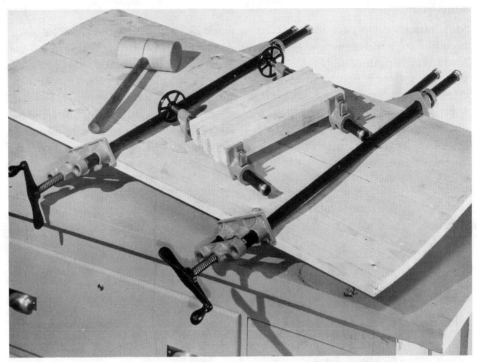

**Fig. 15-17**  *Pictured are pipe-mounted clamp fixtures. A set of fixtures consists of a tail-stop and clamp heads mounted on any conventional pipe. The double-bar design straddles the assembly and opposes the tendency of assemblies like this to buckle under pressure. Regular bar clamps offer the same protection if several are used and placed alternately on opposite surfaces of the slab.*

length of readily available pipe. Thus, with several fixtures that can be used with an assortment of pipe-lengths, the shop will be well-equipped to handle any wide-span clamping chore. Like conventional bar clamps, the tail or the head of the fixtures can be locked at any point so that clamping capacity is from zero to the length of the pipe being used.

The units are made for mounting on ³/₄-inch or ¹/₂-inch pipe that is threaded at both ends. The tail or the head, depending on the design of the fixture, is threaded on at one end of the pipe; a coil-spring stop is used at the other end. Black pipe is recommended—it works better than galvanized pipe and it costs less.

The double-bar design being used in FIG. 15-17 is excellent for edge-to-edge gluing chores. It exerts equal pressure on both sides of the assembly to prevent any tendency of the work to buckle. One of the pipes should be about 3 inches longer than the other so it will be easier to set the tail when the clamp is applied across the work.

## Miter clamps

*Miter clamps*, often called *corner clamps*, work like a vise to hold mitered pieces together in correct alignment (FIG. 15-18). A nice feature of the device is that if you find that the mating edges do not come together as they should, you can use a backsaw to touch up the joint while the parts are clamped. Then, loosen the clamp screws, apply glue, and bring the edges together again. Because the joint is fully exposed, it's easy to add reinforcements like nails or screws or even dowels. Then the joined parts can be removed from the clamp so you can immediately work on other corners or parts. Incidentally, the same device can be used if you wish to form corners with butt joints. The limitation of the clamp is the width of stock it can grip, usually about 3 inches.

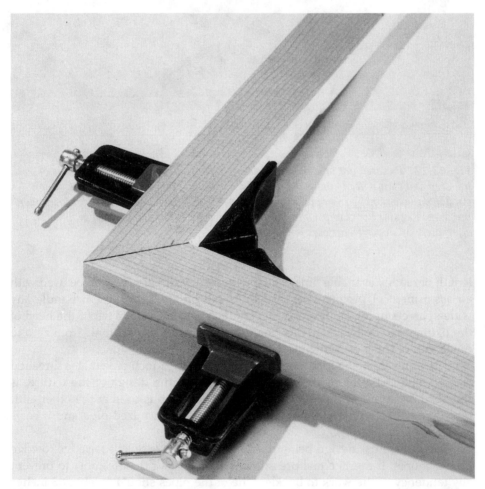

**Fig. 15-18** *A miter clamp is a vise that holds mitered components in correct position for gluing and reinforcing. The joined parts can be removed so other work can be done without delay.*

## Band clamps

Band clamps (FIG. 15-19) are unique in that they are flexible enough to conform to round, square or irregular shapes. A typical light-duty version has a 12- or 15-foot-long nylon band that is 1 inch wide. A heavy-duty band clamp may have a 2 inch wide, pre-stretched canvas band that can be 10 to 30 feet long.

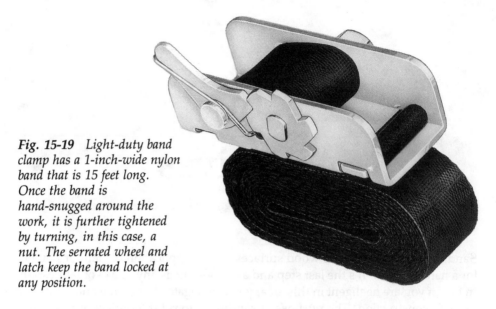

*Fig. 15-19 Light-duty band clamp has a 1-inch-wide nylon band that is 15 feet long. Once the band is hand-snugged around the work, it is further tightened by turning, in this case, a nut. The serrated wheel and latch keep the band locked at any position.*

In practice, the band is placed about the work and pulled as snugly as possible by hand. The final tightening is done by turning a ratchet mechanism with a wrench or screwdriver, whichever applies. A spring-loaded pawl bears against the band at any point to keep it from slipping.

Typical applications for a band clamp include, securing banding to circular forms, holding together rail and leg assemblies for chairs and tables, and keeping segmented projects together until the glue dries. Some band clamps come with steel corner-pieces that are nice to have when assembling projects like picture frames. The corners make it easier to clamp the assembly and they protect both the band and the work.

Band clamps don't have to be limited to in-the-shop chores. Use them for jobs like securing plywood or lumber to your car when returning from the lumberyard, fastening a load on a wheelbarrow, and so on.

# 16

# Abrasives

Sanding is done to prepare wood surfaces for the application of stain or paint or for a natural finish. It's the last step and as important as any phase of fabrication. In fact, if you are negligent in this area, you can negate all the time and effort you put into construction. The purpose of sanding is to rid the project of any marks left by tools and to make all surfaces equally smooth so the beauty of the wood and its grain will be enhanced by the finishing coats. The thought may not apply so much to a project that will receive several coats of paint, but it's not professional to rely on thick coatings to hide imperfections—and paint is not an infallible coverall.

Actually, the bulk of sanding should be done on components before they are put together. Thus, final attention to assemblies amounts to touch-up work—being sure that some tool mark, rough area, or some slight imperfection hasn't escaped your attention.

## Types of abrasives

*Sandpaper* is a cutting tool—paper or cloth that is covered on one surface with sharp particles of a natural or man-made substance. At one time, flint was widely used, but it has been relegated to a back seat by the introduction of harder, more durable materials like garnet and aluminum oxide. Sandpaper (*sand*paper is still used even though the term is no longer descriptive) removes wood by various degrees in relation to the coarseness of the cutting particles on the paper (see TABLES 16-1 and 16-2).

## Table 16-1. Basic Information on Abrasives

| Name | Available grits | Size (inches) | For Wood | Metal | Typical uses |
|---|---|---|---|---|---|
| Flint | Very fine to very coarse | 9″×10″ 4¹/2″×5″ | X | | Rough work—used for finishing chores but lacks toughness and durability |
| Garnet | 220–30 | 9″×11″ | X | | Very good for general woodworking applications |
| Aluminum oxide | 220–30 | 9″×11″ | X | X | Long lasting—good for hardwoods—may be used on non-wood materials |
| Aluminum oxide (cloth) | 120–30 | Belt form for electric sanders | X | X | Cloth-backed belts are very strong and are a number one choice for power sanding |
| Silicon carbide (waterproof) | 400–220 | 9″×11″ | X | X | Excellent for sanding after primer coats and between finish coats—often used with water and other lubricants |

Many abrasives are available in sizes that are just right for power tools like pad sanders—some modern abrasives have self-adhesive backing for pad and disk sanders.

The finer the abrasive, the less obvious the ridge left by each piece of grit will be. A general rule is to work through progressively finer grits until the wood feels satiny smooth, but automatically choosing a coarse grit to begin with is not always the best way to go. The condition of the wood should dictate how to start. It doesn't make sense to obey the general rule if the wood is smooth enough before you begin to sand. In this case, the optimum surface can be achieved by using only fine-grit paper. Most of the wood and wood products of today are offered in respectable shape. The idea is to examine the material and then judge how you can get the job done with the least amount of sanding.

Steps in fabrication often result in edges that are rougher than the material's original condition. So, for example, sawed edges of lumber, especially plywood, will require more attention than adjacent surfaces.

The terms *open-coat* and *close-coat* are used to indicate how much of the surface of the backing material is covered with the abrasive grit. Close-coat products have overall coverage and will produce the smoothest finishes. Open-coat has 50 to 70 percent coverage, which leaves enough space between particles so the paper resists clogging. That's why open-coat paper is a good choice for working on old, rough, or resinous wood and for removing finishes.

## Table 16-2. Sandpaper Grits

| Degree | Grit Grade # | # | Typical uses |
|---|---|---|---|
| Very fine | 400 | 10/0 | Super-fine surface on raw wood—use after applying stain, |
| | 360 | — | shellac, sealers—polishing and smoothing between finish |
| | 320 | 9/0 | cots and for smoothing of the final coat |
| | 280 | 8/0 | |
| | 240 | 7/0 | |
| | 220 | 6/0 | |
| Fine | 180 | 5/0 | Can be used for finishing raw wood before applications of |
| | 150 | 4/0 | stain and sealers |
| | 120 | 3/0 | |
| Medium | 100 | 2/0 | Intermediate smoothing—preparing surfaces for final work |
| | 80 | 1/0 | with fine paper |
| | 60 | 1/2 | |
| Coarse | 50 | 1 | Use when necessary, for first sanding to prepare wood for |
| | 40 | 1½ | final work with finer abrasive |
| | 36 | 2 | |
| Very coarse | 30 | 2½ | For very rough work only—use on wood in-the-rough— |
| | 24 | 3 | often used in place of a file or plane to round edges |
| | 20 | 3½ | |
| | 16 | 4 | |

# Working with abrasives

Smooth and uniform finishes on edges and surfaces are best obtained when the sandpaper is mounted with thumbtacks onto a block of wood that you can grip in your hand (FIG. 16-1). A rigid backing provides a leveling action for broad areas and cuts down ridges and irregularities. A block also allows greater abrasive-to-work contact than you can supply by just using fingers to move the paper. The same block, or a duplicate, can be fitted with a felt pad so the abrasive will conform more readily to contoured surfaces and cylinders. Another type of sanding block that you can make is shown in FIG.16-2. This sanding block requires a little more work to put together than a block of wood, but it has the convenience of applying sandpaper without the use of fasteners. It too, can be fitted with a felt pad. Soft carpeting or even material like foam rubber can be used in place of felt. Think of the pad's thickness in relation to the work. Thick, soft pads will conform more readily to round surfaces and contours.

At times, especially when sanding small components, applying the work to the paper is more convenient. Use a stationary sanding block (FIG. 16-3). Keep the block steady by tack-nailing it to a firm surface or by gripping it in a vise. If you make the block large enough and cover only part of it with sandpaper, you can use clamps to secure it.

Stroking in line with the grain of the wood is the best way to get smooth results. It's okay, in fact it's better, to stroke across the grain or diagonally to it

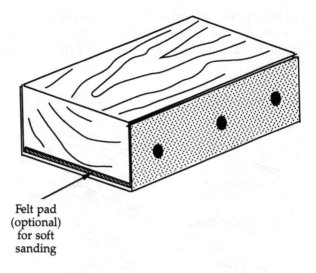

**Fig. 16-1**  *You can make a good sanding tool by wrapping sandpaper around a wood block. The block can be sized and shaped to suit the application.*

Felt pad
(optional)
for soft
sanding

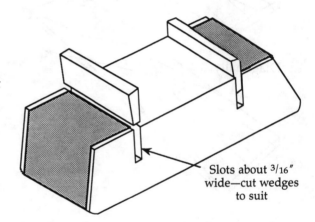

**Fig. 16-2**  *This sanding block design makes it easy to secure the abrasive. Like the plain block, it can be fitted with a soft pad. The pad does not have to be permanently attached. A good size is 2×3¹/₂×6 inches.*

Slots about ³/₁₆″
wide—cut wedges
to suit

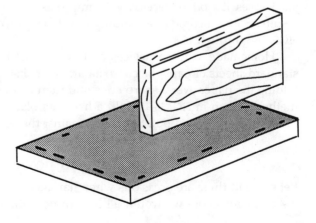

**Fig. 16-3**  *Stationary sanding blocks are handy and especially useful when you must smooth small components.*

when you wish to remove a lot of material quickly. A good procedure, say, when it's necessary to smooth a piece of very rough wood, is to start by working cross-grain, switch to diagonal strokes, and finish by sanding in line with the grain (FIG. 16-4).

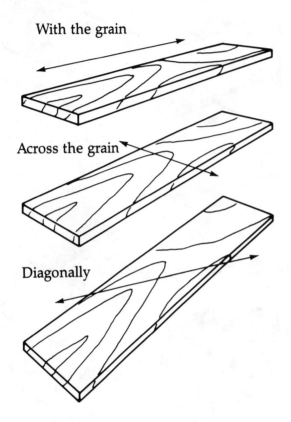

**With the grain**

**Across the grain**

**Diagonally**

*Fig. 16-4  Use cross-grain or diagonal strokes when you must remove a lot of material, but always finish by sanding with the grain.*

Sanding, of course, is not confined to flat surfaces—round corners and edges, contours, ready-made materials like molding, all require attention. In such cases it's often necessary to improvise a method that will lead to best results. Some methods for sanding that have proven worthwhile are shown in FIGS. 16-5 through 16-8.

Homemade sanding devices and even some commercial ones require that standard sheets of paper be cut to a particular size. This can be accomplished by folding the paper over a sharp edge and then tearing it, but it's better to use the method shown in FIG. 16-9. Hold a hacksaw blade or any saw with small teeth firmly in place as you pull the paper against the serrated edge.

## Going to power

Let's face it, there are occasions when hand-sanding is necessary but, generally, it's a tedious chore we would all love to do without. Being able to do the last

**Fig. 16-5** *Smooth round edges that have been formed with a file or plane by using a strip of sandpaper as you would a shoe-polishing rag. Ribbon-type abrasives are available in rolls or you can cut strips from standard sheets.*

**Fig. 16-6** *Sandpaper wrapped around a thin, flexible backing will conform to the contours of molding. Use your fingers to press into concave areas.*

**Fig. 16-7**  *A piece cut from the molding you are working on will make a sanding block that conforms to contours. In this case, the edges of the block have been sawed off so it will fit the major curves.*

**Fig. 16-8**  *Getting into small, concave areas can be accomplished by wrapping the sandpaper around a soft pad so it will conform with the arc. For a tight, sharp corner, use folded sandpaper without a pad.*

*Fig. 16-9*  *A common method used to cut sandpaper.*

chore speedily and with minimum fuss and effort is a happy way to complete a project.

Palm-size *pad sanders*, like the one shown in FIG. 16-10, are among the most popular tools for finishing wood. The units work by vibrating a pad to which the sandpaper is secured. Some move the pad to and fro, but most have an orbital action. When you consider that a typical tool will move the abrasive 13,000 times per minute in $1/16$-inch orbits, you can appreciate that you would need a microscope to discover any swirl marks. Most products work with quarter-size sheets of sandpaper that you can buy ready to use or cut from standard sheets. The tools are light and easy to handle for long periods without fatigue.

Another type of pad sander that has a larger pad, offering a broader abrasive surface, is shown in FIG. 16-11. This unit works with $1/3$-size sanding sheets that orbit at 10,000 strokes per minute. Despite its broad coverage, the model weighs only 3.7 pounds, so using it, with one or both hands, doesn't require a lot of muscle.

While pad sanders are often called *finishing tools* because they can work with very fine abrasives to produce satiny smooth finishes, they are also capable of some heavy-duty applications, depending on the coarseness of the sandpaper used.

When you consider a *belt sander*, you really get into the area of heavy-duty sanding (FIG. 16-12). This tool works with a continuous loop (belt) of abrasive that

**Fig. 16-10** *A palm-size pad sander is a super tool for achieving satiny smooth wood finishes. Most are made for use with quarter-size sheets of abrasive and can get into tight corners.*

**Fig. 16-11** *Many larger-size pad sanders have front handles so they can be gripped with both hands. This model has a skirt around the base to confine sawdust and a bag to capture it.*

**Fig. 16-12** *Belt sanders can be used with all types of abrasives. The sander size is identified by the width of the belt—3-inch and 4-inch belts are most common.*

moves over *drums* that are encased at each end of the machine. One drum is powered to drive the belt, the other is a spring-loaded idler that is adjustable for belt tension and to keep the belt running in line with the rotation of the drums.

The belt sander must be handled a little more carefully than a pad sander. For example, if you were to turn one on and set it down without gripping it firmly, it would travel forward like a tractor. Also, it removes material very quickly regardless of the abrasive grit-size, so it must be moved smoothly and constantly to avoid gouges and other imperfections.

How a sander is adjusted and the method used to attach the abrasive sheets or belts are unique to each tool. For this reason, it is very important for efficiency and safety to study the owner's manual that is supplied with the tool.

# 17
# Projects

You might have many reasons for learning how to use tools. The knowledge enables you to be somewhat independent when faced with household maintenance and repair chores, but the real enjoyment is in constructing projects of your choice—using some of your precious time for something you elect to do. Regardless of whether a project requires a few hours or several days to make, cherish the time for its therapeutic value. Take a few deep breaths and forget the cares of the day. Speed is not part of the process, nor does it contribute to quality projects. There are times when it's nice to take 10 minutes to do a 5-minute job.

The projects that are offered have to be specific in terms of design, size, and construction details, but that doesn't mean that you can't object to any one of the factors. If you like a concept but feel negative about part or even all of its design, adapt it to suit your own creativity. That too is part of the fun.

## For the shop

Most fabrication and assembly work is done on or by a workbench. A shop without a workbench is like a dining room without a table or a kitchen without counters. You can establish one quickly and easily by buying ready-made steel legs and attaching a plywood top and shelf (FIG. 17-1) or you can make your own from scratch. If you opt for steel legs for temporary use, they will not be wasted. You can use them later to make a bench for a stationary power tool.

### Workbench

The design for this workbench is straightforward, practical, and sturdy enough for many years of woodworking (FIG. 17-2). Many workbenches, especially com-

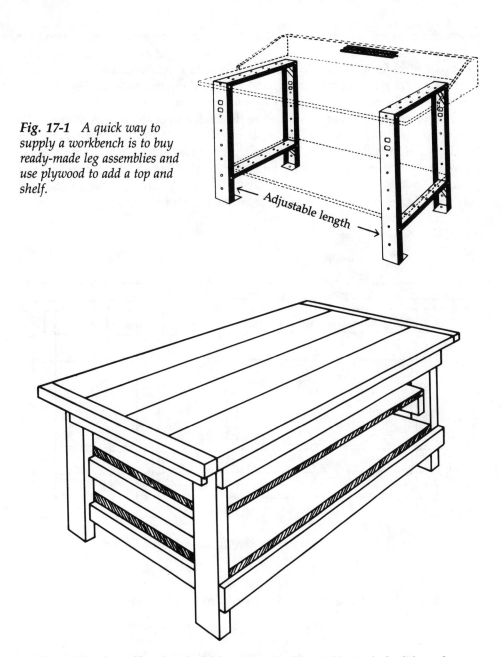

*Fig. 17-1* *A quick way to supply a workbench is to buy ready-made leg assemblies and use plywood to add a top and shelf.*

Adjustable length

*Fig. 17-2* *A workbench to build from scratch. Plywood instead of solid wood can be used for the top. Drawers can be added later.*

mercial ones, are made of hard maple. It's an excellent material to use, but it's expensive and difficult to find at local lumberyards in the sizes you will need. Fir is a reasonable alternative, but choose a select grade or the more costly kiln-dried straight grain. Pine is easier to work with but won't abide too much abuse. A practical compromise is to use pine for the substructure and a harder wood for the top. Construction consists mostly of making straight saw-cuts and following the procedures for forming wide rabbets or end-laps (explained in chapter 13).

Start by studying the plan in FIG. 17-3 and checking the materials list in TABLE 17-1. Parts are listed in actual, not nominal size. Construction begins by sawing the four legs and the six end rails to length. Each end of the rails is rabbeted $3/4$ inch deep × $1^1/2$ inches wide (see details in FIG. 17-4). Mark the legs for the rail locations and then attach them by using glue and two #12 × 2-inch flathead wood screws at each connection. Check connections with a square when assembling to be sure that legs and rails are accurately attached. Be sure that the middle and bottom end rails are placed *inside* the legs; the top end rail *outside*.

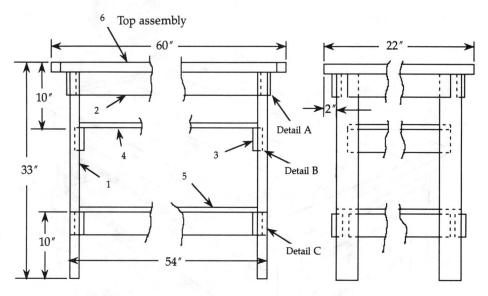

**Fig. 17-3**  *Construction details for the workbench. See materials list for sizes.*

### Table 17-1. Materials List for Workbench

| Key | # pieces | Name | Size (inches) |
|-----|----------|------|---------------|
| 1 | 4 | Legs | $1^1/2 \times 3^1/2 \times 31^1/2$ |
| 2 | 4 | Front rail | $1^1/2 \times 3^1/2 \times 54$ |
| 3 | 6 | End rail | $1^1/2 \times 3^1/2 \times 14$ |
| 4 | 1 | Top shelf | $3/4 \times 14 \times 51$ |
| 5 | 1 | Bottom shelf | $3/4 \times 18 \times 51$ |
| 6 | 4 | Slab pieces | $1^1/2 \times 5^1/2 \times 57$ |
|   | 2 | End pieces | $1^1/2 \times 1^1/2 \times 22$ |

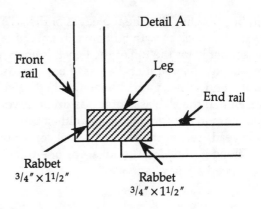

Detail A

Front rail

Leg

End rail

Rabbet
$3/4'' \times 1^1/2''$

Rabbet
$3/4'' \times 1^1/2''$

**Fig. 17-4** *Joint designs for the substructure of the workbench.*

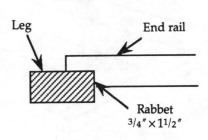

Detail B

Leg

End rail

Rabbet
$3/4'' \times 1^1/2''$

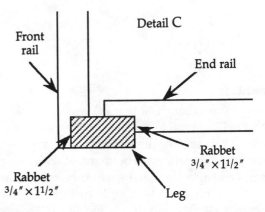

Detail C

Front rail

End rail

Rabbet
$3/4'' \times 1^1/2''$

Rabbet
$3/4'' \times 1^1/2''$

Leg

Next, cut the four pieces required for the front and rear rails, and rabbet them as you did the end rails. When you attach the four parts, using the same system outlined for the end rails, be sure the top edge of the bottom ones and the adjacent of the end rails are on the same plane. Now it's time to add the shelves. Do not cut them to size until you have actually measured on the frame assembly the exact width and length that's required. This is a safety factor that ensures a good fit. Spread glue over the top edges of the rails that the shelves will rest on, then secure the shelves with 5d box nails spaced every eight inches or so.

The assembly for the top of the bench is shown in FIG. 17-5. This is an edge-to-edge glue job that requires the use of bar clamps. If you are equipped to work so, add the end pieces with glue and a single 10d box nail into each slab piece after the glue in the slab assembly has dried. If you like, you can use a sheet of plywood temporarily for the top. In either case, do not attach the top permanently. Instead, secure the top with steel corner braces, using one at each end and two along each side. The idea, for one thing, will allow inverting the top when you need a "new" surface.

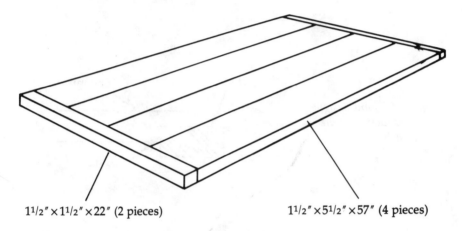

1¹/₂″ × 1¹/₂″ × 22″ (2 pieces)　　　　　1¹/₂″ × 5¹/₂″ × 57″ (4 pieces)

**Fig. 17-5**  *Top assembly. Parts for the slab are joined with glue. The end pieces are glued and nailed.*

### Sawhorse

Like the workbench, a pair of sawhorses can be an asset to any woodworker. They're like portable benches that are usable in or out of the shop. For example, inside they are convenient for making preliminary cuts on panels and long boards; outside they can be spanned with a few boards or a sheet of plywood for use as a temporary workbench or even as a low scaffold.

A sawhorse can be simple or elaborate, but it must be strong. The design shown in FIG. 17-6 and detailed in FIG. 17-7 is as good as any and better than some that are around. The wide top *(beam)* provides more work support than a 2×4, which is often used, and it has enough overhang for securing a clamp-on vise.

Start with pieces of 2×10 and 2×4, 36 inches long. Saw or plane the edges of the 2×4 to a 15-degree angle. You can make the job easier if you do the beveling on a 2×4 that is only about 14 inches long. Then saw it in half to supply separate parts for the leg areas. Attach the piece, or pieces, to the underside of the beam with waterproof glue and ¹/₄ × 2³/₄-inch lag screws.

**Fig. 17-6** *A sawhorse with a board top provides good work support and a ledge that allows the use of a clamp-on vise.*

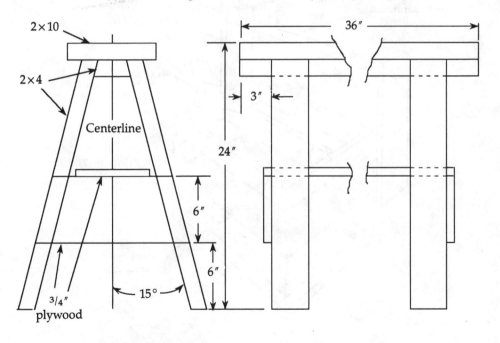

2×10

2×4

Centerline

³/₄"
plywood

15°

6"

6"

24"

36"

3"

**Fig. 17-7** *Construction details for the sawhorse.*

Cut a 2×4 about 25 inches long and place one end against the bevel so you can mark the cut-angle. After sawing, hold the part in place and measure along its length so the project's height will be about 24 inches. Saw to duplicate the top angle and then use the piece as a pattern for three more legs. Attach each leg with glue and two 10d box nails.

Prepare two pieces of exterior grade plywood so they will be 6 inches wide and an inch or so longer than is needed to span across the legs. Attach the parts with glue and 7d nails, then saw the ends so they will conform to the slant of the legs. Measure across the top edge of the braces just installed and then between them, so you will have the exact width and length for the plywood shelf. Attach the shelf with glue and 6d nails. Finish the project with several applications of exterior grade sealer.

### Tool tote

A tool tote, like the basic one shown in FIG. 17-8, is handy for "on-location" chores. It won't hold a full complement of tools but you can base tool selections on the job that needs to be done. Hardware cloth instead of a solid bottom helps to keep waste from accumulating.

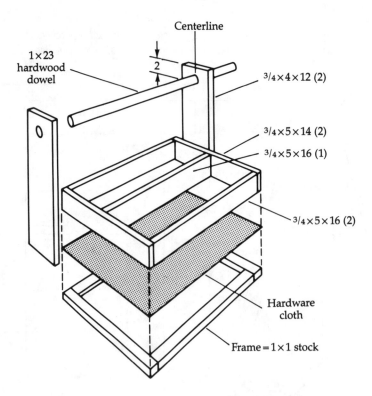

*Fig. 17-8  A tool tote is handy for "on-location" chores.*

Assemble the frame parts and the partition with glue and 7d box nails. Hold the hardware cloth in place with a few staples, then attach the bottom frame with #8×2-inch screws. Be sure to drill adequate body holes through the frame pieces and to locate the screws so they pass through openings in the cloth.

Cut the uprights to size and drill the hole for the handle while the parts are held together with clamps or by tack-nailing. Have the handle in place as you attach the uprights with glue and four #6×1¹/₄-inch flathead screws at each connection. The last step is to install the handle (dowel) permanently by coating the holes with glue and then driving a single 6d box nail through the edge of the uprights, penetrating the dowel.

## For other places

### Trivet

The trivet shown in FIGS. 17-9 and 17-10, is a simple project, but it involves accurate layout and drilling. The project will have more visual appeal if you use contrasting materials (e.g., mahogany for the sides combined with birch or maple dowels). Prepare parts for the sides and then tack-nail together at each end. Use a coping saw to round the ends and then smooth them with sandpaper. Mark

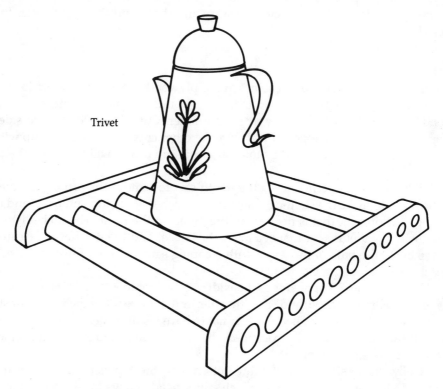

Trivet

*Fig. 17-9  The trivet with contrasting dowels.*

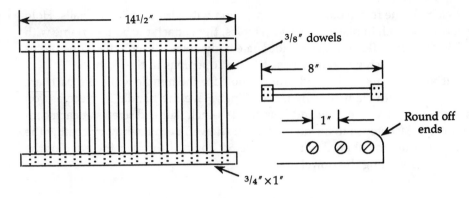

*Fig. 17-10*  *How the trivet is assembled.*

the hole locations very carefully and then drill 3/8-inch holes at each point. This is a good time to make use of the right-angle drill guide that was shown in chapter 9 or, if you have purchased one, to use a doweling jig. In any event, be sure to keep the components firmly on a backup block to avoid the splintering that can occur when the drill bit breaks through the wood.

Separate the parts and install the dowels with glue. The project will be neater if you cut the dowels longer than necessary and then sand them flush after the glue dries.

### Step stool

Maple or birch, lumber core, cabinet grade plywood is a good product for the step stool shown in FIGS. 17-11 and 17-12. It's a handsome material and the solid-wood edges will finish as nicely as solid lumber. Cut two pieces for the sides (part A) and hold them together as you make other cuts so you will end up with twin pieces. This is the best way to ensure that the pieces will be identical and easier to assemble.

With the parts together, use a fine-tooth saw to remove the rectangular area at the front, to make the shoulder cuts for the notches at the top and back, and to execute the long cut that is needed for the rabbet at the front. The rabbet is finished with a shoulder cut that separates the waste, and the notches are cleared by removing the bulk of the waste with a coping saw and then finishing with a chisel. Use a coping saw to form the arch at the base.

Next, cut other components to the widths called for in FIG. 17-12. Start assembly by installing parts B and C with glue and two #6×1½-inch roundhead screws at each connection. If you prefer not to have visible fasteners, counterbore for flathead screws so you can conceal them with wood plugs. The top brace (part D) is just glued in place.

Finally, cut to size and install the bottom and the top steps. Here too, use glue and choose between #6×1½-inch roundhead screws or similar flathead screws that you can conceal with plugs. Be persnickety when sanding the

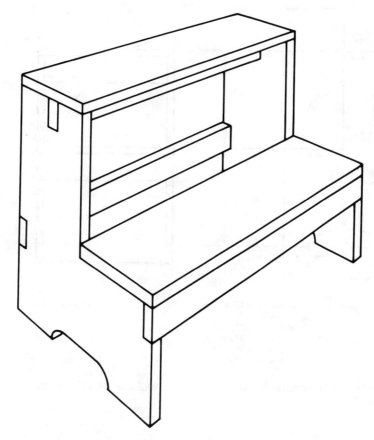

*Fig. 17-11  This step stool is useful in any home or shop.*

exposed edges of the plywood. The smoother they are, the less conspicuous they will be.

### Box furniture

If you can make a box, you can fill a house with simple but attractive furniture (FIGS. 17-13 and 17-14). Boxes can be made in multiple, similar units, or in several compatible sizes that can be stacked without being attached to each other so arrangements can be changed at will. Tables and desks are possible just by introducing slabs of plywood or lumber as part of the design. Install shelves for storage, padding for seats—however far your imagination can take you.

Boxes can be just about any shape or size, and there are many options regarding materials to use. Fir plywood is suitable for service projects, while softwood plywood like clear or knotty pine or redwood, and fancy hardwood plywood that's available in many common and exotic wood species, are better choices when appearance is important. And, of course, there is always solid wood.

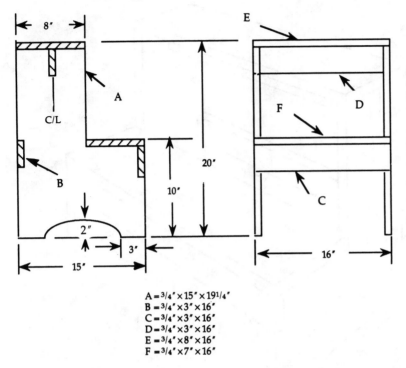

A = 3/4″ × 15″ × 19 1/4″
B = 3/4″ × 3″ × 16″
C = 3/4″ × 3″ × 16″
D = 3/4″ × 3″ × 16″
E = 3/4″ × 8″ × 16″
F = 3/4″ × 7″ × 16″

**Fig. 17-12** *The assembly drawing for the step stool also lists the material requirements.*

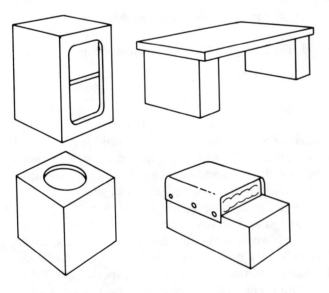

**Fig. 17-13** *Examples of box furniture.*

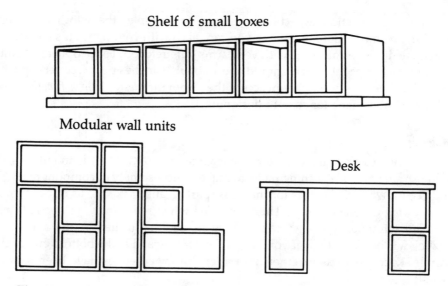

Shelf of small boxes

Modular wall units

Desk

*Fig. 17-14  Seeing boxes as modular units can lead to many ideas. Plywood slabs add to possibilities.*

The choice of joints to use should be influenced by the material you have chosen and by the function of the project (FIG. 17-15). The size of the box, especially when it will serve for storage or display, can be established by determining what will eventually be placed in it. There are some situations where size, especially height, can't be arbitrary. For example, the height of a dining table or card table should be 29 to 30 inches. A coffee table should not be more than 14 to 17 inches high. The average height of an end or lamp table is 24 inches. Information about an acceptable size for any piece of furniture you plan to make is easy to obtain. Just check existing pieces in the house or in a retail store. These are average sizes, but you can make changes to suit your own preferences and the areas where the projects will be used.

*Fig. 17-15  These are joints that can be used for box constructions. Choose the easiest one that is compatible with the purpose of the project.*

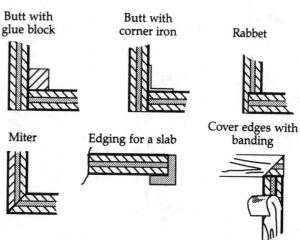

Butt with glue block

Butt with corner iron

Rabbet

Miter

Edging for a slab

Cover edges with banding

There are practical aspects to design. For example, the width of a desk shouldn't be much more than what you can reach with your hand. It's length can match the distance you cover with your arms outstretched. For people to sit comfortably at a dining table, you should allow about 16 inches per place setting with about 8 inches in between. If you accept the axiom that *design follows function*, you will be in good shape for custom designing.

**Magazine rack**

A good construction sequence for a magazine rack (FIG. 17-16) is to cut to size, then use glue and 6d finishing nails, to make a subassembly of components B, C, and D (FIG. 17-17). Cut pieces for the ends (part A) and make the layout shown in the drawing on one of them. Then, as usual when twin units are needed, join the parts temporarily so they can both be shaped and drilled in one operation. Sawing will be easier to do if you bore holes for the radii at the bottom end of the handle. Keep the parts together until after the sawed edges have been sanded smooth.

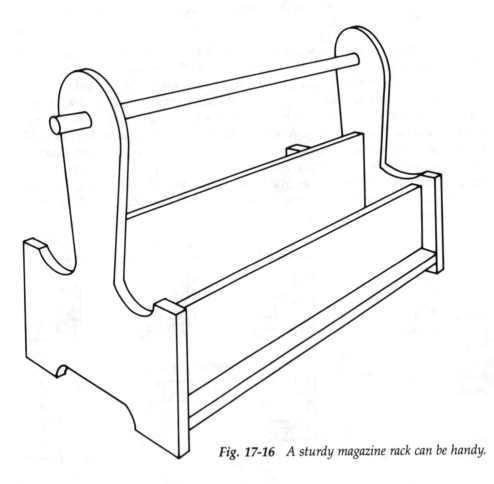

*Fig. 17-16  A sturdy magazine rack can be handy.*

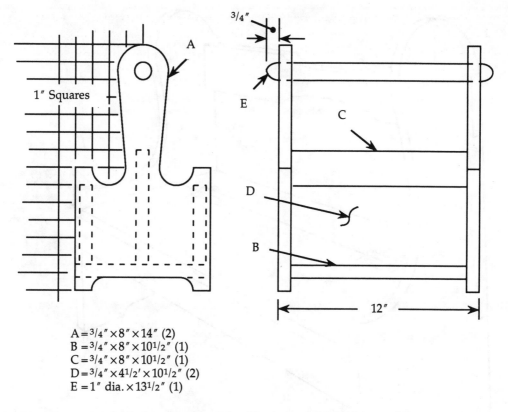

1" Squares

A = 3/4" × 8" × 14" (2)
B = 3/4" × 8" × 10¹/₂" (1)
C = 3/4" × 8" × 10¹/₂" (1)
D = 3/4" × 4¹/₂' × 10¹/₂" (2)
E = 1" dia. × 13¹/₂" (1)

*Fig. 17-17   Assemble the magazine rack with glue and 6d finishing nails.*

Add the ends to the subassembly with glue and 6d finishing nails. Use a nail set to sink the nails ¹/₁₆ inch or so below the surface of the wood. Then, fill the holes with a wood dough that matches the project material. The last step is to round off the ends of the 1-inch diameter dowel used for the handle and to install it with glue. A single 6d nail driven at each end so it penetrates the dowel will provide extra security.

### Storage bench

The bench shown in FIG. 17-18 has a design similar to a deacon's bench but with the added feature of providing for some storage. It isn't overly large and meant for long-term comfortable seating, but can be used in an entry and even a bedroom for keeping reading matter and for a quick seat when putting on socks or shoes. Construction details are in FIG. 17-19; material requirements are listed in TABLE 17-2.

One approach, as far as materials, is to use cabinet grade, lumber core plywood for the wide pieces and compatible solid wood for narrower components. The project can be constructed with all lumber if you prepare slabs that are wide

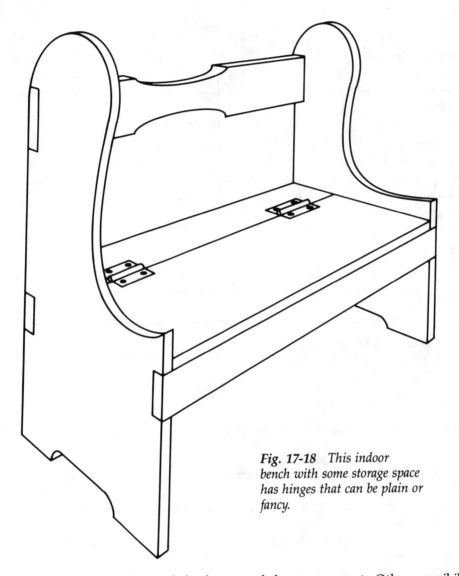

**Fig. 17-18** *This indoor bench with some storage space has hinges that can be plain or fancy.*

enough for the sides and the bottom of the storage seat. Other possibilities include glued-up slabs of various widths or extra wide boards, available through supply catalogs or at your local wood supply center.

Start the project by holding together the two pieces required for the sides and making a careful layout of the top and bottom contours and of the location for the notches for the backrest and the ends of the storage seat. Cut curved areas with a coping saw or a fine-tooth keyhole saw, staying a bit outside the lines. Use sandpaper to smooth rough edges. Make the shoulder cuts for the notches with a backsaw, removing the bulk of the waste with a coping saw. Remove the waste that remains with a chisel or file and do final smoothing with sandpaper wrapped around a wood block.

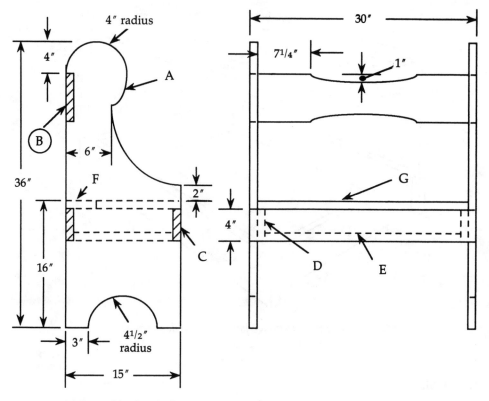

**Fig. 17-19**  *Assembly details for the indoor bench.*

**Table 17-2. Materials List for Indoor Bench**

A = 3/4″ × 15″ × 36″ (2)     E = 3/4″ × 13¹/2″ × 27″ (1)
B = 3/4″ × 6″ × 30″ (1)       F = 3/4′ × 4″ × 28¹/2″ (1)
C = 3/4′ × 4″ × 30″ (2)       G = 3/4″ × 11″ × 28¹/2″ (1)
D = 3/4″ × 4″ × 13¹/2″ (2)

Put together the parts for the storage seat as a subassembly (FIG. 17-20), using glue and 6d finishing nails. The crucial dimension is the total length of the bottom, ends, and hinged top (Parts D, G, and E). The front and back parts can extend a bit more than necessary so their ends can be sanded flush after components are assembled. Remove the hinged seat and, after coating all mating areas with glue, connect the ends to the subassembly. Without the hinged seat in place, it's possible to use C-clamps or handscrews to keep the parts joined until the glue dries. Pipe clamps, if available, are also suitable for the chore. Keep the components under clamp pressure while you shape and install the backrest with glue and 6d finishing nails.

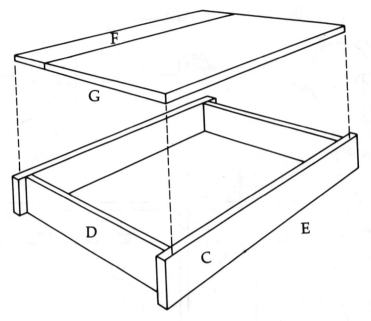

*Fig. 17-20* *The seat and storage box for the indoor bench are put together as a subassembly.*

## Patio table

The design of the table in FIG. 17-21 is often adopted as a special means of displaying prized potted plants. Its rather dainty appearance does make it suitable for the purpose.

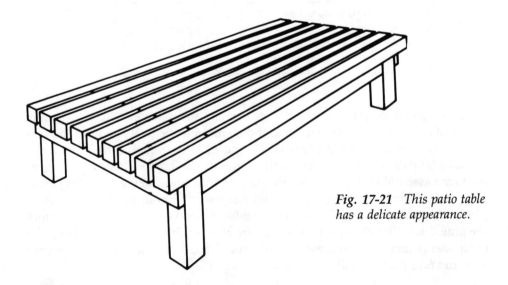

*Fig. 17-21* *This patio table has a delicate appearance.*

First, cut pieces for the legs and the rails (C and D in FIG. 17-22) and assemble them with waterproof glue and two #8×1³/4 inch roundhead screws at each joint. Cut the stretchers (E) to length and add them to the leg assembly as shown. The same size screws are used again here, but be careful to locate them so they don't run into those already installed.

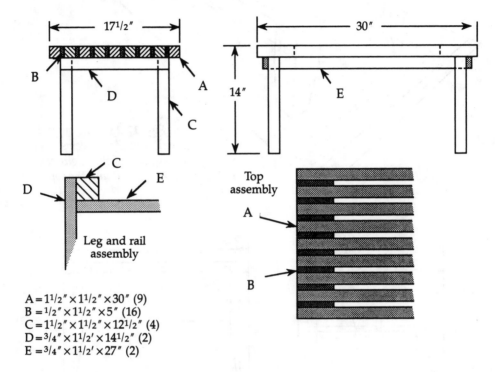

A = 1¹/2" × 1¹/2" × 30" (9)
B = ¹/2" × 1¹/2" × 5" (16)
C = 1¹/2" × 1¹/2" × 12¹/2" (4)
D = ³/4" × 1¹/2' × 14¹/2" (2)
E = ³/4" × 1¹/2' × 27" (2)

*Fig. 17-22  Assembly details for the delicate patio table.*

Next, prepare all the parts required for the top. A good way to do the assembling is to start by using glue and two 4d box nails to attach a spacer (B) at each end of a slat (A). Add a second slat with glue and 5d box nails. Follow the same program until the assembly is complete. Put the parts together carefully so you will end up with a flat surface.

You can attach the top with minimum fuss by using small corner angles—one at each end and one at a midpoint along the sides.

### End table

The project shown in FIG. 17-23 has a *floating* surface—the top appears to occupy a separate space because of the gap between it and the legs. Study the plan in FIG. 17-24 and check the material requirements in TABLE 17-3 before you begin working. Choose a cabinet grade plywood for the top and the shelf and compatible lumber for other components.

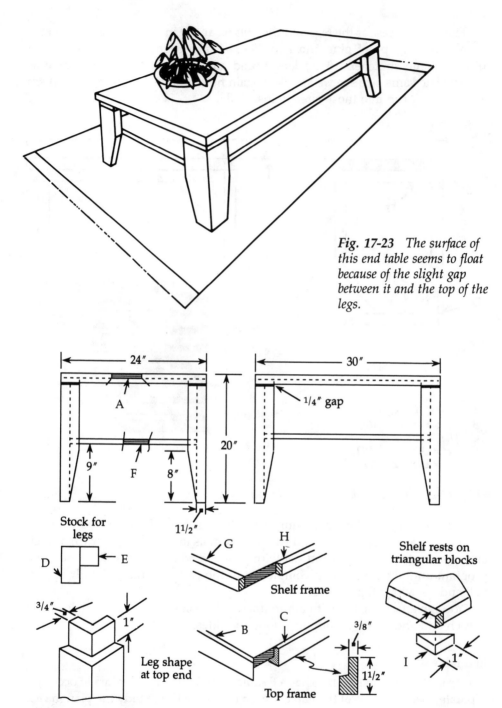

**Fig. 17-23** *The surface of this end table seems to float because of the slight gap between it and the top of the legs.*

24"

A

20"

9"

F

8"

1½"

30"

¼" gap

Stock for legs

D

E

3/4"

1"

Leg shape at top end

G

H

Shelf frame

B

C

Top frame

3/8"

1½"

Shelf rests on triangular blocks

I

1"

**Fig. 17-24** *These plans show how the end table is assembled. Study the details before beginning construction.*

### Table 17-3. Parts Required
### for the Outdoor Bench

| Key | Name | #pieces | Size (inches) |
|-----|------|---------|---------------|
| A | Top | 1 | $3/4 \times 23^{1}/4 \times 29^{1}/4$ |
| B | Top—frame | 2 | $3/4 \times 1^{1}/2 \times 24$ |
| C | Top—frame | 2 | $3/4 \times 1^{1}/2 \times 30$ |
| D | Leg piece | 4 | $1^{1}/2 \times 3 \times 19^{1}/4$ |
| E | Leg piece | 4 | $1^{1}/2 \times 1^{1}/2 \times 19^{1}/4$ |
| F | Shelf | 1 | $3/4 \times 20 \times 26$ |
| G | Shelf—frame | 2 | $1/2 \times 3/4 \times 20$ |
| H | Shelf frame | 2 | $1/2 \times 3/4 \times 27$ |
| I | Shelf support | 2 | $3/4 \times 1 \times 1$ |

Start by joining parts D and E as shown in FIG. 17-24. The joint does not require more than glue, but be certain that mating surfaces make overall contact. The top of the legs are shaped to the form shown in FIG. 17-24 by cutting mating end-laps that turn a 90-degree corner. Use a backsaw to make both the shoulder and cheek cuts. Saw the tapers required at the bottom end of the legs, but stay a bit outside the cutline so you can smooth rough edges with sandpaper.

Next, cut the plywood required for the shelf, then frame it with parts G and H. Start with the end pieces, cutting them $1/8$ inch or so longer than necessary so they can be sanded flush after they are attached. Use glue and 4d finishing nails to attach them. Follow the same procedure to install the side frame members.

At this point, it's a good idea to assemble the legs and the shelf. This way you can check dimensions on the assembly to be sure of preparing the top of the table to exact size. Prepare the supports for the shelf by cutting two pieces $3/4$ inch $\times 1$ inch $\times 1$ inch and sawing them so you will have four triangular parts. Mark their locations on the legs and attach them with glue and brads. The brads don't play much of a part here; it's the glue that supplies the strength so be sure the blocks fit tightly in the corners of the legs. Put the shelf in place after applying glue at its four corners and to the top of the supports. Use bar clamps or a band clamp to keep the assembly together until the glue dries. Check FIG. 17-25 to see how a stretcher is used between the legs. This part is not in the materials list because it's better to determine its size on assembly. Use a piece that is $3/4$ inch $\times 1^{1}/2$ inch $\times$ the distance between the legs.

Cut the plywood for the top and the pieces that will be used to frame it. The latter parts are rabbeted as shown in FIG. 17-24 and attached like those on the shelf, but in this case the corners are mitered. The best procedure for each piece is to miter one end and then place it in position so you can mark for the miter at the opposite end.

Apply glue to the top of the legs and the surface of the stretcher. Put the top in place. Drive a couple of #6 $\times 1^{1}/4$-inch flathead screws through the stretchers to pull the top firmly into position.

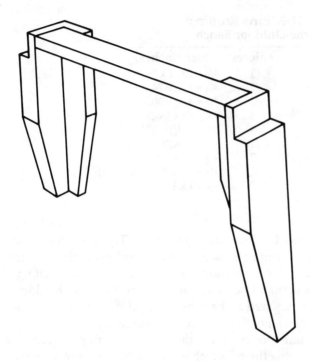

*Fig. 17-25* *The stretcher between the legs of the end table is not in the materials list. Use 3/4 inch × 11/2 inch material. Determine its length on assembly.*

## Plant containers

Plant containers are worthy projects, fun to make and use, and fine candidates for gift-giving to fellow gardeners. Heart redwood and cedar are preferred materials, but other species will do if treated to withstand the abuse of soil, moisture, and weather. Wood can be treated with preservatives like Copper green and Cuprinol but avoid products containing pentachlorophenol, which is toxic to plants. Use waterproof glue in joints and employ fasteners that are galvanized. Other applicable fasteners are aluminum nails and brass screws.

Start the plant container pictured in FIGS. 17-26 and 17-27 by cutting the ends (part B) to size, then sawing the semicircular shape at the bottom end. Prepare the bottom piece (part C) and attach it to the ends with waterproof glue and two 1/4 inch × 4 inch lag screws. Place the bottom so it extends 1 inch beyond the sides of the end parts. The last step is to prepare the sides (part A) and to attach them with glue and 7d galvanized nails. Drill several 1/2-inch drainage holes through the bottom and cover them with squares of aluminum screening before you fill the container with soil. A good idea that applies to all containers is to run a bead of caulking along all the inside seams to guard against moisture entering the joints.

## Display shelf

Begin the display shelf in FIGS. 17-28 and 17-29 by cutting two pieces for the sides to their actual size. Before shaping the parts, check the suggestions in FIG. 17-30.

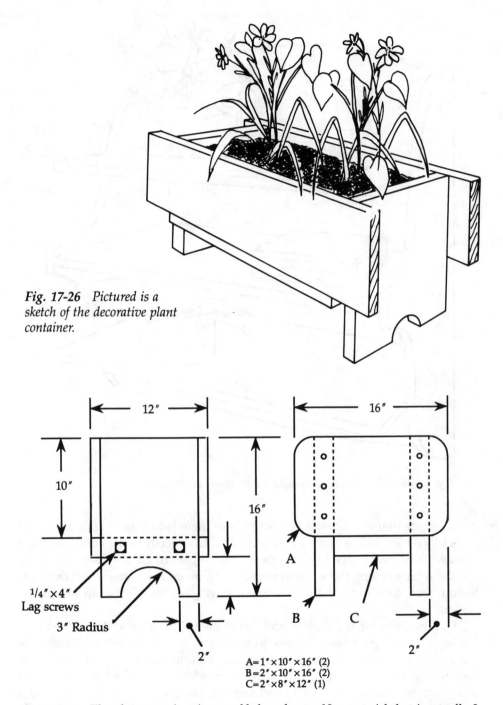

**Fig. 17-26** *Pictured is a sketch of the decorative plant container.*

12″

10″

16″

16″

¹/₄″×4″
Lag screws

3″ Radius

2″

A

B    C

2″

A=1″×10″×16″ (2)
B=2″×10″×16″ (2)
C=2″×8″×12″ (1)

**Fig. 17-27** *The plant container is assembled as shown. Use material that is actually 2 inches thick for the ends and the bottom. Attach the sides with 7d nails and use waterproof glue on all joints.*

**Fig. 17-28**  *The display shelf adds a nice touch to the wall.*

If you decide to use dadoes, it is wise to form them before sawing curved areas especially if they will be formed on a table saw. Go directly to the curve-cutting if you decide on butt joints. In either case, make a pattern for only one half of the profile. After marking the top area of the sides, invert the pattern and mark the bottom area. Stay outside the line when sawing so the edges can be sanded smooth.

Cut the parts for the shelves and install them with glue and either nails or screws, depending on the joint design you chose to use. Measure between the sides of the project before you cut the top and bottom components (B) to be sure they will be the right length. Install the parts with glue and 6d finishing nails driven through the side members and shelves. The project is wide enough so it can be secured to a wall at studs with two screws through the top piece. Remember that the distance between the centers of wall studs is 16 inches. Use a level when you mount the project to be sure that it will be horizontal.

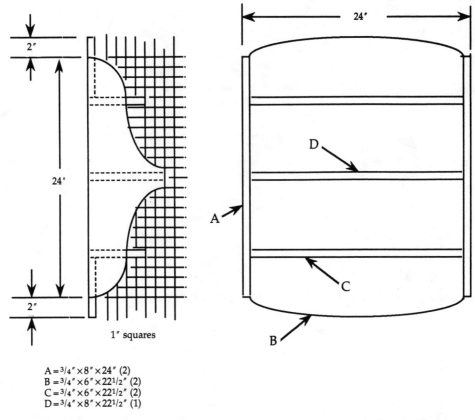

1″ squares

A = $^3/_4'' \times 8'' \times 24''$ (2)
B = $^3/_4'' \times 6'' \times 22^1/_2''$ (2)
C = $^3/_4'' \times 6'' \times 22^1/_2''$ (2)
D = $^3/_4'' \times 8'' \times 22^1/_2''$ (1)

**Fig. 17-29** *Listed are construction details and material requirements for the display shelf. Do not cut the top and bottom parts to length until after the sides and shelves have been assembled.*

**Fig. 17-30** *Two ways to install the shelves in the display unit: (top) a butt joint reinforced with #6 × 1¹/₂″ flathead screws hidden with plugs; and (bottom) a dadoed shelf attached with 6d finishing nails hidden with wood dough.*

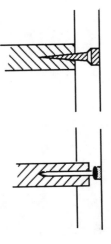

# Glossary

**anti-kickback fingers**  A safety device incorporated in the guard of tools like the table saw and radial arm saw. Small, pivoting arms with serrated edges, normally ride on the surface of the work but will dig in to hold the work should the rotation of the saw blade tend to throw the material back toward the operator.

**auger bits**  A hole-forming cutter normally used in a *hand brace*. The bits have a screw point that pulls the cutter into the wood as the brace is turned.

**awl**  A small, sharp instrument that looks like an ice pick. Uses include starting holes for screws and marking dimension points and lines.

**bench hook**  A board of arbitrary size with a strip of wood nailed across one end, used as a substitute for a vise to secure small pieces that must be sawed or planed.

**bevel**  An angular cut that removes the entire edge of a workpiece. Also, a tool for checking or marking angles.

**bit brace**  A handtool for boring large holes. Its *chuck* is designed to grip the tapered end of *auger bits*. It has a U-shaped handle that drives the bit into the wood when rotated clockwise and retracts the bit when the rotation is reversed.

**blade projection gauge**  A device used on a table saw to determine the distant the blade projects above the saw's table. Many woodworkers make their own, but they are available commercially.

**blind holes**  Any hole that does not pass completely through the material; for example, a 1/2-inch-deep hole in 3/4-inch wood.

**board foot**  A standard unit for measuring lumber. A board foot is 1 inch thick × 12 inches square or the equivalent. A piece of lumber 1 inch thick × 6 inches wide × 24 inches long also measures a board foot. To determine the board feet in a piece of lumber, multiply its thickness (in inches) by its width (in inches) by its length (in feet); then divide by 12. A piece that is 2 inches × 6 inches × 16 feet equals 16 board feet.

**body hole**  The hole that is required to accommodate the diameter of the unthreaded portion of a screw. Often called *shank hole*.

**box nails**  Box nails are similar to *common nails* but have slighter bodies and smaller heads. Thus, they are often used instead of common nails when splitting might be a problem. In essence, box nails are suitable for light construction and in-the-shop work.

**butt joint**  The simplest wood connection. The edge of one part is placed against the edge or surface of another piece. The mating areas are not modified in any way.

**cabinet lip**  The form often used on the edges of cabinet doors. The edges are L-shaped so the door is recessed part way into the cabinet's frame. (See *rabbet joint*.)

**carriage bolt**  A heavy-duty fastener with a square shoulder under an oval or round head. The shoulder digs into the wood and keeps the bolt from turning as the nut is tightened.

**chamfer**  An angular cut similar to a *bevel*, but it does not remove the entire edge of the stock.

**chippers**  Components of a power tool accessory used to produce cuts that are wider than a saw blade can form. (See *dado assembly*.)

**chuck**  A device on tools, such as hand and power drills, that adjusts to grip the plain end of the hole-forming bit being used. A special key is used to tighten the chuck on power tools.

**close-coat**  Sandpaper that has abrasive particles packed tightly together. (See *open-coat*.)

**combination blade**  A general-purpose saw blade with teeth designed to cut either across or parallel with the grain direction of wood.

**combination square**  A measuring and marking device with a head that slides along a 12-inch steel blade. The head is shaped so that it can be used to mark lines 45 degrees or 90 degrees from an edge.

**common nails**  Nails with large, flat, circular heads used extensively for heavy-duty constructions, such as house framing, where strength is more important than appearance.

**compass**  An adjustable tool used to mark arcs or circles. Some are made so the marker can be either a steel point or a pencil.

**compass saw**  A handsaw with a slim blade that tapers from handle to end. Practical tool for sawing curves and holes and for cuts that can't be accomplished with a conventional saw.

**counterbored hole**  Hole with an upper area that is large enough for a fastener to be driven below the surface of the wood. The hole is then filled with a wooden plug so the fastener is concealed.

**countersunk hole**  Hole with a shallow, conical shape at its top end. The form suits the head-shape of screws that are driven flush with the surface of the wood. The screws are usually referred to as *flathead*, or simply *FH*.

**creep**  Inaccuracies that can occur because of the tendency of a table saw blade to pivot the workpiece about the forward edge of the *miter gauge*. The condition applies mostly when making angular cuts. (See *miter joints*.)

**crosscut**  A saw cut made squarely across the grain direction of the wood.

**cross miter**  An angular cut made across the grain direction of the wood. This type of cut is called a *bevel* when made parallel with the grain.

**cross-ply construction**  A design of plywood in which alternating plies of thick or thin veneers are bonded at right angles to each other.

**dado**  A U-shaped cut made across the grain of the wood.

**dado assembly**  A table or radial arm saw accessory used to make cuts that are wider than can be accomplished with a saw blade. The tool consists of two saw blades and an assortment of *chippers*. The number of chippers used between the blades determines the width of the cut.

**dadoing**  Making U-shaped cuts.

**divider**  A compass-type tool that usually has two integral steel points, used to mark off distances.

**drill stops**  Small accessories used on drill bits to control how far the bit penetrates; used for *stopped* or *blind* holes.

**edge grain**  Interchangeable with *vertical grain* to describe softwood lumber sawed so the growth rings, visible on the end of the board, form an angle of 45 degrees or more with the surface of the lumber.

**edge-to-edge joint**  The connection used to assemble separate pieces of wood to form a wide panel. An edge-to-edge joint is actually a *butt joint* since the mating edges are not usually modified in any way.

**end grain**  The grain pattern visible on the end of a board.

**expansive bit**  A hand brace bit with an adjustable cutter used to cut large holes of a variety of diameters.

**feather**  A slim strip of wood used to reinforce a joint; usually applied to *miter joints*, where the feather fits a groove cut across the joint line.

**file card and brush**  A device used on files to prevent accumulation of waste material that clog the teeth.

**files**  Various handtools used to shape or smooth wood or metal. The files most applicable for woodworking are called *rasps*.

**finishing nails**  Slim nails with small heads designed for sinking below the surface of the wood so that they can be concealed, usually with a type of plastic wood.

**finishing tools**  A variety of implements used for final touches on wood products. Files and sandpaper, for example, fit this category.

**flat grain**  Softwood lumber sawed so that the growth rings, visible on the end of the board, form angles of less than 45 degrees with the surface of the lumber. The saw cuts are tangent to the annual rings. The pattern of the surface grain appears as ovals or V-shapes.

**flex tapes**  Measuring tools with flexible steel blades that slide in or out of compact cases. Modern versions allow the blade to retract automatically and have locks to hold the blade in an extended position.

**folding rule**  Measuring device that consists of 6-inch sections hinged together so they can be extended or folded. Usual maximum length is 6 or 8 feet; also called *zig zag* rule.

**gouge**  Chisel with a concave or V-shaped cutting edge, used for digging out wood or forming grooves.

**grinding wheel**  A device used extensively for sharpening tools.

**groove**  A U-shaped cut made parallel with the grain of the wood. *Dado* and *groove* have become interchangeable.

**hand drills**  Various types of hand tools used with drill bits, or *points*, to form holes. Maximum hole-size capacity is $1/4$ inch or $3/8$ inch, depending on the model.

**handscrews**  A type of woodworking clamp with heavy, hardwood jaws joined by twin threaded rods with opposing screw action. Since the rods can be adjusted separately, the clamps can grip parallel or nonparallel surfaces.

**hardboard**  A dense, strong manufactured panel material made of compressed wood fibers. Commonly available in 4-foot-×-8-foot panels and in various thicknesses, hardboard is good material for the insides of cabinets and furniture. Also available in various forms as wall paneling.

**hardwood**   A botanical term that refers to lumber produced from broad-leaf deciduous trees. Common hardwoods include birch, maple, oak, cherry, and poplar. Poplar, a hardwood, is actually "soft" in terms of fabrication.

**jointer/planer**   A power tool used to smooth the edges and sometimes surfaces of boards. The closest equivalent in handtools is the *plane*.

**kerf**   The cut made by a conventional handsaw or powered circular saw.

**keyhole saw**   A slim, tapered saw that ends in a sharp point so it can be used to make internal cutouts; available in sets of various size blades that fit a single handle.

**kickback**   The action of a workpiece being thrown back toward the operator. Kickback can happen on a table saw when the work binds between the saw blade and the rip fence. (See *anti-kickback fingers*.)

**lag screws**   Heavy-duty screw fasteners with square or rectangular heads. They are driven with a wrench and are used mostly for heavy construction. Smaller sizes are often used for projects such as garden furniture and plant containers.

**lap joint**   The joint formed when two boards that cross or meet at an end are joined surface-to-surface. *Half-laps* and *end-laps* are formed when identical notches or L-shaped cuts that are half the thickness of the stock are made in the mating pieces. The latter designs are stronger and have a better appearance than the simple lap joint.

**lead hole**   The part of a hole drilled for a screw that accommodates part of the length of the screw's threaded area. (See *pilot hole*.)

**lumber**   Broad term for wood that has been sawed from a log into a size and form suitable for use.

**machine bolts**   Fasteners with square or hexagonal heads and smooth shanks above the threaded area, that are turned with a wrench.

**marking gauge**   Essentially, a marking device with a sharp steel pin on the end of a wooden bar, or *beam*, that slides in a lockable head. A typical application is marking lines parallel with the edge of boards. A strip of pencil lead can be substituted for the steel pin.

**miter**   A saw cut made obliquely across the grain of wood. (See *miter joints*.)

**miter box**   A handmade or commercial accessory that helps achieve accuracy when sawing miter cuts.

**miter box saw**   Special saw with fine teeth that is usually supplied with a commercial miter box.

**miter gauge**   A table saw accessory used to guide wood for crosscutting and making miter cuts. The head of the gauge can be rotated left or right from zero to 45 degrees.

**miter joints**   The connection between two pieces that have similar angular cuts, such as the corners of square or rectangular frames. When the angular cuts are 45 degrees, the angle between the inside edges of the frame is 90 degrees.

**miter square**   A tool used for checking the squareness of lumber and for measuring and marking right angles. The blade end of the handle has an edge cut at an angle so the tool can be used for checking or marking 45-degree angles.

**mortise-and-tenon**   A classic woodworking joint that consists of a square or rectangular projection (tenon) on one part that fits a corresponding cavity (mortise) in the mating piece. Most times, the mortise is limited in depth so the end of the tenon won't be visible.

**oilstone**  A tool used to finish sharpening of cutting tools such as knives or chisels. Oil is used to keep ground-off particles of steel from clogging the pores of the stone.

**open-coat**  Sandpaper that has open areas between particles of abrasive grit. It allows sanding of soft materials with less danger of clogging the abrasive.

**particleboard**  Paneling made of wood chips bonded under pressure. Various types are called *chipboard* and *flakeboard*. Special values are strength and resistance to warping and dimensional changes. Often used for doors, tops of projects, and as a substrate for plastic laminates.

**penny**  Originally used to indicate the price of 100 nails, penny now indicates nail sizes; usually abbreviated as the letter "d." For example, a 2d nail is 1 inch long and a 6d nail is 6 inches long.

**pilot hole**  The part of a screw-hole that suits the threaded portion of a screw. Also, a hole drilled part way through a board to receive a nail that might cause splitting if it were driven in the usual way. The diameter of the pilot hole is always less than that of the nail.

**pinion**  A small wheel with teeth that fit into the teeth of a larger wheel. On a hand drill, the large wheel turns the pinion that, in turn, causes the chuck to rotate.

**planes**  A variety of handtools used to smooth and square the edge of a board or its surface; also used to *bevel* or *chamfer* edges and to reduce the width or thickness of lumber.

**ploughing**  Another term for grooving, or making a U-shaped cut parallel with the grain of the wood.

**points per inch (PPI)**  On hand saws, the PPI are counted from tooth point to tooth point. The number of teeth per inch is always one less than the number of points.

**punch**  A handtool used to form an indent at a dimension point, often the first step in a drilling operation. The indent keeps the drill bit from moving off the mark.

**push drill**  The smallest hand drill. Pushing the handle up and down causes the drill bit to rotate. It works with bits up to about $^{11}/_{64}$ inch.

**push stick**  A safety device used instead of fingers to move workpieces. On a table saw, a push stick is used on ripping operations when the distance between the blade and the fence is too narrow for safe use of hands.

**quarter-sawed**  Lumber produced by first sawing a log into quarters before boards are cut. Saw cuts are made parallel to the vertical centerline of the quarter section. Quarter-sawed boards are less likely to warp, and they have an attractive grain pattern, but they are more expensive since the sawing method wastes much of the log.

**quarters**  The thickness of hardwoods; $^1/_4$ equals $^1/_4$ inch. Thus, $^5/_4$ means $1^1/_4$ inch, $^3/_4$ means $^3/_4$ inch, and so on.

**rabbet joint**  A wood connection in which one part is L-shaped and receives the end of the mating piece.

**rasps**  Woodworker's files, with large, widely spaced teeth that remove wood quickly and are less likely to clog than regular files.

**ready-mades**  Commercial items that woodworkers can use as is, including legs, spindles, posts, wheels for toys, dowels, moldings, and so on. Often referred to as *specialty items*.

**reinforcement irons**  Ready-to-use hardware that can hold parts together or reinforce joints, including items such as *metal braces, mending plates,* and *corner irons*. Reinforcement items are available in bulk or in packages that include the necessary screws.

**rip**  Saw cut made parallel with the grain of the wood.

**rip fence**  Adjustable accessory used when making a rip cut on a table saw. The distance between the saw blade and the fence determines the width of the part being cut.

**ripsaw**  Handsaw with special teeth that are efficient when sawing parallel with the grain of the wood. The saw has deep spaces (gullets) between the teeth to easily throw off the large waste chips the saw produces.

**S4S**  Lumber term meaning that a board has been planed on surfaces and edges (four sides).

**set**  Condition of alternate teeth on a saw blade being bent in opposite directions. The *kerf* made by the blade is wider than the blade, so it can cut without binding.

**softwood**  Botanical term indicating lumber than has been cut from needle-bearing trees (conifers). Cedar, pine, redwood, and fir are examples of softwoods.

**spiral-ratchet screwdriver**  Handtool that makes it easy to drive or withdraw screws just by pushing its handle up and down. The tool is adjustable so it can turn left or right or be used like a conventional rigid screwdriver.

**splines**  Strips of wood used to reinforce joints, including edge-to-edge joints and miter joints. Splines are strongest when the grain direction runs across the width. Plywood and hardboard, which have strength in all directions, are good materials for splines.

**splitter**  Part of the guard on a table saw, the splitter's job is to keep the *kerf* from closing and thus binding the blade.

**squares**  Various types of measuring and marking tools. (See *combination square* and *miter square*.)

**steel square**  An L-shaped measuring and marking tool usually equipped with 24-inch and 16-inch blades. The tools are engraved with a host of information such as figuring board measure, finding circumferences, angles for miter joints, and more. Steel squares come in a variety of types, among them *framing* and *carpenter's* squares.

**stopped**  Indicates a hole or other cavity that does not go through the stock. Stopped and *blind* are used interchangeably.

**Surforms**  Stanley handtools used to shape, shave, and plane wood. Some look like conventional files, others resemble hand planes. The cutting blades look almost like old-fashioned cheese graters. Cutting teeth are widely spaced and have their own waste ejection hole so that clogging is seldom a problem.

**swaged edges**  The cutting edges on the chippers of a dado assembly, which are wider than the gauge of the cutters so that they clean out the waste material between the outside blades.

**T-nuts**  Cylinder-shaped hardware with internal threads and prongs that penetrate the wood to keep the item from turning. They provide a means of establishing steel threads in nonmetal materials like wood, plywood, and particleboard.

**tenoning jig**  A special table saw accessory, often homemade, that provides safety and accuracy when making some of the cuts required for a tenon. It provides support for narrow components that must be held on edge when moved into a saw blade.

**threaded inserts**  Small, cylinder-shaped hardware that has internal and external threads. They are turned into a hole drilled in wood to provide steel threads in material like lumber, plywood, or particleboard.

**torque**  A force that produces a twisting or rotating motion. In a sense, turning a screwdriver produces the torque needed to drive a screw.

**try square**  A measuring and marking tool similar to the *miter square*, but lacking the angle cut in the handle that would allow 45-degree angles. Usually, its handle is about two-thirds as long as its blade. The blades range from 6 to 12 inches long.

**turning chisels**  Specially shaped chisels used when shaping wood in a lathe. They have longer handles and shorter blades than conventional wood chisels.

**twist drills**  Common hole-forming cutter that function best when driven with a power drill. Twist drills usually have the same diameter from end to end, but large ones might have reduced shanks so they can be gripped in $1/4$-inch or $3/8$-inch chucks.

**whetstone**  See *oilstone*.

**wing-type**  The driving end of a screwdriver blade that is designed to turn conventional slot-head screws. Often called a *standard* blade and tip.

**wire brads**  Small, thin, light-duty nails that have heads like *finishing nails* so that they can be driven below the surface of the wood and concealed. They are graded by length—from $1/2$ to $1^1/2$ inches—not by the penny system that applies to other nails.

**woodworker's vise**  A gripping device usually installed at one end of a workbench. Its steel jaws are faced with replaceable wooden plates so parts that are held won't be marred. Large ones have 10-inch-wide jaws that can open to as much as 12 inches.

# Index

# Other Bestsellers of Related Interest

**COUNTRY ELEGANCE: Projects for Woodworkers**—Edward A. Baldwin

Add a cozy country mood to your home with this collection of challenging and rewarding project plans that you're sure to like—no matter what your skill level! This book presents step-by-step, illustrated instructions or 30 original country furniture designs for every room in your home. Projects are as practical as they are attractive, and range from small knick-knacks to large furniture pieces. 256 pages, 241 illustrations. Book No. 3768, $14.95 paperback only

**THE TABLE SAW BOOK**—R. J. De Cristoforo

*"R. J. De Cristoforo is the outstanding tool authority in the world."* —*Popular Science*

This book is a complete and practical approach to basic and advanced table saw functions. Detailed instructions and hundreds of illustrations are included for crosscuts, rips, miters, tapers, chamfers, dadoes, compound angles, and more. 352 pages, 500 illustrations. Book No. 2789, $16.95 paperback only

**SHAPING WOOD: A New Woodworking Approach**—Douglas Hackett

Now you can create marketable, art-gallery-quality sculptured wood pieces safely and quickly in your home shop. This book offers diverse projects that you can make even if you don't have a large shop or expensive machinery. It provides helpful tips on safety, design, and project applications, and, to assist those with less experience or a limited tool supply, it suggest methods for performing various woodshaping tasks. 180 pages, 260 illustrations. Book No. 3930, $14.95 paperback only

**COUNTRY CLASSICS: 25 Early American Projects**—Gloria Saberin

If you like to work with wood, you can easily make authentic reproductions of Early American antiques by following the plans in this guide. Each project, selected for its unique charm and simplicity, includes a photo of the finished piece, historical information about the item, materials list, instructions, working plans, and construction tips. A special section of full-color photographs is also included. 184 pages, 198 illustrations. Book No. 3587, $12.95 paperback only

**GARDEN TOOLS AND GADGETS YOU CAN MAKE**—Percy W. Blandford

This book boasts project plans for just about any garden convenience or accessory you can think of! All of them will make gardening more enjoyable, productive, and easier—you'll be amazed at the money you can save by making your own garden tools. Step-by-step instructions and detailed illustrations accompany each project. Included are small handtools, boxes, bins, climbing supports, carts, buildings, and more. 260 pages, Illustrated. Book No. 3194, $11.95 paperback only

**GIFTS FROM THE WOODSHOP**—R. J. De Cristoforo

Whether you're a master craftsman or novice woodworker, you'll find something challenging in this collection of practical and attractive gift projects. You'll find instructions for building kitchen aids, plant hangers and stands, wind chimes, bird houses and feeders, toys, picture and mirror frames, shelves and racks, decorative plaques, and much more. All projects can be made using basic handtools. 240 pages, 290 illustrations. Book No. 3591, $15.95 paperback, $24.95 hardcover

**A HOME FULL OF FURNITURE: 79 More Projects for Every Room**—Percy W. Blandford

Blandford, long noted for producing high-quality woodworking designs, provides you with complete plans and instructions for 79 new furniture projects, grouped around rooms in the home. Plans included are: portable side stand, corner shelves, room divider, umbrella stand, hanging telephone table, plant stand, folding hall table, Shaker rocking chair, and an octagonal coffee table. Almost all of the pieces can be made with the most basic tools. 352 pages, 248 illustrations. Book No. 3500, $16.95 paperback, $25.95 hardcover

**REFINISHING OLD FURNITURE**—George Wagoner

Bring back the natural beauty and luster of a time-worn dining table, rocking chair, desk, or any other classic piece with the detailed, step-by-step instructions and working illustrations in this guide. You'll discover how to choose the proper finish, make simple repairs, select the best refinishing methods, and care for and touch up your projects. 192 pages, 96 illustrations. Book No. 3496, $13.95 paperback only

# Other Bestsellers of Related Interest

**WOODWORKER'S JACKPOT: 49 Step-by-Step Projects**—John A. Nelson

This book compiles a range of woodworking designs from small to large, simple to complex, ordinary to unusual. You will enjoy making and using the selection of kitchen projects, folk art projects, toys, projects incorporating country hearts, weekend projects, and antique reproductions. Each is presented with a materials list, complete step-by-step instructions, exploded assembly drawings, and a photograph of the finished product. 240 pages, Illustrated. Book No. 3154, $16.95 paperback only

**WOODWORKER'S 30 BEST PROJECTS**—Editors of *Woodworker* Magazine

A collection of some of the finest furniture ever made can be found within the pages of this project book. Designed for the woodworker who has already mastered the basics, the projects presented in this book are for the intermediate- to advanced-level craftsman. Each furniture project comes complete with detailed instructions, a materials list, exploded views of working diagrams, a series of step-by-step, black-and-white photos, and a photograph of the finished piece. 224 pages, 300 illustrations. Book No. 3021, $14.95 paperback only

Prices Subject to Change Without Notice.

## Look for These and Other TAB Books at Your Local Bookstore

### To Order Call Toll Free 1-800-822-8158
(24-hour telephone service available.)

or write to TAB Books, Blue Ridge Summit, PA 17294-0840.

| Title | Product No. | Quantity | Price |
|-------|-------------|----------|-------|
|       |             |          |       |
|       |             |          |       |
|       |             |          |       |
|       |             |          |       |

☐ Check or money order made payable to TAB Books

Charge my ☐ VISA ☐ MasterCard ☐ American Express

Acct. No. _____ Exp. _____

Signature: _____

Name: _____

Address: _____

City: _____

State: _____ Zip: _____

Subtotal  $ _____

Postage and Handling
($3.00 in U.S., $5.00 outside U.S.)  $ _____

Add applicable state and local
sales tax  $ _____

TOTAL  $ _____

TAB Books catalog free with purchase; otherwise send $1.00 in check or money order and receive $1.00 credit on your next purchase.

*Orders outside U.S. must pay with international money order in U.S. dollars drawn on a U.S. bank.*

**TAB Guarantee: If for any reason you are not satisfied with the book(s) you order, simply return it (them) within 15 days and receive a full refund.**                                                              **BC**